D0025230

TEACHING IN JAPAN

TEACHING IN JAPAN
A CULTURAL PERSPECTIVE

NOBUO K. SHIMAHARA

ROUTLEDGEFALMER

NEW YORK   LONDON

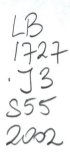
HARVARD UNIVERSITY
GRADUATE SCHOOL OF EDUCATION
MONROE C. GUTMAN LIBRARY

Published in 2002 by
RoutledgeFalmer
29 West 35th Street
New York, NY 10001

RoutledgeFalmer is an imprint of the Taylor & Francis Group.

10 9 8 7 6 5 4 3 2 1

Library of Congress Cataloging-in-Publication Data
Shimahara, Nobuo.
   Teaching in Japan : a cultural perspective / Nobuo K. Shimahara.
      p. cm. — (Reference books in international education ; 54)
   Includes bibliographical references and index.
   ISBN 0-8153-3512-1
      1. Teachers—Training of—Japan. 2. Teachers—In-service training—Japan. 3. Educational change—Japan. I. Title. II. Series.

   LB1727.J3 S55 2001
   371.1'00952—dc21

                                                    2001031773

Printed on acid-free, 250-year-life paper.
Manufactured in the United States of America.

To: Yasuko, Erika, and Mark

TABLE OF CONTENTS

Series Preface

This series of scholarly works in comparative and international education has grown well beyond the initial conception of a collection of reference books. Although retaining its original purpose of providing a resource to scholars, students, and a variety of other professionals who need to understand the role played by education in various societies or world regions, it also strives to provide accurate, relevant, and up-to-date information on a wide variety of selected educational issues, problems, and experiments within an international context.

Contributors to this series are well-known scholars who have devoted their professional lives to the study of their specializations. Without exception these men and women possess an intimate understanding of the subject of their research and writing. Without exception they have studied their subject not only in dusty archives, but have lived and traveled widely in their quest for knowledge. In short, they are "experts" in the best sense of that often overused word.

In our increasingly interdependent world, it is now widely understood that it is a matter of military, economic, and environmental survival that we understand better not only what makes other societies tick, but also how others, be they Japanese, Hungarian, South African, or Chilean, attempt to solve the same kinds of educational problems that we face in North America. As the late George Z. F. Bereday wrote more than three decades ago: "[E]ducation is a mirror held against the face of a people. Nations may put on blustering shows of strength to conceal public weakness, erect grand façades to conceal shabby backyards, and profess peace while secretly arming for conquest, but how they take care of their children tells unerringly who they are" (*Comparative Methods in Education*, New York: Holt, Rinehart and Winston, 1964, p. 5).

Perhaps equally important, however, is the valuable perspective that studying another education system (or its problems) provides us in understanding our own system (or its problems). When we step beyond our own limited experience and our commonly held assumptions about schools and learning in order to look back at our system in contrast to another, we see it in a very different light. To learn, for example, how China or Belgium handles the education of a multilingual society; how the French provide for the funding of public education; or how the Japanese control access to their universities enables us to better understand that there are reasonable alternatives to our own familiar way of doing things. Not that we can borrow directly from other societies. Indeed, educational arrangements are inevitably a reflection of deeply embedded political, economic, and cultural factors that are unique to a particular society. But a conscious recognition that there are other ways of doing things can serve to open our minds and provoke our imaginations in ways that can result in new experiments or approaches that we may not have otherwise considered.

Since this series is intended to be a useful research tool, the editor and contributors welcome suggestions for future volumes, as well as ways in which this series can be improved.

Edward R. Beauchamp
University of Hawaii

Preface

Teaching in Japan: A Cultural Perspective is intended for an English-speaking professional audience, including college students and professors as well as classroom teachers, with an interest in what it is like to be a teacher in Japan. It offers the reader the latest perspective on teaching in Japan and an ethnographic view of how Japanese teachers construct teaching. This volume is composed of two parts. Part One addresses the following three major topics: the culture of teaching, teacher preparation and social change, and professional development. Part Two consists of three chapters originally published in *Learning to Teach in Two Cultures: Japan and the United States* (Shimahara & Sakai, 1995). These three chapters, which have been edited for this book, focus on how beginning teachers learn to teach, the influence of Japanese pedagogy on beginning teachers, and their enculturation into teaching.

Part One explores salient characteristics of teaching, reforms in teacher preparation prompted by social change, and strategies for professional development. It represents an up-to-date analysis of teaching in Japan based on data gathered in the 1990s and teaching documents. Part Two is a detailed ethnographic account of teaching as reflected in the process of learning to teach. It illustrates not only how beginning teachers learn to teach but also examines deeply rooted teaching practice in Japan— the Japanese culture of teaching. Thus these two parts are complementary and offer a broad and integrated view of teaching.

The data used in this volume are drawn from several research projects. The first three chapters are based on the data I collected in: 1) a 1994-1996 collaborative ethnographic project, 2) a 1995 national survey on teachers' lives, and 3) a 1998 ethnographic study, as well as a large corpus of teaching documents. The collaborative ethnographic project was directed by Hidenori Fujita at the University of Tokyo and me. Following the planning initiatives we undertook during 1993-1994, our project was launched in the spring of 1994 and continued through 1996. Fujita directed a large-scale national survey on teachers' lives administered in the fall of 1995, and survey data were analyzed in the following year. The sample included 1,019 elementary teachers and 1,034 middle school teachers representing a total of 93 schools in the following eight prefectures: Aichi, Fukushima, Fukui, Fukuoka, Nagano, Shizuoka, Tokyo, and Yamagata. In the text I will refer to this survey as the Professional Actions and Cultures of Teaching, or PACT, survey (Fujita et al. 1996).

Our project was one of the international studies of teachers' work in changing social contexts involving a research network of scholars from eight industrialized countries, studying Professional Actions and Cultures of Teaching (PACT). PACT was directed by Any Hargreaves at what was then known as the Ontario Institute for Studies in Education and Ivor Goodson at the University of Western Ontario in Canada. Participating countries included Australia, Canada, Israel, Japan, Norway, Sweden, the United Kingdom, and the United States.

The majority of our time from April 1994 to March 1995 was spent collecting ethnographic data through intensive observations and extensive interviews at four elementary schools and three middle schools located in the Ota, Shinagawa, and Shinjuku wards in Tokyo and one elementary and middle school in Kariya City, Aichi Prefecture. In addition, we videotaped a variety of school events and classroom activities to offer a microethnographic analysis of typical events and teaching. Our approach was designed to focus on ongoing events in a natural setting, the linkages between these events and their social and cultural context. We were interested in capturing social actions in the classroom and school setting as they occurred, and we paid special attention to the meanings of these actions to the actors. We inductively sought patterns of actions and identified cultural principles that govern everyday life in the classroom and school setting, as well as relationships between events in the classroom and the school setting at other levels of the system. Interviews were employed to elicit teachers' views of teaching, student guidance, life-course, and accounts of events.

The 1998 study focused on teacher professional development at both the elementary and secondary levels in Tokushima Prefecture. This research was conducted for six months in 1998 to augment the database generated in Tokyo during 1994-1995. I visited a total of sixteen elementary, middle, and high schools in the prefecture for classroom observations and interviews with teachers and administrators; two prefectural education centers in Tokushima and Hiroshima; and the National Education Center in Tokyo, where I collected documents on leadership development. My observations in Tokushima included fourteen study meetings of teachers organized at three levels: in-house, municipal, and prefectural.

The last three chapters resulted from the comparative ethnographic project that I directed during 1989-1991. It examined how beginning teachers learn to teach in Japan and the United States. We extensively observed and interviewed beginning teachers at three elementary schools in Tokyo for one year in 1989, when a national internship program was introduced; and American beginning teachers at two elementary schools in a mid-Atlantic state for one and a half years. Further detail on the methodology is presented in *Learning to Teach in Two Cultures: Japan and the United States* (Shimahara & Sakai, 1995), as the study culminated in this volume.

I would like to acknowledge the generous support I received that made my participation in these projects possible. In 1989, the Japan Society for the Promotion of Sciences invited me to serve as a visiting professor at the University of Tokyo. During my professorship at the university I conducted research on Japanese beginning teachers. The Japanese National Institute of Multimedia Education offered me a research professorship in 1994-1995, which enabled me to participate in the PACT project in Japan. The PACT project also received a grant from Japan's Ministry of Education in 1994. Naruto University of Education offered me a research professorship in 1998 to conduct the project in Tokushima.

Finally, I would like to express my deep appreciation to Professor Edward Beauchamp at the University of Hawaii, the editor of this series, for his valuable suggestions and support that made the publication of this volume possible.

Nobuo K. Shimahara

January 2001

Part One

Teaching and current Issues

CHAPTER I

Introduction: The Background

The primary purpose of this volume is to take a fresh look at teaching at the elementary and middle-school levels in Japan. It will address two questions: What sustains teaching? And what is pressing teaching to change? As an educational anthropologist my interest is in examining the relationship between culture and education. This volume presents a cultural perspective on these questions based on ethnographic and other related data that I have gathered over the past ten years in Japan.

The first part of this book considers salient characteristics of contemporary teaching, national reforms aimed at changing the way that teachers are prepared, and professional development. The second part presents an ethnographic account of how Japanese beginning teachers learn to teach. This account mirrors teaching in general and specifically illuminates what novices are expected to learn in order to become teachers and how they are enculturated into teaching. Although this ethnographic analysis is based on a case study of a small number of beginning teachers, it sheds lights on the culture of teaching in Japan: teachers' shared beliefs, sociocultural knowledge, and time-honored practices. Although this analysis is embedded in the data collected in 1989-1990 and published in 1995 (Shimahara & Sakai), in my view it remains valid and helps explain the Japanese culture of teaching. Since 1990, I conducted two major ethnographic research projects for a total of a year and a half (Shimahara, 1997, 1999)—one year in 1994-1995 and a half-year in 1998—and data from these projects suggest that teaching in Japan has changed very little over the past decade. The government has introduced important reforms to change teacher preparation since the mid-1980s, but whether these reform initiatives will effect important change in classroom practice remains to be seen. Thus far, no study has shown significant change in Japanese teaching practice.

Nevertheless, major social change inevitably affects teaching. Over the past two decades students have been driving Japan's school reforms, including teacher education overhauls. Education reform initiatives have been a response to problems created largely by teenagers who attend secondary (middle and high) schools and whose behaviors reflect the penetrating influences of social change on their lives.

When a national school reform task force (National Council on Educational Reform, 1988) started a series of restructuring initiatives in the mid-1980s, Amano (1986) a perceptive sociologist, made this observation:

> The most immediate reason why reform is necessary now is the troubled rela-
> tionship between the children who are the main actors in the educational
> process and the system itself. A reexamination of that relationship, not so much
> of educational institutions or of education's role in society, is the key issue....
> The strong support for reform derives from the totally new perception of the
> changes occurring in children, on the one hand, and of the relationship between
> children and the educational system, on the other. (p. 2-3)

We will explore teaching in Japan against the politically charged backdrop of education reforms over the past two decades. The overall purpose is to provide a fresh analysis of teaching in the context of contemporary social change. We will examine the culture of teaching at the elementary and lower secondary levels. It is a stabilizing, powerful force that provides a collective ethos and a framework for teaching in which the knowledge of teaching is embedded. Our attention is focused on the interface between stabilizing forces and driving forces for change. Our exploration of teaching calls for a critical analysis of the characteristics of teachers' everyday work, the organizational structure of schooling, and the intensification of teaching as well as an inquiry into how teachers adapt to changing students and changing society. Further, we explore strategies for teacher preparation reforms and professional development, which are crucial factors in providing both continuity in teaching and adaptability to change.

As a brief background to this volume, we will now discuss several relevant strands of events in post-1945 teaching in Japan, followed by a brief analysis of teachers' opinions about their careers, and then an overview of the volume, including chapter synopses as a guide to the reader.

STRANDS IN JAPANESE POSTWAR EDUCATION

The first strand in Japanese postwar education is the introduction of an education system, including the preparation of teachers, which completely replaced the prewar nationalistic, authoritarian school system. In early 1946, the United States Mission on Education was invited to Japan to recommend education reforms (see Ministry of Education, 1980). The mission drew on the American education system as a model for formulating its recommendations, which delineated the initial policy and basic structure of postwar education in Japan. The Education Reform Committee, appointed by the Japanese government as a counterpart to the American mission, played a vital role in reviewing the Americans' recommendations and drafting final recommendations for reforms for legislation.

The Education Reform Committee's work led to the establishment of a uniform system of coeducation offering six years of elementary, three years of lower secondary (middle school), three years of upper secondary (high school), and four years of college education—the first nine years being compulsory. The American mission of 1946 repudiated the centralized structure of school governance and called for greater community and teacher initiative. It recommended, among other pivotal ideas, that elected boards of education as well as parent and teacher organizations be established. The mission's report also recommended a complete revamping of the pre-1945 teacher education system, which provided nationalistic, narrow occupational training deficient in specialized, intellectually rich knowledge. Based on that report, the Education Reform Committee recommended a new organization of teacher education to the government with emphasis on college-level general education. Teacher education was to be incorporated into the university education system and to integrate three principal areas: broad education in the arts and sciences, study in subject fields, and professional study. The committee also recommended an "open system of teacher education," enabling any college or university to offer a teacher education program without direct control by the Ministry of Education. This system eventually led to the development of certification programs by the vast majority of institutions of higher education in Japan.

In 1947, the legislature enacted a national teacher certification law and the Ministry of Education was granted the authority to oversee its implementation. Meanwhile, each local prefectural board of education gained the authority to certify and appoint public school teachers at all levels.

The education reforms introduced in the late 1940s came under intense fire throughout the 1950s, and consequently many of these reforms were altered by the conservative government. The 1950s was a reactionary decade epitomized by a movement toward reestablishing the standardization and central control of schooling. The government initiated a number of administrative and legislative measures to accomplish the return, which resulted in a series of intense and prolonged confrontations between the government and its opposition, which consisted of the left-wing Japan Teachers Union, academic organizations such as the Japan Pedagogical Association, and other interest groups (Kaigo, 1975). Although the basic structure of formal education remained true to the postwar model, the curriculum and school governance underwent significant transformation in this conservative era. By the end of the 1950s, the government had grasped the reins of the nation's schools by centralizing the control of schools. It was in this context that the Ministry of Education embarked on reeducation of teachers in the late 1950s.

In 1958, the Ministry of Education announced a sweeping curriculum revision for Japan's schools, which included introducing moral education at the elementary and lower secondary levels as an independent area of teaching. Overall, this revised curriculum was designed to promote Japan's industrial development in the 1960s. At the same time, the Ministry of Education issued an administrative measure to make the national course of study binding; it had previously been regarded only as an advisory guideline by textbook writers and schools. With this measure, the Ministry of Education firmly established a national curriculum and tightened control of the textbook authorization process.

In the 1950s, the Ministry of Education began to assume greater control not only of teachers but also of teacher education. As early as 1958, the Central Council of Education (1958), an influential body that made policy recommendations to the minister of education, issued a report on enhancing teacher education. The report sprang from the ministry's concern with what it feared to be deteriorating teacher education in the nation. The council was unambiguously critical of the postwar liberalization of teacher education, which, in its opinion, had downgraded certification standards. Since the early 1960s, the Central Council of Education and another standing advisory council, the Teacher Education Council, have periodically made policy recommendations on teacher education to the Ministry of Education. These recommendations have addressed the needs for: improving professional studies, especially clinical experience, for preservice students; establishing internships for teachers and professional development programs; and developing colleges whose primary purpose is to prepare teachers. These policy concerns, including revisions of teacher certification, were again addressed during the 1980s, which led to major legislative action to change teacher education and to introduce one-year mandatory internships for beginning public school teachers (see chapter 4).

The second strand is the theme that postwar Japanese education has come full circle. Japanese education has been guided by two contrasting paradigms of development. The first one is the so-called "catch-up" ideology that drove industrial and social development from the dawn of Japan's modernization in 1868 for nearly one hundred years. The goal of this ideology was to catch up with the West, and it dictated the structure and orientation of schooling. In the postwar era, except its short early phase in the 1940s, the Ministry of Education's central goal was efficient, uniform education and egalitarianism in elementary and secondary education. This approach, however, has been under attack over the past two decades. The second paradigm of development is the post catch-up ideology, which emerged in the 1970s and 1980s as Japan caught up with the West in terms of economic and industrial development. Its rhetoric is not about efficiency, uniformity, and drivenness; instead it is represented by diversity, individual differences, freedom, and personal motivation and interest. The rhetoric epitomizes the ideological orientation of postwar education around 1950.

Let us look at postwar curriculum changes that reflect the second strand. Japan's national curriculum has been reviewed and revised every ten years in light of social, technological, and economic changes (see Shimahara, 1992). The first revision took place under the strong influence of American education during the Occupation. The new curriculum emphasized experience-based and student-centered learning and promoted problem-solving methods. The Ministry of Education issued an official course of study as a guide for teachers and local schools to build their curricula. During those years, the Ministry allowed teachers considerable freedom to determine curricula relevant to their local schools. The experience-oriented curriculum was widely criticized, however, with the chief contention being that student performance had deteriorated.

Accordingly, the Ministry reviewed that curriculum in the early 1950s and, in 1958, made a fundamental revision for the elementary and secondary levels that took effect in the early 1960s. Having gained firm control over the nation's schools through legislation and administrative measures in the 1950s, the ministry issued a course of study that became binding and established more rigorous standards to ensure that commercial textbooks matched the Ministry's goals. The primary focus of the revised curriculum was on improving moral education, academic achievement, science and technical education, and vocational education. As a result, a knowledge-centered curriculum displaced the experience-oriented curriculum and simultaneously quashed local adaptations. The 1960s witnessed an industrial and economic expansion unparalleled in Japanese history. Responding to the demands of industry, in 1968 the Ministry of Education announced its third comprehensive revision of the curriculum to improve scientific and technical education and enhance students' adaptability to a changing society. The revision called specifically for upgrading math and science education. The revised curriculum built on exceedingly high expectations of student performance, however, failed to coincide with the actual abilities and skills of high school students at a time when ninety percent of youth were enrolled in high school (Kinoshita, 1983; Yamaguchi, 1980; Yanagi, 1984).

In response to the perceived rigidity and excessive requirements of the previous curriculum reform, the ministry revised the national curriculum in the late 1970s, this time emphasizing flexibility and diversity to "humanize" student life at school. This revision marked the shift back toward the immediately postwar curriculum policy. Subsequent curriculum reform in the late 1980s accelerated this course, further accommodating students' needs, individual differences, and choice. The Ministry of Education announced the latest curriculum reform in 1998, which will take effect in the early 2000s. This reform reduces curriculum content by thirty percent, mainly in consideration of students' abilities to follow the curriculum and the reduction of school time from six to five days a week. It is said to emphasize basic education, student initiative in learning, and freedom in student life at school. It will introduce "comprehensive study" at all levels to encourage students to take initiative in organizing research projects focused on specific issues such as environmental, community, and international topics. Comprehensive study is the rebirth of the experience-based curriculum introduced in the early years of Japan's postwar education.

The two most recent curriculum reforms underscore problem-solving strategies in teaching and learning, or what is officially referred to as a "new view of academic competence" (see chapter 4). This view gives emphasis to students' intrinsic motivation and problem-solving approaches in learning. But again, such a view of student competency is not new in Japan, because it was introduced in the early phase of postwar education under the American influence. In short, the second strand, that

Japanese education has come full circle, thematically characterizes Japan's education reform initiatives.

In a third strand of the postwar history of Japanese, the confrontation between the Ministry of Education and the Japan Teachers Union (JTU) takes center stage. The Ministry's views have invariably represented the conservative government, whereas JTU's policy position symbolized the left-wing ideology of the Socialist and Communist parties since its formation in 1947 through the 1980s. The largest union in the country, JTU enrolled more than 86 percent of the teaching force late in the 1950s, a decade during which there were intense and even violent confrontations between JTU and its allies on the one hand and the conservative government on the other, as the latter attempted to gain greater control of teachers and introduce a variety of controversial measures, such as moral education and a binding national course of study. Indeed, the history of post-1945 education could be written as a history of disputes and showdowns between the government and the union on every major educational issue for over three decades. These issues included, for example, national testing, teacher evaluation, textbook authorization, a national course of study, school management, the national anthem, the national flag, government-led school reforms, and internships. Hence, the government's education policy has been restrained as well as constrained and mediated by the opposition marshaled by the union.

For example, union critics of government-sponsored inservice education raised a crucial political question regarding its purpose: What does it serve? Teruhisa Horio (1988), a former intellectual spokesman for JTU and a former professor of education at the University of Tokyo criticized government-led inservice education as early as 1971:

> [Government-sponsored inservice training] threatens to make our teachers' desires for personal advancement directly dependent upon the power of a centralized system of administrative control. Thus, to realize their desire for higher positions within the organization of the school, teachers will increasingly have to perform successfully within government-sponsored programs of in-service training (*kenshu*). Moreover, as only those teachers who have already been deemed ideologically deserving of such training will be given the opportunity to participate in the necessary in-service programs [organized at the national level], the organization of elites within the school system will increasingly come under the direct control of the Ministry of Education. (p. 247)

A significant change in this pattern of confrontation started to occur in the 1980s, as the union's influence over teachers and the government started to diminish as a result of declining membership. Moreover, JTU split into two separate organizations over internal ideological conflicts in 1989: a moderate mainstream union, which continues to represent JTU, and a left-wing minority union. That change of power balance in favor of the Ministry of Education enabled the government to pass major legislation in the 1980s without significant opposition, such as a teacher certification reform and long-coveted internships for beginning public school teachers. In the past the union had been vehemently opposed to these government measures as an attempt to control teachers.

As of 1995, only 34 percent of the teaching force belonged to the JTU, while 43 percent of teachers were not affiliated with any union. At its 1995 annual convention, JTU decided to create a partnership with the Ministry of Education to promote education. The dramatic shift in the relationship between the major foes in the history of postwar education has eviscerated debate on critical educational issues, as effective opposition to government policy has all but disappeared. For example, when the Ministry of Education announced an initiative to reform teacher education in 1998 it became a law with little debate. Additionally, JTU's voice has barely been heard concerning the revised curriculum that will take effect in 2002.

The fourth strand in postwar Japanese education is the story of adolescents whose anti-school behavior has become a national preoccupation since the late 1970s. It is no overstatement to suggest that students have had more impact on educational change than any other group since the late 1970s. The legitimacy of teaching was challenged by students when incidents of student violence against teachers and school authorities became daily events at middle schools throughout the nation in the late 1970s and early 1980s. Fujita (1989) aptly comments:

> In any organization, legitimacy is the key to its maintenance and successful function. This is particularly the case in an educational organization. In such an organization as school, legitimacy relies on two mutually related factors: self-evidentness and communality. Self-evidentness here means that activities, both their modes and contents, are believed as self-evident and unquestionable, while communality means that activities are supported as necessary and reasonable by the people of a community concerned.... In the last ten years or so [the 1980s], both self-evidentness and communality seem to have been weakened, and hence the legitimacy of school education has been undermined. (p. 137)

Consequently, the traditional pattern of authoritarian control of students began to give way to less authoritarian forms of student management and teaching. Adolescents' needs, values, and respect for authority changed significantly as a result of economic affluence, social differentiation, the information age, and the internationalization of work and life. Their needs and values became multifaceted, and their compliance with adult expectations and control became increasingly context-dependent and subject to negotiation. In other words, adolescents' authority orientation changed markedly. Hence, teachers had little choice but consider teaching and student guidance strategies that reflected students' demands and interests. In recent years students have been resorting to a new form of disruption—creating classroom disorder—as an expression of their dissatisfaction and resistance to deep-seated conventional methods of didactic teaching and passive learning as well as rigid classroom management. Classroom disorder has been widely reported in the mass media as *gakkyu hokai*, a popular journalistic depiction of "classroom crisis." *Gakkyu hokai* is evident not only in general public schools but also in selective schools. For example, in 1998, a social studies teacher at a middle school affiliated with Naruto

Education University, regarded as a selective and prestigious school in Tokushima Prefecture, commented:

> One of the reasons why students become disorderly is that they do not understand the lesson because the content of the course of study is high. If students do not understand what is taught, they get bored and disruptive. More important, the basic cause of disorderly behavior is embedded in society that imposes pressure on entrance exam preparation.

The sustained, comprehensive education overhaul launched by the prime minister's initiative in 1984 was impelled in large part by the urgency of responding to students' anti-school behavior. Likewise, succeeding school reforms have followed suit. Japanese adolescents are important actors in changing schools, teaching, and the curriculum. Although adolescents are a vital cause for educational change, educational reforms are slow. Hence tension between adolescents and teachers continues largely unabated.

These four strands of postwar educational events constitute a broad background against which today's problems in Japanese education are explored in this volume. Next we will present a preliminary survey of teachers' opinions to capture briefly how they view their lives and work.

TEACHERS' VOICES

What is it like to be an elementary or a middle school teacher in Japan? This question is embedded in inquiries into teachers' lives, an approach becoming popular in the United States and Europe (see Goodson, 1992; Huberman, 1989). Teachers' life stories and life histories provide a context for gaining a good understanding of their work. As Goodson (1992) defines, "the life story is the 'story we tell about our life'; the life history is a collaborative venture, reviewing a wider range of evidence" [including a historical context] (p. 6). He argues that we must find ways "to sponsor the teacher's voice" (p. 12) to understand his or her work. Let us listen to teachers' voice as presented in our national PACT survey on teachers' lives (Fujita, et al. 1996).

How do Japanese teachers structure their everyday lives? One of the characteristics of teachers' lives in Japan is that they work long hours. As my research participants noted, teachers have no free time for lunch due to the responsibility of supervising students during lunch, and they can legally leave school around 3:50 P.M. However, teachers' actual work pattern is quite different from the official definition. The majority of teachers in one of the elementary schools we studied in Tokyo typically arrive at school by 8:00 a.m. and leave around 7:00 p.m. After children leave school around 3:30 p.m, teachers usually remain in school to participate in meetings, discharge non-instructional duties, check students' work, and prepare for lessons. In our study schools at the middle school level, teachers spend a significant amount of time on extracurricular activities and student guidance, which includes preparing students' applications for high schools. Our PACT survey reveals a similar national pattern of teachers' time allocation in their daily lives: nearly two-thirds of elementary and middle school teachers arrive at school between 7:30 and 8:00 a.m; and 35 percent of them leave school around 6:00 p.m., with another 35 percent leaving school by 7:00 p.m. It becomes evident that the majority of teachers work between ten and eleven hours at school every day. They typically wake up around 6:00 a.m. and go to bed between 11:00 and 12:00 p.m. Not surprisingly, on weekdays at home, 54 percent of the teachers spend one hour or less on school work while 20 percent spend little time on school work.

With respect to teaching load, 15 percent of elementary teachers teach 21-25 hours weekly while 54 percent teach 27-30 hours. 45 percent of middle school teachers, on the other hand, teach sixteen to twenty hours, and 34 percent teach 21 to 25 hours. Elementary teachers must teach all academic subjects, while middle school teachers teach specialized subjects. The overwhelming majority of teachers—76 percent at both levels—agree that their daily life is very busy.

What are Japanese elementary and middle school teachers' priorities in teaching? The PACT survey shows that their top priority is classroom instruction followed by the creation of a classroom community. 41 percent of elementary teachers place the first priority on instruction, while 29 percent emphasize classroom management. Likewise, classroom instruction is the first priority for 48 percent of middle school teachers, followed by classroom management, chosen by 17 percent. What emerges from these data is the fact that while similar percentages of teachers at both levels prioritize instruction, classroom management is the second priority for more elementary teachers than middle school teachers, reflecting different characteristics of teaching at the two levels. For example, an elementary teacher takes charge of students permanently located in a given classroom, in contrast to the middle school level where a teacher is assigned to instruct a particular subject and teaches different classes of students throughout the day. Building a classroom community is considered key to effective teaching, but most especially at the elementary level. Nonetheless, classroom management is considered important at both levels. Chapter 2 addresses this topic further.

Japanese schools are cooperatively managed by teachers. Both elementary and middle school teachers view cooperative management as a major source of stress, and an area of their work that supports classroom instruction only indirectly. Further, middle school teachers must address students' violence, bullying, and resistance to authority. They regard handling these problems as particularly stressful. Moreover, teachers' self-image is affected by the perceived decline of teacher authority. Eight of ten teachers at both levels believe that teacher authority is challenged by students and parents and that, overall, teacher authority has declined. Another source of tension is supervision of extracurricular activities, which are invariably emphasized at the middle school level. Two-thirds of middle school teachers devote a significant amount of time—a couple of hours daily at least—to the supervision of club activities. This issue will receive more attention elsewhere in this volume. Generally, there is much more stress and tension in teachers' work at the middle school level than the elementary level.

Teachers' stress at work in part stems also from their own conception of teaching. More than two-thirds of both elementary and middle school teachers believe that teaching is a holistic undertaking and must address all aspects of students' development (see chapter 2). Only one-fifth of teachers at both levels disagree with this conception of teaching. Self-sacrifice is an important element in teaching in the opinion of the majority of teachers—85 and 89 percent at the elementary and middle school levels, respectively. More than 80 percent of teachers at both levels feel that their work is as intensive as that of busy corporate employees. Nine out of ten teachers further believe that teachers require a sense of mission to be effective and to stay in teaching.

In teachers' opinions, teaching in Japan is predicated on overwork and self-sacrifice. Nearly 90 percent of teachers feel they are chronically tired. As a whole, however, 95 percent of teachers consider teaching to be rewarding. Only a handful of teachers disagree with this view. Moreover, a little over 50 percent of them believe that they have some degree of autonomy in teaching, an important feature of their work. The fact that teaching demands overwork and self-sacrifice does not lead to rejecting teaching as an unattractive occupation on the part of most teachers. In fact, only 30 percent of elementary and middle school teachers have even considered quitting, despite the difficulties. Over half of the teachers surveyed insist that they can make teaching successful as long as they have a sense of mission in teaching and enthusiasm for the work. Their view is supported by the belief that they can teach any student as long as they devote enough time and effort to teaching him or her. 65 and 60 percent of elementary and middle school teachers, respectively, share this belief.

Related to this shared premise of teaching is a strongly-rooted ethos that all normal children can develop the ability to learn well. This ethos attributes achievement to effort, not to innate ability. Therefore, differences in student achievement are thought to be a consequence of individual diligence and self-discipline. This attribution paradigm ignores innate ability as a criterion for assessing student performance, and accounts for the tradition in Japanese compulsory schools of consciously avoiding ability grouping. While this ethos still persists, 60 percent of middle school teachers now support the introduction of some type of ability grouping in selected subject areas.

Are teachers economically satisfied? One-third of both levels of teachers feel that they are content with their compensation while the remaining two-third are not. Likewise, one-third of them believe that they have relatively high social esteem, but the remainder—the majority—do not share the same opinions. Incidentally, according to a 1975 survey (Tominaga, 1979), elementary principals and teachers ranked 9th and 18th respectively in public esteem out of 82 occupations. Elementary teachers enjoyed higher prestige than civil and mechanical engineers, and white collar employees in large firms (U.S Department of Education, 1987).

In summary, Japanese teachers work for long hours each day. Teaching is intensified by the fact that they must undertake a broad range of such non-instructional responsibilities as cooperative school management based on a division of labor, supervision of club activities, and handling rising problems of student violence, bullying, and resistance to authority. Teachers share the view that teaching demands self-sacrifice as well as emotional and moral commitment. Notwithstanding these daunting issues, teaching is still rewarding for the vast majority of teachers. They believe that they can improve teaching if they have the desire to do so.

OVERVIEW OF THE BOOK

This volume comprises seven chapters. Following this introductory chapter, chapter 2 presents a broad view of the culture of teaching in Japan, focusing on several dimensions that reflect deep-seated Japanese practice. This chapter explores the culture of teaching at the elementary and middle school levels, with particular attention to five themes: teaching as a holistic undertaking, ethnopedagogy, teaching as craft, cooperative management, and intensification of teaching. These themes are closely related and make teaching in Japan distinctive. The culture of teaching as the accumulated experiential wisdom of teaching is a driving as well as conservative force. While it provides a guiding framework for teaching, it constrains teachers in adapting to change. The efficacy of the culture of teaching against the background of extensive social and economic change in Japan is now at issue. Yet teachers are disinclined to press for change in their taken-for-granted practice.

Chapter 3 deals with professional development or *kenshu* and Japanese strategies to promote teaching. Both teachers and the government promote initiatives in teacher development. Teacher-initiated *kenshu* is strong and deeply rooted in the Japanese culture of teaching, which stresses peer collaboration. Another equally important area of *kenshu* is teacher networking at the national level to promote professional development. This bottom-across approach is widespread throughout the country, and school-based professional development is particularly popular at the elementary level. Government initiatives, on the other hand, are characterized as being driven by a top-down structure in which the Ministry of Education formulates national policy on inservice education for teachers. These government programs began in the 1960s to compensate for what was considered inadequate postwar teacher preparation and to improve the teaching force. There are several types of *kenshu* programs developed by the government: leadership development offered by the National Education Center; internships for beginning public school teachers with a supervised, reflective induction into teaching; prefectural programs organized by the local education center to promote career objectives; and long-term *kenshu* through graduate study.

There are some salient issues in professional development. "Study lessons" that teachers organize to improve teaching, a primary initiative in school-based *kenshu*, are short in providing an empirical and theoretical basis for sustained, methodical refinement of practice. They are not explicitly designed to test theory and research findings. Government *kenshu* programs, on the other hand, tend to be fragmentary and are often viewed as impositions because they are formulated from above and mandatory. Teachers have little sense of ownership of professional development.

Chapter 4 turns to teacher preparation and social change. Postwar teacher education remained by and large unchanged for nearly four decades after the late 1940s. The significant restructuring of teacher education began only in the late 1980s in response to problems resulting from immense social transformation, which had started in the 1960s. As mentioned earlier, a central driving force for the restructuring of teacher education is Japanese youth who relentlessly challenged traditional school authority and resorted to violence as a way of displaying resistance to traditional schooling. The first major restructuring initiative was launched by a national task force in the mid-1980s with a strong backing by the conservative government. Reformers introduced some significant changes in the preparation of teachers, initiating advanced certification and higher requirements for teaching. Japan also finally began to place more emphasis on graduate preparation of teachers. The second major restructuring of teacher education got under way in the late 1990s to strengthen professional education for preservice students. Confronted by persistent problems of adolescent behavior, reformers resorted to ethnopedagogy to cope with them, representing a shift toward teacher education with an emphasis on a therapeutic pedagogy. Various reform initiatives since the 1980s pointed in the same direction, emphasizing the imperative to recognize students' diversified needs and the centrality of students' learning nested in intrinsic motivation.

Chapter 5 offers a descriptive account of the routines that beginning teachers at the elementary level develop, followed by an analysis of both their understanding of teaching and their strategies for learning to teach. Learning to teach is a complex, intersubjective process that occurs in multiple social settings at the school. Beginning teachers are active participants in this process of constructing the social reality of teaching, which involves intense engagement in seeking advice from experienced teachers and developing strategies in response to demands and problems. The culture of teaching into which new teachers are socialized influences both the process and outcomes of learning to teach. The influence of experienced teachers on beginners figures potently in this process. Beginners learn the cultural knowledge of teaching through casual conversations with and observations of experienced teachers. This mode of learning to teach has more influence on beginning teachers than the national internship program for beginning public school teachers introduced in 1989.

Chapter 6 explores the themes and assumptions of teaching that beginning teachers incorporate into their teaching. Beginning teachers hold beliefs that are isomorphic to those of experienced teachers regarding expectations for students, classroom management, and control of students. Teaching is characterized by the inclusion at the elementary level of the cognitive, moral, expressive, and social dimensions of children's development. Central to teaching is ethnopedagogy, which assumes that ligature is basic to the enhancement of children's orientation toward schooling. It is believed to be the foundation of the Japanese style of classroom management, with its emphasis on interpersonal relations and group harmony. Japanese teachers believe that control over students can be achieved by properly developing students' habits and putting a priority on practice over the codification of rules. In the first year of teaching, beginning teachers are extensively exposed to the inclusiveness of schooling and ethnopedagogy—salient characteristics of Japanese culture of teaching— tacitly transmitted to neophytes in the process of occupational socialization.

Chapter 7 focuses on the occupational socialization of beginning teachers, with particular attention to the perspectives on teaching that they develop, including their approaches to problems in teaching, collegial relationships, and relationships with parents and the community. Beginning teachers learn how to teach by participating in the social construction of teaching. They are actively involved in the reproduction of teaching, which is possible through an intersubjective process in which they interpret the relevance of the knowledge of teaching to which they are exposed. There is extensive face-face interaction among teachers, making interpersonal relations a pivotal factor in everyday school life. The beginning teachers' occupational socialization is a process in which the transmission of cultural knowledge of teaching plays an important role in individual teachers' decisions on teaching strategies.

Finally, this volume ends with some concluding remarks. They epitomize a critical reflection on educational reforms in Japan, the new emphasis on therapeutic pedagogy in teacher education, limits of ethnopedagogy in teaching, problems in teacher development, and remedies for the intensification of teaching.

CHAPTER 2

Culture of Teaching in Japan

A culture of teaching is an elusive notion, yet it captures both salient and latent characteristics of teaching. For two decades, Western scholars—especially Americans—have researched culturally unique features of Japanese schools, finding distinct contrasts to schools in their own countries. Publications by Cummings (1980), Rohlen (1983), Duke (1986), White (1987), Tobin and colleagues (1989), Peak (1991), Stevenson and Stigler (1992), and Lewis (1995), for example, epitomize the interest in Japanese education. These scholars have significantly contributed to the understanding of Japanese educational practice by making what is familiar to the Japanese strange. Likewise, it is a purpose of this volume to make explicit the Japanese culture of teaching, which is usually taken for granted by Japanese teachers and remains hidden in everyday teaching. We will use the term "teaching" to refer to teachers' professional actions.

The literature indicates that teaching hardly possesses a shared technical culture (for example, Sarason, 1971; Lortie, 1975). Moreover, the fact that teachers differ considerably in age, experience, social background, gender, academic preparation, competence, subject matter, and the level of teaching, does not provide a cogent, empirical basis for a consensual definition of the culture. These problems contribute to the difficulty of conceptualizing teaching as an occupational culture (Feiman-Nemser & Floden, 1986). But teachers do share work-related beliefs, knowledge, and practice. What Waller (1967) calls stereotypes are developed on the basis of observation of habitual teacher behaviors. His observation relates to Hammersley's (1980) notion of "typifications of situations and lines of actions" in teaching. Jackson (1990) speaks of "themes" that characterize teachers. Likewise, Hargreaves (1980) addresses the occupational culture of teachers in terms of themes that each have micro-macro linkages between the workplace and its environment. McPherson (1972) and Schofield (1982), on the other hand, describe teachers' beliefs as an ideology. Another view is that the culture of teaching is embedded in teacher reference groups, as pointed out by Pollard (1982).

The culture of teaching is multidimensional, but we will confine our focus to several related dimensions that reflect deep-seated Japanese practice. This chapter explores the culture of teaching in Japan at the elementary and middle school levels, with particular attention to five themes: teaching as a holistic undertaking, ethnopedagogy, teaching as craft, cooperative management, and intensification of teaching. These themes are closely interrelated and, in our view, make teaching in Japan distinctive. For other frameworks to examine the culture of teaching in Japan, the reader may review the recent works of Inagaki and Kudomi (1994) and Kudomi (1994), which offer a composite view of teaching.

TEACHING AS HOLISTIC UNDERTAKING

One of the prominent themes of teaching in Japan, in contrast to teaching in the U.S. or U.K., is its holistic character. In the United States emphasis at the elementary and middle school levels is decidedly on the cognitive process of teaching and learning, whereas in Japan it is more broad, encompassing the cognitive as well as social, moral, and expressive dimensions of students' experience (Shimahara and Sakai, 1995). The inclusiveness of teaching makes Japanese schooling distinct when viewed from Anglo-American perspectives and is deeply embedded in the culture of teaching. Teachers see the holistic nature of their work as essential to Japanese pedagogy and integral to their culture of teaching.

The holistic approach to schooling is symbolized by the inclusive goals of education as stated in school catalogs. For example, one elementary school aims to foster:

- robust and healthy children
- children who think deeply and are creative
- empathetic and cheerful children with a sensitive heart
- cooperative and diligent children
- children who get along well and help others

The goals of one middle school are to develop:

- robust and strong students whose human nature is enriched by creativity
- students who take initiative, have cheerful dispositions, and are healthy
- students who are rational and live just lives
- diligent students who can perform responsibly without hesitation

These educational goals are very broad and perhaps elusive. Yet what lies beneath these goals is a belief in a kind of teaching that can address the cognitive, moral, expressive, and physical dimensions of students. As an American observer of Japanese education puts it (Sato, 1996): "In fact, knowledge transmission is secondary to a more comprehensive emphasis on developing *ningen* (human beings), the primary teaching goal expressed by principals, teachers, and parents" (p. 123). Although each school phrases its goals somewhat differently, the above lists are typical of the goals of Japanese schools throughout the country. Compare the above goals with those of an American elementary school in New Jersey (Shimahara & Sakai, 1995):

> We recognize the importance of our children as individuals with specific needs, and we strive to provide a strong educational program that meets those needs at each step of development…. In order to implement this philosophy, we focus on the following goals:
>
> - to provide a strong foundation in math, reading, and language arts
> - to help children to explore and investigate the world through science and social studies
> - to help each child communicate in the most effective ways possible through oral and written languages (p. 58)

In contrast to the Japanese goals of schooling, these goals are framed in cognitive and instrumental terms and are very concrete.

To realize the broad goals of teaching, Japanese teachers promote school programs that encompass a wide spectrum of student activities and teacher responsibilities. These programs include: academic lessons, physical education (the responsibility of the classroom teacher at the elementary level and of a specialist at the middle school level), moral education, supervision of lunch service, school cleaning, club activity, swimming, home visits, and such school events as ceremonial events, retreats, excursion trips, and athletic and music festivals. The Ministry of Education's course of study, the binding official guideline for the national curriculum, defines the school curriculum as consisting of academic subjects, moral education, and "special activities," which include most of these non-academic activities. Teaching at the elementary level is most inclusive in that elementary teachers are expected to implement all the activities. Elementary teachers design teaching broadly, on the assumption that it is multifaceted. This conception of teaching is embedded in what is called *zenjin kyoiku* or whole-person education (Sato & McLaughlin, 1992). It is assumed that personal habits, motivation, and interpersonal relations are important parts of teaching that teachers are expected to address. Further, teachers' routine responsibilities also include fostering children's social development through social interactions.

Unlike elementary teachers, who are responsible for teaching all subjects except upper-level music and arts and crafts, middle school teachers specialize in particular subjects; but like elementary teachers, they are also responsible for whole-person education. In our national PACT survey (Fujita et al, 1996), 79 and 76 percent of elementary and middle school teachers reported respectively that they address students' entire personal development in teaching.

Ninth-grade homeroom teachers are extensively involved in placing students in high schools—a very heavy responsibility when combined with a normal teaching load. Because high school education is not compulsory in Japan, ninth graders must seek admission to high schools through entrance examinations. Placing students in high schools requires a prolonged process of guidance, which begins immediately after the summer vacation and lasts until February when students take entrance exams. It involves consultation with students and parents, performance assessment based on school records and tests, selection of high schools, and preparation and filing of applications. To provide effective student guidance based on personal knowledge of students, homeroom teachers are usually expected to teach the same group of students from seventh through ninth grade. This teaching as a holistic undertaking is supported by the design of the curriculum.

Student guidance or life guidance is another important area of inclusive teaching at both the elementary and middle school levels. The student guidance committee, composed of teachers, addresses a variety of concerns on student life both in and out of school; it also addresses student government, school cleaning, and other student-related health and safety issues. Every aspect of student lives is supervised by the committee. As part of student guidance, middle school homeroom teachers counsel students on bullying, violence, and other types of behavioral and emotional problems. In the U.S., this would be the domain of specialized counselors at both the elementary and secondary levels. Since the late 1970s, when students' behavior problems became a source of teachers' fixation, the homeroom teacher's responsibility has often become onerous. Yet teachers assume that responsibility as being intrinsic to their work—an assumption that it is an integral part of teaching, revealing a characteristic of the Japanese culture of teaching.

Counseling, part of student guidance, falls to the homeroom teacher or a group of teachers. It entails immediate interventions in incidents, investigations, consultations with parents, and resolution of problems. Teachers view counseling as time-consuming and emotionally draining, but only in extraordinary situations are incidents referred to outside specialists.

Student guidance was an extraordinarily demanding responsibility in one of the middle schools we studied. Teachers described it as a very disruptive school where student violence was disproportionate and uncontrollable in recent years, reminiscent of the early 1980s when the nation was gripped by widespread adolescent rebellious behavior. Student violence peaked in 1993 at the school and started to decline in 1994, reflecting the changing student culture and improved trust between teachers and ninth graders. Thus, when we were studying the school, teachers still appeared weary, jaded, and incredulous about improvement. When student violence was frequent, members of the student guidance committee took turns at patrolling the school every day; during special events, such as a sports festival, parents also volunteered to patrol the school to assist teachers. In addition, members of guidance committees at many middle schools patrol hot spots on a regular basis during the summer vacation to check student behavior (see LeTendre, 1996).

Club activities are encouraged at both the elementary and middle school levels. The national course of study defines clubs as collective activities organized to enhance cultural, athletic, and creative dimensions of student life at school. While at the elementary level club activities are normally offered once a week, at the middle school level they are much more extensive, taking place daily, even on Saturday and sometimes Sunday. Teacher supervision of club activities, however, is voluntary in principle.

Middle school teachers attach great importance to extracurricular club activities as a unique way for them to develop close relationships with students and get to know them better. The academic coordinator at the aforementioned middle school, for example, viewed these activities as "significantly contributing to the development of students' interests and their initiatives in organizing and promoting their own activities." He served as the coach of the guitar club, which won many awards for outstanding performance in local and national competitions. He devoted two hours to the club each Tuesday, Thursday, and Saturday. Likewise, over 50 percent of the teachers provided their time for club activities three or four times a week after school, though some were more willing than others.

At another school, club activities are an everyday event for one hour in the morning before school begins and two hours after school is over. Although this school represents a somewhat extreme case, findings from our national PACT survey (Fujita et al, 1996) indicate that 75 percent of middle school teachers and 22 percent of elementary teachers coach club activities. It is evident that club activities are very popular at the middle school level and that teachers are willing to spend a substantial amount of time on them every week. In comparison, elementary teachers' involvement in clubs is rather limited.

Why are clubs so popular with teachers and students alike? There is a widespread belief that clubs mold students into better persons. As a teacher respondent pointed out, students' voluntary participation in clubs teaches them not only particular skills but also the importance of rules and commitments, and how to function in a hierarchical organization. In other words, clubs offer a vital opportunity for adolescents to be socialized in a rule-bound, but also enriching and fun, setting. A ninth-grade homeroom teacher explained: In contrast to the elementary school where children learn interdependence through *fureai* or interaction, the middle school emphasizes students' independence and sociability. Clubs provide space for initiative and relationships. Teachers encourage disruptive and rebellious students to participate in clubs in the hope that they will learn to work with others and follow the rules. As pointed out earlier, it is often through clubs that teachers gain personal knowledge of students based on the interpersonal relationships with them. Put differently, clubs provide a very useful vehicle for student guidance. LeTendre (1996) aptly suggests: "Understanding oneself in a Japanese school takes place in a group—a team readying for a sports festival or a choir practicing for the choral context" (p. 291).

Let us turn to another unique feature of middle school education that addresses holistic teaching: staff organization. In the U.S. and U.K. teachers are organized into departmental units by specialty. In such a structural arrangement, subject-matter subcultures are likely to develop. In contrast, Japanese teachers at the middle school level are organized into grade units cutting across subject boundaries to deal with common problems and tasks pertaining to a particular grade level. From an organizational point of view, the grade-based structure places priority on students' needs, the satisfaction of which requires faculty coordination and commitment, rather than on faculty needs for discussing and developing curriculum materials in particular subject areas. Although Japanese middle school teachers have subject-area groups that can address such needs, they meet infrequently, partly because the curriculum in each subject area is standardized nationally, which negates much need for curriculum material development and coordination. In comparison, in the U. S. and U.K., teachers have the responsibility of constructing the curriculum, which necessitates strong departmental initiative by subject area.

In middle schools, faculty are grouped into three grade units, each of which constitutes a functionally separate entity coordinated by a senior teacher. The ninth-grade unit of teachers, for example, addresses as its common objectives a wide gamut of tasks: student guidance, placement of students in high schools, school events, counseling, and supplementary drills for entrance exams. Consequently, each grade unit constitutes a strong subculture based on close interaction on a daily basis, geographical proximity within the staff room, and shared work and perspectives.

It is to be expected that the Japanese notion of teaching as a holistic undertaking is more readily integrated into the functional pattern of teachers' work at the elementary level than at the middle school level, where teaching responsibility is undifferentiated. As we have seen, however, at the middle school level teaching is differentiated only in terms of classroom teaching. Teachers broadly address the other area of schooling as a collective undertaking to be shared and promoted. In this sense, teaching is viewed at both levels as encompassing the cognitive, social, emotional, moral, and physical development of children.

The rationale for teaching as a holistic undertaking is grounded in the Japanese belief that schooling is an inclusive process emphasizing personal development and experiential learning (Fukuzawa, 1996; Sato, 1996). The basic assumption underlying holistic teaching is that teaching is centered on the development of character and that character can be inculcated by providing students with proper guidance and well-directed tasks (LeTendre, 1996). As mentioned earlier in this chapter, the school curriculum consists of academic instruction, moral education, and special activities. The last category is very broad, and the national course of study offers official justification for holistic teaching. Holistic teaching provides the overlapping layers of social contextualization for personal development through experiential learning.

ETHNOPEDAGOGY

The second theme of the Japanese culture of teaching is ethnopedagogy (Shimahara & Sakai, 1995). Ethnopedagogy is a theory of teaching grounded on time-honored shared beliefs embodied in the Japanese culture. Teachers use these beliefs to develop relationships of trust with students and encourage, inspire, and exhort them to meet their expectations. The tenets of ethnopedagogy are fundamental at all levels of instruction, though they are more saliently expressed and shared among teachers at the elementary than the middle school level as teaching shifts its focus from inclusive child-centered orientation to specialized academic subjects in middle schools.

Ethnopedagogy is a folk theory of teaching shared among Japanese teachers as a frame of orientation. It is not identified as a research-based concept or as a field of study in teacher education and scholarly circles. Instead, it is intrinsic to the craft of teaching formulated by practitioners and reproduced through self-discovery, teacher discourse, and inservice education. The significance of ethnopedagogy resonates among the mentors of beginning teachers, administrators, and officials of boards of education and the Ministry of Education. This reveals that it is a cultural concept widely accepted throughout Japan and learned independently of teacher education at college. Likewise, Japanese teachers' cultural knowledge, identified here as ethnopedagogy, is a broadly-espoused ethos of teaching in the schools we studied. Teachers are a fiduciary agent of ethnopedagogy and often interpret teaching competence in terms of its application to the motivation of children.

Ethnopedagogy concentrates on ligature—close interpersonal relations—as the primary condition for effective teaching and learning. This central concept of ethnopedagogy is often referred to as *kizuna* or *kakawari*. Kizuna is believed to foster empathy and what is characterized as "touching of the hearts." It is "attachment" (Rohlen, 1989), a notion ubiquitously stressed in Japanese culture.

As our elementary teacher participants told us, the starting point of ethnopedagogy is the appreciation of the feelings by teachers that shape children's lives—particularly their emotional commitment to children, which leads to the fostering of the bond between teachers and children. The attachment that evolves from this bond is marked by shared feelings of inclusiveness and trust. Teachers believe that effective teaching is enhanced by this ligature and that developing it often takes precedence over technical competence in teaching. Because the ligature creates an environment of trust, it enables teachers to inspire children to meet their expectations. Additionally, the significance of the ligature in Japanese education means that the most important teacher aptitude is believed to be an affection for children and an understanding of their hearts. Thus, priority is placed on the emotional foundation of teaching.

Teachers speak of *kokoro*—the heart—as a basis of education. For example, a veteran elementary teacher declared: "My focus is on educating children's *kokoro*, an important concern throughout my teaching career. Another is to foster their ability to empathize with others, *omoiyari*. I want to create a classroom environment where every child feels comfortable and secure." A first-grade teacher also asserted that the teacher's heart and sensitivity is a critical attribute of teacher competence and that "my challenge is to broaden my receptivity to children, to accept and understand all children."

Likewise, teachers and administrators at middle schools highlight the ligature between students and teachers as a basis of order in the school. Teachers share the view that developing both personal knowledge and strong bonds with students are critical in gaining their trust. Hence, as mentioned earlier, it is common practice for teachers to teach the same group of students for three uninterrupted years, from seventh through ninth grade. Teachers can thus "grasp [understand] children's *kokoro*" through the relationships they develop over an extended period. In the view of a principal, "reading the students' *kokoro*" is critical in offering effective guidance.

Teachers' repeated references to *kokoro* suggest its ontological status in the universe of a child's experience. Self-identity and relationships with the world, including peers, families, and teachers, are thought to be revealed through the heart. In this sense, the heart is "the centerpiece for self-development that places empathy and consideration of others as integral to self-identity" (Sato, 1996, p. 123). In other words, *kokoro* is the primary window through which a child's identity and universe are communicated and understood, a "root image" of the interpersonal world.

Ethnopedagogy is commonly embodied in elementary classroom management. Let us explore several tenets of classroom management to identify ethnopedagogy's role (Shimahara, 1998). First, teachers design classroom management to provide a process and a structure in which children learn to become members of a group. The group is the most potent context in the children's lives, a context in which cognitive and non-cognitive experiential learning occurs. Elementary teachers we studied unambiguously pointed out that unless children are smoothly socialized within the group, it is difficult to promote effective teaching and learning in the classroom. Their classroom management techniques highlight the importance of harmonious development of the heart and the body through participation in group life. Children are expected to develop emotional dispositions to group life and the skills to organize groups, to participate in their activities, and to learn appropriate roles in classrooms.

Second, a critical task of classroom management, in teachers' view, is to create a community where the heart, empathy, emotional security, and trustful relations are promoted. Japanese socialization is potent, enduring, and pervasive in accentuating emotions throughout childhood (Hess & Azuma, 1991; Azuma, Kashiwagi, & Hess, 1981; De Vos, 1973), again stressing the primacy of *kokoro* as a central concept in Japanese education.

Third, building a classroom community is in large measure predicated on children's participation in self-management. Children's active involvement in building a classroom community is considered an important part of schooling, and so teachers prioritize building students' skills in self-management. Self-management involves setting goals for the class, assigning division of work, and performing such duties as cleaning, lunch service, and student monitoring. Children sign up for different kinds of activities (called *kakari*), such as library, assembly, physical education, bulletin board, treasures for classroom activities, study coordination, and the like. Two monitors, a boy and a girl, are usually in charge of duties, including conducting a brief morning meeting and an afternoon reflection meeting, cleaning the chalkboards, writing entries in the class diary, and calling the class to attention at the beginning and end of each period.

There is a significant degree of similarity in elementary and middle school class-room management. Elementary and middle school classrooms are organized in sim-ilar fashion: students have homerooms, which are assigned to teachers whose primary responsibility is to develop a classroom community. Student and faculty organiza-tions in middle school are alike, placing priority on student needs and tasks in the homeroom: both are grouped in grade and homeroom units. Like elementary teach-ers, homeroom teachers in middle school are responsible for supervising their home-rooms and a host of activities providing student guidance, placing students in high school (in case of ninth graders), monitoring lunch service and cleaning, organizing participation in retreats and excursion trips, sports and music festivals, and the like.

To promote a classroom community, each homeroom in middle school empha-sizes student participation in self-management, which entails creating classroom goals and assigning the division of work—tasks and assignments identical to those in elementary school. Student monitors write classroom diaries describing daily activities and events, which are shared with the homeroom teacher; these diaries pro-vide an emotional connection between students and the teacher. Homeroom teach-ers also encourage students to write personal journals focused on their lives, which are also submitted to the teachers for their comments. Student journals provide an interpersonal context where both the student and the homeroom teacher can pro-mote *kakawari* or bonding. As an eighth-grade female homeroom teacher put it, "I want my students to feel I am part of their lives," emphasizing the prominence of trustful relationships between her and her students. She attributed the primary cause of student rebellion against school authorities, which often occurs in her school, to the absence of trust and communication between teachers and students.

A middle school head teacher explored the significance of *kakawari* in another context. Students at the middle school level are heterogeneously grouped through-out Japan to provide equality to all students during compulsory education, and teachers follow a didactic method of instruction, putting emphasis on transmission of knowledge rather than on the reflective and interactive learning typical in ele-mentary schools. This emphasis stems in part from pressures generated by high school entrance examinations, which require that teachers transmit knowledge to students tested in the examinations. Consequently, classrooms have not only aca-demically slow students but also unmotivated and rebellious students who often dis-rupt lessons unless they are controlled. This is a common problem, resulting in what the Japanese mass media characterize as a "classroom crisis." The head teacher, how-ever, viewed the primary cause of student resistance as the absence of *kakawari* between the classroom teacher and rebellious students. She was confident that these students could be integrated into an orderly classroom under proper guidance when there is *kizuna*, or attachment, between students and their instructors. Thus, Japanese teachers are likely to interpret such a problem in the framework of ethnope-dagogy, instead of considering different student groupings or unconventional instructional methods to meet unmotivated students' needs.

Why do Japanese teachers attach great importance to *kizuna*, *kakawari*, and group life? Their ethnopedagogy simply reflects the cultural emphasis on the relationship of the individual to the group, which in turn reflects how the Japanese define themselves. The Japanese see themselves as part of a network of human relations and pay specific attention to others' behaviors, feelings, and opinions. As Kiefer (1976) aptly observes, "The Japanese tend to include within the boundaries of [the] concept of self much of the quality of the intimate social groups of which the individual is a member" (p. 281). This explains why the Japanese develop what Lebra (1976) calls social preoccupation, a tendency to be highly sensitive to social interactions and relationships. Thus, "the identification of self and other," Smith (1983) suggests, "is always indeterminate in the sense that there is no fixed center from which, in effect, the individual asserts a non-contingent existence" (p. 81). For example, the "individuality" that is celebrated in school programs is viewed as developing from harmonious relationships between individual children and their peers within a context of social interaction.

Befu (1986) points out that it is personal interdependence and interconnectedness that determine who one is. The Japanese do not see their selves as distinct from all others and immutable, as Americans do (Hsu, 1963). "Personhood," which Befu calls a preferable term to "self" to identify the image of a Japanese person, involves not only grounding oneself in a network of interpersonal relations, but also moral commitment to others, reciprocity of relational commitment, and extension of trust. *Kizuna* is an exemplification of such interpersonal relations and trust.

As noted above, ethnopedagogy is actualized in classrooms that require student self-management.This reflects the Japanese cultural ideology that emphasizes individual responsibilities and obligations (De Vos, 1973; Dore, 1987). That ideology remains potent in contemporary Japan and is the underpinning of what characterizes Japan as a role-oriented society (Azuma, 1994). Individuals not only are dedicated to performing their roles but also identify themselves in terms of those roles in a particular institutional setting (Nakane, 1972). The Japanese achieve social self-realization by fulfilling a role that they assume as part of an interconnected network.

In summary, ethnopedagogy is embedded in the cultural definitions of personal identity, interpersonal relations, empathy, and role performance. Viewed this way, ethnopedagogy is not a cultural formulation unique to teaching. Rather, it reflects the broader cultural definition of the relationships between the individual and the group and the emotional qualities that mediate the relationships.

TEACHING AS CRAFT

We turn to the third theme of the culture of teaching: teaching as craft. Teaching is learned, transmitted, and reformulated as a craft in Japan, and Japanese teachers commonly view craft knowledge as embedded in teacher-generated experience and knowledge—a form of professional expertise based on the accumulation of pedagogical wisdom. This notion of teaching is predicated on three premises. First, knowledge, skills, and the frame of orientation requisite for teaching are intrinsic to the culture of teaching shared and modified through practice. Second, the content of professional development is derived from the shared repertoire of practice, rather than from research and academic scholarship. The conception of teaching based on craft knowledge places relatively little emphasis on theoretical and scientific bases for teachers' work. Third, teaching as craft fosters the view that informal teacher learning and formalized professional development via inservice education are the best vehicles for conveying craft knowledge.

Customarily, craft is understood as an apprenticeship through which occupational practice from the past is perpetuated. In the past, craft as a metaphor for teaching has more often than not represented a habitual practice. The recent American literature on teaching that focuses on reflective practice in the classroom, however, contributes to the construction of teaching embedded in craft knowledge, which underscores teachers' reflective judgment in understanding and enhancing classroom practice. It is significant that teaching as craft received important attention in the American Educational Research Association's 1992 *Review of Research in Education* (Grant, 1992). Craft knowledge as accumulated wisdom complements research-generated knowledge for teaching.

Grimmett and MacKinnon (1992) view craft knowledge of teaching in terms of what Shulman (1987) calls "pedagogical content knowledge." Their delineation of craft knowledge of teaching includes pedagogical knowledge with emphasis on skills, competencies, and dispositions which are developed in response to the practical demand for making teaching effective. Craft knowledge is an experientially-grounded repertoire constructed by teachers to deal with evolving events in the classroom. Additionally, teaching as craft involves reflective practice. Schön's (1983, 1987) work focused on reflection-in-action has had a highly impressive impact on the field of teaching (see Schön, 1991; Clift, Houston & Pugach, 1990). Reflection-in-action is an epistemological process in which practitioners focus on dealing with practical problems inherent in uncertain and conflicting situations. It consists of reflective performance and solving problems to which scientific knowledge cannot be directly applied. Schön rejects technical rationality as the sole epistemology of practice that views professional knowledge as the application of theory and technique derived from scientific knowledge. In brief, new meaning is now being attributed to craft knowledge, defining it in the context of reflective practice.

Likewise, teaching as craft in Japan does not simply represent a habitual practice. In a very significant sense, it is developed, modified, and transmitted through reflective practice. The postwar history of teacher education, which stimulated initiatives for professional development and the promotion of teaching as craft, will be reviewed first in this chapter. In 1947, based on the recommendations made by the American Mission of Education, Japan underwent drastic school reforms, including a new teacher education system with emphasis on the liberal arts, that replaced teacher training conducted at prewar normal schools. An "open-certification system" was introduced, in which colleges and universities could participate in teacher education without direct control by the Ministry of Education. By the 1970s, the new system had led to a proliferation of teacher education in which more than two-thirds of Japanese colleges and universities participated. Also under this new system, requirements for certification remained minimal until the mid-1980s with respect to professional studies and clinical experience. For example, only fourteen credits in professional studies and two weeks of student teaching were required for secondary certification. In other words, although formal teacher preparation became a popular program attracting large numbers of college students, it provided an insufficient grounding in teaching.

The primary responsibility of universities has been commonly viewed as providing preservice education. Only in the 1990s did the number of universities that offer advanced degree programs for full-time teachers begin to increase. Once preservice students have completed their educations, however, most of them become disconnected from universities and education professors. Our research participants invariably fell into this category. Likewise, most university professors are rarely involved in studying and improving teaching at the elementary and secondary levels. Their scholarship is often unrelated to practice in the classroom. This is most apparent during student teaching, when the university supervisor generally serves as a liaison but not a mentor or researcher, while the cooperating teacher assumes total charge for exposing student teachers to the culture and practice of teaching.

In the postwar context of deteriorating teacher education, creating opportunities for teacher development became vital. Both teachers and government responded to the call for initiatives to promote teacher development. Professional development that draws on the shared repertoire of practice—that is, the culture of teaching—assumed centrality in promoting teaching as craft. *"Kenshu,"* which refers to professional development activity, is the common vehicle for teachers to promote teaching. Another term used to refer to *kenshu* is inservice education or *genshoku kyoiku*. Because chapter seven focuses on professional development, it is sufficient here to discuss how it highlights teaching as craft.

There are several types of *kenshu*, two of which will be mentioned here. The first is school-based professional development, which is a peer-driven model of *kenshu*. This is the most popular type of *kenshu* and is extensively developed throughout the country, especially at the elementary level. A "study promotion" committee at each school organizes professional development activities for faculty. In essence, school-based *kenshu* focuses on improving teaching through a series of systematically organized "study lessons" on a particular theme, such as science education. These lessons involve extensive peer planning and collaboration, and are presented to students for observation and critique by peers. They are designed to provide the opportunity for reflection-in-action, in which craft knowledge of teaching is examined and reformulated. The peer-driven model of teacher development is also widely subscribed to by municipal and prefectural associations of teachers. The latter designate particular schools every year where study lessons are organized for observation and analysis by members of the associations. This model draws on peers as resources, collaborators, and professional referees. In short, peer teachers are central in promoting teaching as craft.

Government-sponsored *kenshu* is also extensively developed across the country. Prefectural boards of education offer a broad range of obligatory and optional courses and seminars. The obligatory courses target the professional competencies of teachers who are at specific stages in their teaching careers while optional courses focus on particular issues and interests. Internships for beginning teachers are part of government-sponsored *kenshu*; the prefectural boards of education are responsible for implementing the out-of-school component whereas the mentors, who are senior teachers in the interns' schools, organize the in-house component focused on instructional improvement. These *kenshu* programs largely conform to the model of teaching as craft described above. They are organized by instructional supervisors or *shido shuji* at the prefectural education centers; these people are teachers who are on leave from school to serve as staff members of the centers. Basically, they are teacher peers whose experiences as teachers and views of professional development have strong influence in the selection of topics, course materials, and resource persons in *kenshu* programs. In fact, instructional supervisors draw extensively on other experienced and skilled teachers, school administrators, and researchers at research institutes who represent familiarity with and a strong background in teaching as resource persons for each center.

Craft knowledge is embedded in teachers' biographies. Knowles (1992), for example, emphasizes that biography is critically important for understanding the formation of a teacher role identity and thinking about his or her classroom practice. Canadian researchers draw on a broad genre of studies of teachers' lives to situate teacher education in social contexts, using teachers' voices to offer active accounts of teaching from their personal perspectives (Goodson, 1995). In exploring how teaching as craft is embedded in a broad context of Japanese teachers' lives, we have found motifs that mark salient features in teachers' lives. Using the life-course interviews with both elementary and middle school teachers, we will illuminate these motifs.

The first motif is an induction into teaching mediated by informal mentoring, which occurs in the context of everyday teacher discourse. Our participants remarked that senior colleagues strongly influenced their early careers, especially in the schools where they first started teaching. Senior colleagues are seen as a source of pedagogical knowledge and skills—the cultural knowledge of teaching upon which beginners depend to improve their teaching. While there is no formal status distinction among teachers, experienced teachers are expected to assume mentor roles to guide less experienced colleagues. Informally shaped mentoring relationships are an important part in early teachers' lives.

This leads to the second motif, a supportive environment. That environment has a pivotal impact on teachers, especially in the first several years. Our respondents recalled that they were given more freedom to concentrate on their classrooms than were experienced teachers with additional responsibilities; this freedom enabled them to explore teaching strategies with little constraint. They also suggested that a sense of camaraderie created by their senior colleagues was an essential condition for teacher development.

The third motif is the influence of networking with colleagues, especially teachers from other schools, on professional development. Interactions with colleagues in *kenshu* meetings outside one's own workplace is viewed as a source of intellectual as well as emotional stimulation. These interactions entail the social construction of teaching and contribute to self-confidence. They result in the development of a reference group that helps to define individual teachers' beliefs, attitudes, and values.

Critical events constitute the fourth motif. These are events, defined in the context of personal experience, which augment teachers' professional development and enhance confidence by encouraging self-reflection and construction of metaphors for teaching. Many of the teachers interviewed recalled such consequential events. For example, one elementary teacher mentioned that the birth of her child was a very positive experience in her career. Raising her child enabled her to gain a deep, enduring insight into child psychology that she would not have learned sufficiently otherwise.

The fifth motif relates to changes that occur in teachers' roles during their professional careers. These shifts represent an extension of roles and relationships, which contributes to professional development. For example, Japanese teachers are periodically transferred to different schools to provide them with a broad exposure to a variety of schools and to ensure the equality of resources allocated to schools. These transfers sometimes correspond to distinct phases in a teacher's career. Elementary and middle school teachers perceive the first several years of teaching as a stage of coping and exploring, concerned solely with teaching in the classroom. The second phase of development entails broadening their perspectives on teaching and assuming a variety of responsibilities, including important committee work. Their involvement in in-house professional development becomes more substantive and focused. The third phase involves the assumption of leadership roles in a third or fourth school, such as chairperson of the study promotion committee or coordinator of school programs. At the middle school level, grade-level coordinators, especially the ninth-grade coordinator, play a significant role. Teachers' views in this phase are broadened to encompass oversight of the entire school. They spend a substantial amount of time promoting schoolwide activities. Teachers who reach this level in their careers are typically in their forties and considered veterans.

The sixth motif is the impact of peer-driven *kenshu* on teachers' lives. This type of *kenshu* assumes centrality for many teachers in their professional development. Its contribution to their development looms much larger than it does to teachers in the United States, where graduate education as a means to enhance teaching qualifications and professional development is more common and widespread than the other types of teacher development initiatives. The degree to which Japanese teachers and schools are involved in *kenshu*, however, varies considerably, as discussed in chapter eight. To illustrate teacher participation in *kenshu*, let us refer to a first grade teacher who is in her mid-forties. At her first school, she participated in a study program offered by the Tokyo Municipal Research Institute (*Token*) for one year. In her second school, she joined a privately-organized study group that focused on the teaching of the Japanese language, which was promoted through discussions and study lessons.

Subsequently, she was chosen as a study member by *Token* and granted a one-year leave from her school to study children's self-expression. In her present school, she is in charge of the Japanese program and represents her school in the district Japanese Language Association of Teachers. It meets twice a month and sponsors study lessons at selected sites throughout the district. In addition, she actively participates in a study program on science education at her school, which also requires planning and organizing study lessons.

These overlapping motifs shed light on how teaching as craft is embedded in teachers' lives. They reveal how teachers are enculturated into the culture of teaching and also recreate it. Informal mentoring, camaraderie, teacher roles, and professional development initiatives color and enrich teachers' lives.

COOPERATIVE MANAGEMENT

The culture of teaching is a complete representation of the typified teacher actions and beliefs that inform teaching. We have included in this cultural portrait teaching as a holistic undertaking, ethnopedagogy, and teaching as craft. We now address the fourth theme, cooperative management of schools by faculty, which is related to teaching as a holistic undertaking. Cooperative management is part and parcel of teachers' work in Japan and displays both a marked contrast between teaching in Japan and in the U. S. and a remarkable parallel between the cooperative management of the classroom by students and of the school by teachers. Both students and faculty assume particular responsibilities that constitute *kakari,* or assigned roles. *Kakari* make up a matrix in the division of assignments. Student and teacher cooperative management is designed to build a classroom community and a school community, respectively. Teacher cooperative management epitomizes how teachers view teaching: teaching is holistic, comprising all dimensions of schooling, and teachers are involved in every aspect of students' lives at school. In an elementary school principal's view, school management is composed of four types: educational, personnel, administrative, and facility. Teachers are charged with educational management, and the principal discharges the remaining three types of management.

Central to cooperative "educational" management is *komu bunsho* or faculty division of work, which details the "system of school operation" in every school, as presented below. All teachers are charged with specific responsibilities as identified in the division of work chart, which outlines the infrastructure of management of schooling. In contrast to Japanese schools which are characterized by the diffuse responsibilities of teachers, there is no such structure of work in American schools, where personnel roles are clearly delineated.

To appreciate the salient characteristics of cooperative management, we now review the organizational structure of the Japanese school. The principal is positioned at the head of the organization and is assisted by the head teacher; below these two administrators the organization is a horizontal structure of the teaching staff,

which plays a key role in the operation of the school. The division of work presented in tables 1 and 2 is typical in Japanese schools and includes several common
departments: academic programs, professional development (subsumed under school
programs in the above middle school), special activities, life guidance, and health.
Each department has subdivisions, and except for business management, which is
run by business staff, all other departments are staffed by teachers who are expected
to provide a broad range of planning, paperwork, and implementation. For example,
the department of school programs entails many subdivisions that plan and coordinate curriculum, school events, instruction, moral education, ordering textbooks,
acquisition of audiovisual and computer equipment and books, and the like. Each
school has several schoolwide coordinators who contribute to daily operation of the
school: coordinators of school programs, professional development, life guidance,
special activities, and health.

Table 1: System of School Operation at a Japanese Elementary School

Principal						
Head Teacher						
Faculty Meeting			Operation Committee			
Dept. of School-Community Relations	Dept. of Health	Dept. of Life Guidance	Dept. of School Programs	Dept. of Professional Develop-ment	Dept. of Special Activities	Dept. of Subject Study
PTA Activities, Public Relations	Health, Hygiene	Life Guidance Within and Outside School, Hazard Prevention, Safety, Cleaning, Counseling	Curriculum, School Events, Textbooks, Attendance	*Kenshu* Programs	Student Government, Club Activities, School Events, Classroom Activities	Japanese, Social Studies, Math, Science, Music, Life Science, PE, Arts/Craft, Home Economics

These coordinators constitute the school operation committee, the most vital committee in the school, which is chaired by the coordinator of school programs and
includes the principal and head teacher. The primary functions of the committee are
to review and plan various programs and events at its weekly meeting and to advise
the coordinator of school programs. The coordinator of school programs is pivotal in
cooperative management and is responsible for coordinating and integrating all academic and non-academic activities at the school, encompassing class schedules,
school events, special activities, and a broad range of activities proposed by faculty
committees. The principal appoints this coordinator, a competent veteran teacher,

from among the ranks of the teaching staff. The academic coordinator works very closely with colleagues as well as administrators on a daily basis. Regarded as the third most influential position after the principal and the head teacher, the coordinator has a heavy workload in addition to a normal teaching assignment, overseeing the operation of the entire school.

Table 2: System of School Operation at a Japanese Middle School

Principal				
Head Teacher				
Grade-level Coordinators	Faculty Meeting	Operation Committee	Coordinators of Specialized Subjects	
Dept. of Business Administration	Dept. of Life Guidance	Dept. of School Programs	Dept. of Special Activities	Dept. of Health
	Student Guidance, Health, Counseling	Curriculum, Prof. Development, School Events, Moral Ed. Textbooks, Library, Audio-visual Equipment, Computer Technology	Student Government, Classroom Assembly, Club Activities, Student Placement, Artistic Events	Health Guidance, Health Check-up, School Lunch, Beau-tification Guidance, etc.

In a school where professional development is a priority, the coordinator of professional development is an influential position. She is also appointed by the principal, which reflects the schoolwide significance of her role. She heads the committee of *kenshu* programs, and her responsibility is to organize and implement *kenshu* programs. At the middle school level, where student guidance is a critical concern because of frequent student violence and disruptive behavior—which occurs more often in middle schools—the guidance coordinator plays a very vital role.

A school is substantially run by the teaching staff in Japan, and everyday operation of the school is accomplished by faculty self-management. Participation in cooperative management is taken for granted as part of teachers' lives in school, and very few complain about it. Holistic teaching and cooperative management are the linchpin of schooling at the elementary and secondary school levels and epitomize the deeply-rooted Japanese notion of how teaching is constructed and managed. In this regard, cooperative management exemplifies the culture of teaching, as does holistic teaching.

INTENSIFICATION OF TEACHING

We now explore the intensification of teaching, the fifth theme characteristic of the Japanese culture of teaching. Intensification of teaching has been a common concern in the U.S. and U.K. since the 1980s (Hargreaves, 1994; Apple, 1989). It refers to an increasing loss of teacher autonomy caused by prescribed programs, mandated curricula, and step-by-step methods of instruction, combined with pressure to respond to various innovations and diversification of students' academic and social needs. In the American and British contexts, the intensification of teaching accelerated in significant part as a result of school reforms to improve student performance, which mandated higher academic standards and newly introduced state or national tests in the 1980s and 1990s.

In contrast, it is in large part the culture of teaching that intensifies teaching in Japan. In other words, the pressure comes from within. Teaching is "intensive" because teachers are expected to adhere to the collectively-defined ethos of teaching. Intensification of teaching, however, is a more salient phenomenon in middle schools than elementary schools. At the middle school level it is caused by pressure stemming from teachers' work outside classroom teaching discussed earlier, including cooperative management, placement of students in high schools, club activities, and student guidance. Especially, student behavior problems loom larger over the past two decades and substantially contribute to the intensification of teachers' work. As social change impacts middle schools, it creates more problems, and teaching becomes even more intensified. Thus, teachers' responsibilities constantly generate pressure on them to perform labor-intense routines that require extensions of their roles and in turn entail more work.

A vignette from an interview with a ninth-grade teacher who served as the grade-level coordinator at his school illustrates what he called the "unending work" of teachers and illustrates the intensification of teaching:

> In our work, there is neither beginning nor end because it just continues. So I am extremely busy. It would be the best to complete everything at school, but it is impossible. I have to bring my work home and spend one or two hours on it every day. And on top of that I also use weekends to work on it. To be frank, I spend 50 percent of my time on paperwork and the remaining time on instruction and related work. We cannot complete paperwork during our free periods at school and even after school. As a result, I have to bring it home. I often wonder if we can do it more efficiently. But, I feel we cannot make education more efficient.

This teacher's comments refer to his work placing students in high schools. During the busy months of placement work from November through January, he often left his school as late as 8:00 p.m. as did many of his colleagues. He declared that intensification of teaching he described is their "*shukumei*" (lot), or what ninth homeroom teachers are expected to undergo, but he did not challenge this expectation because it is deeply-seated in the culture of teaching.

Intensification of teaching is also highlighted by *shido*, which calls for teachers' involvement in every aspect of students' lives at school. In teachers' vocabulary, *shido* is an elusive folk term that refers to a broad range of teacher activities: formal instruction, guidance, induction, training, supervision, directing, and scaffolding. But the technical definition of *shido* is "to teach." Teachers consider every situation where a teacher-student relationship is present as involving *shido,* which, as Sakai (1998) suggests, is a major source of intensified teaching. Adapted from Sakai's work, the following is an inventory of situations in which teachers invoke *shido* (1998, p. 242):

A. Instruction
　1. *Shido* refers to teaching students to learn; teaching subjects, reading comprehension, physical education, and self-expression, etc.
　2. *Shido* involves supervision of students in self-organized activities, such as preparation for a music contest.
B. Student Guidance
　1. *Shido* is employed in student guidance, cleaning, inspection of student uniforms, entering and leaving the classroom, leaving school, and lunch service.
　2. *Shido* is invoked to explain why teachers reprimand students who violate school rules.
　3. *Shido* is invoked when advice is given to students in incidents of refusal to attend school, violence, and bullying.
C. Student Placement
　1. *Shido* is given to place students in high schools and employment.
　2. *Shido* is offered in selecting a high school for admission.
　3. *Shido* is given to students in preparing for entrance examinations.
D. Supervision
　1. *Shido* refers to coaching for club activities and athletic and music festivals.
　2. *Shido* is given for retreats, excursions, nature classrooms, and ceremonies.

The above widely-varied application of the term *shido* reveals its pervasiveness in holistic teaching and illustrates how the intensification of teaching results from teachers' adherence to holistic teaching.

Elementary school teachers embrace holistic teaching, but intensification of teachers' work is not as pervasive at the elementary level as the middle school level. Unlike middle school teachers, elementary teachers are not accountable for several labor-intensive areas of work, including placement of students in high schools, club activities, student guidance on behavior problems, and preparation of students for high school entrance examinations. Each area requires an intense and prolonged commitment of middle school teachers. The difference in teachers' accountability between the two levels elucidates the relative lack of intensification of teaching at the elementary level. Our research suggests that intensification of work at the elementary level is by and large a function of teachers' participation in professional development initiatives. If schools actively promote professional development, teachers' work becomes intensified. For example, one of the schools studied in Tokyo has a reputation as a study school, and the Ministry of Education designated it as a pilot school twice since 1989 to explore life science, a newly introduced area of study for first and second graders and science education for upper graders. During the four years in which the school served as a pilot school, teachers frequently remained at school until 9:00 p.m. for collaborative research and planning of study lessons, which teachers and instructional supervisors from Tokyo and other prefectures were invited to observe.

All in all, intensification of teaching is a general phenomenon at both levels. It is confirmed by evidence from our national PACT survey data (Fujita et al, 1996) which indicate that the majority of Japanese teachers spend at least ten hours at school every day, from 8:00 a.m. to 6:00 p.m. 70 percent of elementary and 80 percent of middle school teachers leave school even later, between 6:00 and 7:00 p.m.; 50 percent of the latter group leave school between 7:00 and 8:00 p.m. These figures reveal that the majority of middle school teachers daily spend eleven to twelve hours at school performing their duties.

In conclusion, we have noted above that teachers' intense work largely stems from the culture of teaching, which places emphasis on holistic teaching and cooperative management. But it is not entirely self-perpetuated. The Ministry of Education and the local board of education fail to provide resources to alleviate the intensification of teaching. For example, middle school teachers continue to perform student placement in high schools and student guidance, which are largely the province of specialized staff in the U.S. Classroom teachers in Japan are not trained specialists, but are expected to perform these additional duties guided by ethnopedagogy without additional training. The Ministry of Education has offered little support either to lighten teachers' workload or to better equip them for their *shukumei*.

FINAL REFLECTIONS ON THE CULTURE OF TEACHING

This chapter has explored the primary characteristics of the culture of teaching in Japan: its salient themes include holistic teaching, ethnopedagogy, teaching as craft, cooperative management, and intensification of teaching. Teachers' everyday work is informed by the culture of teaching; it makes teaching in Japan unique. Inservice education or *kenshu* assumes centrality in teacher development and in the enhancement of teaching as craft. Teaching is holistic at both the elementary and middle school levels, emphasizing experiential learning. Teaching is grounded in ethnopedagogy, pronouncing the importance of trust and ligature as the linchpin of teaching. Cooperative management is key to running the Japanese school.

The culture of teaching as the accumulated experiential wisdom of teaching is a driving as well as a conservative force. While it provides a guiding framework for teaching, it constrains teachers in adapting to change. The efficacy of the culture of teaching against the background of extensive social and economic change over the past two and a half decades in Japan is now at issue. Yet teachers are disinclined to press for change in their taken-for-granted practice. For example, in a reflection of the deeply-seated concepts of teaching, middle school teachers are still charged with student guidance and placement in high schools. The Ministry of Education recently started to place specialized counselors in school districts to address student behavior problems, but the ministry's initiative is very slow and does not substantially alleviate intensification of teaching. Coaching of club activities, which is a traditionally established part of teachers' extracurricular activities, is also a significant source of constraint. Those practices, however, remain the province of classroom teachers notwithstanding increasing intensification of teaching at the middle school level.

Despite the cohesiveness of Japanese educational policy and practice, which gives it many advantages, there are some cracks in that facade. Our national PACT survey (Fujita et al, 1996) indicates that 85 and 89 percent, respectively, of elementary and middle school teachers believe teaching requires self-sacrifice; over 80 percent of these teachers reported that they are chronically fatigued—very significant evidence that cannot be overlooked. Despite the imposition of such non-instructional responsibilities on teachers, neither teachers nor the government has developed effective strategies to lighten teachers' workloads. This, in our view, is attributable to their faith in the efficacy of the tenets of the established culture of teaching no less than to funding constraints.

A word on another related issue. Middle school teachers tend to capitalize on ethnopedagogy, with its emphasis on bonding, to control unmotivated and disruptive students in the classroom, while still adhering to their conventional didactic method of teaching. Our observation of teaching in Japan suggests that the traditional teaching method has hardly changed at the middle school level, which turns off even motivated students. One may question if this strategy based on ethnopedagogy is effective in generating enduring positive effects for these unmotivated students. It seems essential to reconsider some of the premises of ethnopedagogy in addressing problems stemming from contemporary social change.

A final issue relates to teaching as craft, a concept well established in Japan. Both teachers and government have actively promoted initiatives for professional development to advance teaching as craft. These initiatives, however, tend to reproduce teaching rather than transform it, by virtue of the fact that they are mostly formulated within the existing framework of the culture of teaching. Indeed, the dominant pattern of *kenshu* remains unchanged.

As social change immensely affects schooling, the efficacy of the culture of teaching is tested. The challenge that the Japanese culture of teaching faces is how teachers can transform it to respond effectively to social change.

CHAPTER 3

Teacher Education and Social Change

Postwar teacher education remained substantially unchanged for nearly four decades after 1949, when Japan's postwar school system was established. The significant restructuring of teacher education began only in the late 1980s in response to problems resulting from immense social transformation. That restructuring was orchestrated by the National Commission on Educational Reform (NCER), which launched a highly visible, sustained educational reform campaign in 1984, an initiative authorized by the national legislature and directed by the prime minister. During its deliberations on the future of Japanese education, NCER issued four reports, the last of which was made public in 1987.

NCER noted that Japanese education was suffering from a "grave state of desolation" caused by pathological conditions in society and the schools (NCER, 1986a). The development of such conditions, in its view, led to increasing public criticism and distrust of public education and teachers. The Japanese term for desolation is *kohai*, referring to a state of desertedness and deterioration; use of this word rendered an emotionally charged indictment that revealed Japan's deep concern with an emerging crisis in education. The state of desolation, according to NCER, was manifest in a persistent syndrome of juvenile delinquency among students, including bullying, refusing to attend school, and behaving violently at school. Intense competition in entrance examinations for both high schools and colleges contributed to the problem by hindering adolescents' creativity and personal development.

In the Commission's (1986a) words:

> During recent years, there has been increasing public criticism expressing distrust of our schools, teachers and the education sector as a whole. We must face the harsh reality of the problems in our schools and serious state of dilapidation or "desolation" of our educational system which they signal.... A general diagnosis must first be made of the grave social illness now afflicting our educational sys-

tem, the "desolation" whose symptoms include bullying, school violence, and excessive competition in entrance examinations. (p. 4, the English version of the report)

The Commission's recommendations have driven the restructuring initiatives in teacher education over the past decade and a half. NCER formulated a basic framework for subsequent educational reforms, including redesigning teacher education. The purpose of this chapter is to explore reform initiatives in teacher education in Japan as a response to contemporary social change and consequent issues.

The 1980s was a decade marked by major school reforms in advanced industrial countries. School reform issues in these countries are embedded in their unique historical, political, economic, and cultural contexts. Across these contexts, however, teacher education has surfaced as a common international interest. In the U. S., for example, the nationwide school reform movement of the 1980s was stimulated and orchestrated by the publication of *A Nation at Risk*, a report of the National Commission on Excellence in Education (1983) that declared: "Our society and its educational institutions seem to have lost sight of the basic purposes of schooling, and of the high expectations and disciplined effort needed to attain them" (pp. 5-6). It reminded the nation that America's international competitiveness was eroded by "a rising tide of mediocrity" in schools. The National Commission indicted the profession of teaching for its shortcomings, including the fact that "teacher preparation programs need substantial improvement" (p. 22). *A Nation at Risk* has left a lasting legacy of initiatives to redesign education at the institutional, local, and state levels.

The movement to improve teaching in the U.S. in the 1980s was bolstered by two reports, among others, in response to national reform campaigns: *Tomorrow's Teachers*, issued by The Holmes Group of education deans (1986), and *A Nation Prepared: Teachers for the 21st Century*, issued by the Carnegie Task Force on Teaching as a Profession (1986). Responding to the National Commission's call for high academic standards for teachers, both reports emphasized the need for enhanced academic preparation of teachers at both the undergraduate and graduate levels. The Holmes Group's (1990) subsequent report, *Tomorrow's Schools: Principles of the Design of Professional Development Schools*, led to the establishment of over 300 professional development schools across the country. Meanwhile, the Carnegie Task Force report resulted in the establishment of a National Board for Professional Teaching Standards: a voluntary system to assess and certify teachers who meet its standards. It is a professional board governed mostly by teachers, and has developed the highest national standards for certifying exemplary veteran teachers in the nation.

In the U.K., meanwhile, the National Education Act enacted in 1988 led to the development of a national curriculum and subsequent restructuring of schools and teacher education in the 1990s (Maguire & Ball, 1995; McCulloch, 1998). Consequently, new routes to teacher certification were introduced: the "licensed teacher scheme" and school-centered initial teacher training. The former is designed for men and women without a bachelor of education degree, who are required to receive training in the school setting for two years to obtain teacher certification, while the latter is for those with a college degree, who must undergo training in the same setting for one year to be certified. Thus, the central venue of teacher education has shifted from schools of education to schools, representing a dramatic change in teacher education in the U.K. (see Takano, 1998).

SOCIAL CHANGE AND CONSEQUENT PROBLEMS

Postwar Japan has transformed in several phases, as described in economic historian Takafusa Nakamura's (1998) *A History of Showa Japan 1926-1989*. The first major transformation occurred in the second half of the 1960s: the Izanagi Boom, which was named after a god in the earliest mythological account of Japan's emergence. This five-year extended economic expansion from 1965 to 1970—with economic growth rates in excess of 10 percent a year—led to the rapid structural transformation of Japanese manufacturing, particularly the heavy and chemical industries. That transformation marked a shift in economic growth from the production of basic materials, such as steel and ethylene, to the manufacture of finished products, such as ships and automobiles. The rapid economic development of the 1960s had been set in motion by an ambitious income-doubling plan launched by Prime Minister Hayato Ikeda in 1960, which resulted in a rise in personal income of over 10 percent a year in the early 1960s. The rate of economic growth was even greater during the Izanagi Boom, outstripping West Germany's gross national product in 1968; and annual pay increases for workers averaged almost 15 percent during the boom (Nakamura, 1998, p. 388). As Japanese exports exploded, Japan ranked second to the United States in gross national product.

The income doubling plan was an audacious economic policy that dramatically transformed not only Japanese industry, but also Japanese society. This social transformation accelerated an unprecedented educational expansion that helped to accomplish universal high school education. This development marked the onset of Japan's "internationalization," which became a popular term in the following decade. It also accelerated social mobility and caused severe labor shortages even though swift urbanization was shifting population from the rural, agricultural regions to the Pacific industrial belt. Land transportation also shifted, from railroads to automobiles, as express highways were constructed. Increasing affluence was evident in the possession of automobiles, which became commonplace in the first transformation period, not to mention the presence of washing machines, vacuum cleaners, and color TV sets in ordinary homes; telephones also became a common item for the first time. As high school and college enrollments exploded, the proportion of the household budget for education increased to 20 and 30 percent of spending in families with high school and college students, respectively (Nakamura, 1998, p. 391).

Japan's astonishing change, however, met with some domestic resistance. While rapid economic growth brought with it higher incomes and a higher standard of living, the Japanese started to react against its adverse effects: rising prices, pollution, and alienation resulting from urbanization and an automobile-driven society.

Notably, rapid growth of the heavy and chemical industries created widespread pollution and social protests, and these side-effects inflicted stresses and strains on people. The Izanagi Boom provoked the younger generation's reaction against social complacency, which had developed under the politics of high economic growth (Nakamura, 1998). Widespread campus unrest began in 1969 at the University of Tokyo. As Nakamura wrote, youth anger was directed against "the nature of Japanese society, obsessed as it was with the economy and with industry and apparently offering no alternative to a life of enslavement as cogs in the corporate machine" (p. 398).

Another significant transformation in the structure of industrial production occurred shortly after the oil crisis of 1972, with the emergence of a new pattern of production. The heavy and chemical industries' production reached a peak around 1973; thereafter micro-electronics, electric machinery, precision engineering, transportation machinery, and other fields of advanced technology and sophisticated processing led Japanese industry. For the first time, tertiary (service) industry surpassed secondary (manufacturing) industry in 1975 (Tominaga, 1990, p. 406). This represents the second major social transformation in postwar Japan, attained by the combination of a decline in the old pattern of production and a revolution of micro-electronics coupled with the expansion of service industries (Tominaga, 1990). This transformation marked the onset of an information age, with information technology playing a key role in society. It was accompanied by an augmentation of the nation's affluence in the late 1970s and the 1980s and the internationalization of work and business. The Japanese per capita income in 1987 reached $15,770, the third highest in the world, and the annual rate of per capita increase from 1981 to 1987 was 7.7 percent. These vast changes in the Japanese culture in the 1960s, 1970s, and 1980s were the context in which stubborn problems in schooling developed.

The rapid economic growth of the 1960s and 1970s stimulated an unprecedented expansion of high school and college enrollments. Industry was desperate for ever greater numbers of better-trained young people. Reflecting the tenor of those times, enrollment of middle school graduates in high school increased from 57.7 percent in 1960 to 81.6 percent in 1970 and 94 percent in 1979; similarly, high school graduates' entry rates into college rose from 10.3 to 23.6 to 37.4 percent in the same years. Meanwhile, the Curriculum Council, an advisory body to the minister of education, began to research and deliberate upon the content of a third postwar curriculum reform in 1965. The council submitted its recommendations in 1967, and in 1968 the ministry announced its third comprehensive revision—one intended to improve scientific and technical education and to enhance students' adaptability to a changing society (Kinoshita, 1983; Yamaguchi, 1980).

A wag once observed that anything worth doing is worth doing to excess, and that comment has some applicability to Japanese education in the late 1960s and 1970s. High school enrollments rose above 90 percent in the early 1970s, causing a number of problems. For example, a disconcerting lack of continuity became apparent between the curricula of elementary and secondary schools. In addition, critics pointed out that high school curriculum requirements had been pulled out of thin air in response to postwar industry and technology; they failed to coincide with the abilities, skills, and readiness of secondary school students. Awareness of these problems led to another curriculum revision to "humanize" student life in school, which took effect in the early 1980s.

The dramatic expansion of enrollments in high schools led to strains and stresses in student life at both the middle and high school levels, stemming from a lack of material and human resources, an absence of articulation between compulsory (elementary and middle school) and high school education, students' failure to meet academic requirements, and the intense pressure of high school and college entrance examinations (see Imazu, 1996). As educational sociologist, Ikuo Amano (1986) aptly remarked:

> [There developed a] troubled relationship between the children who are the main actors in the educational process and the system itself. . . . Student dissatisfaction with the education system began to take concrete form around the beginning of the 1970s. . . . Student activism in the universities was vigorous, even violent. . . . Eventually the situation returned to normal, but "antischool" attitudes and behavior began to surface among junior and senior high school students. Disillusionment and dislike of school, refusal to attend school, violence, lapses in scholastic performance, and dropouts are manifestations of that protest. (p. 2)

In the postwar period, as in the prewar times, education was viewed as the most powerful means to achieve social mobility. This ethos was realized through the times of rapid economic growth in the 1960s and 1970s. However, when affluence was attained and high school and college enrollments reached 94 and 37 percent, adolescents became complacent and lost aspirations for social mobility (Amano, 1986; Fujita, 1997). Yet overheated entrance examination pressure, stress on educational credentialism, and uniform schooling, which were instrumental in promoting Japan's drive to catch up with the West, remained unchanged. Consequently, a serious gap opened between adolescents' declining aspirations and the school system's drive to excel.

School violence, student turnover, bullying, and juvenile delinquency reached a new peak in the late 1970s and early 1980s (Imazu, 1996; Fujita, 1997; Jijitsushin, 1998). As the mass media began to report daily on those worsening conditions in secondary schools, Japan became obsessed with these problems.

Figure 1: Trends in School Violence, Bullying, and Truancy
(Source: Jijitsushin (1998). *A Databook of Educational Statistics*. Tokyo: Jijitsushin. Pp. 72-87)

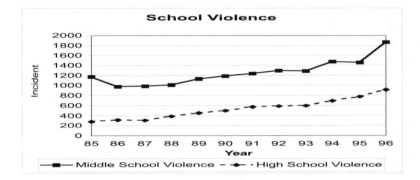

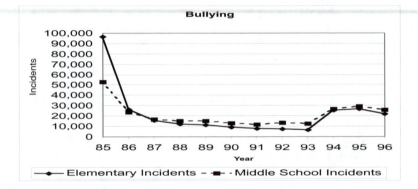

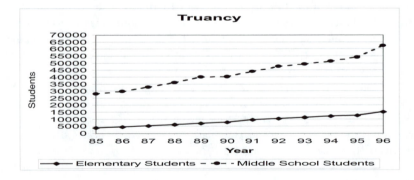

Bullying, school violence, and student absenteeism have been persistent problems over the past two decades. The incidence of bullying was high in 1985, declined considerably for the next eight years, and started to climb again in 1994. Bullying occurs more often among elementary and middle school children than high school students. School violence, which includes peer violence and violence against teachers, has also been on the rise, and two and a half times as high at the middle school level as at the high school level. Especially salient is the fact that nearly 30 percent of school violence at the middle school level is directed against teachers. Student resistance to school authorities, including violence against teachers, started to become notable in the middle of the 1970s and reached a peak around 1980. Meanwhile, student truancy has been on the rise since the mid-1970s in elementary and middle schools, and it is four times as high at the middle school level as at the elementary. Student truancy is defined as absence from school for more than fifty days during the school year. Major reasons cited by middle school students for their absenteeism include laziness, fatigue, lack of motivation to study, peer relations, and emotional disorder, and among them laziness and lack of motivation to study are the two most notable factors. It is evident that student truancy does not suggest adolescents' active resistance to school but that its reasons are socially induced emotional causes of "school refusal" (Morita, 1991, pp. 149-212). High school dropout rates are low by international standards, but they sound an alarm in Japan when they exceed 2 percent. Over the past two decades, they have been consistently above 2 percent, except for a few years in the early 1990s.

RESTRUCTURING DRIVE IN THE 1980S

Against the background of social change and its concomitant problems, the government undertook a major educational restructuring initiative in the middle of the 1980s. In 1982, when the Nakasone cabinet was first formed, the nation's desire for school reform was growing apace. Prime Minister Nakasone had long been interested in education from a nationalist perspective and promised a "total clearance of the postwar political accounts," of which educational reform was a part (Schoppa, 1991). During the 1983 general election campaign he issued his own "Seven-Point Proposal for Educational Reform," which included improving teacher quality (Nakasone, 1984, pp. 214-215). As his and other groups' initiatives and public perceptions of school problems rendered support for his educational reform campaign, he garnered multiparty backing in the national legislature to create a supercabinet-level educational reform task force independent of the Ministry of Education. The bill to establish the National Council on Educational Reform (NCER) passed in the national legislature in the summer of 1984. NCER had four divisions responsible for education: education for the twenty-first century; activating educational functions of society; reforming elementary and secondary education; and reforming higher education. The third division also addressed teacher education reforms.

We will briefly review the reports produced by the Ministry of Education's advisory councils prior to the establishment of NCER. In 1978, the Central Council of Education (1978) issued a brief report on enhancing "teachers' competence." It addressed two central issues that were recycled from previous reports, but were perhaps significant in terms of the new context in which reform was being contemplated. The first was how to rectify Japan's watered-down teacher education, regulated by the postwar open-certification system (see chapter 1). The Council recommended that professional studies be enhanced, including student teaching, and endorsed the 1972 Teacher Education Council's recommendation to require eight and six weeks of clinical experience for elementary and secondary preservice students, respectively. Further, the Central Council of Education urged the Ministry of Education to consider one-year internships for beginning teachers. The second issue was to bolster certification standards. Following the Central Council of Education's report, the Teacher Education Council (1983) proposed a framework for certification standards that eventually resulted in legislative action to overhaul Japan's certification system in 1987 (Teacher Education Council, 1987).

Reformers indicted teachers as a major contributor to deteriorating schools. Thus, what the Japanese call *shishitsu*—the quality of teachers—became the subject of polemics during the reform campaign of the 1980s. The perception that teacher quality was in need of improvement and that teacher education must be overhauled were perpetuated among school administrators, government bureaucrats, and conservative politicians in the national legislature. An increased incidence of adolescent anti-school behavior in the early 1980s reinforced these widespread perceptions. NCER suggested ways to improve teacher quality in its second report. They included: restructuring of teacher education and the certification system, one-year internships for beginning teachers, an alternative route to certification, improving teacher hiring procedures, and enhancement of professional development (National Council on Educational Reform, 1988). Although teacher education was the last item in Nakasone's seven-point proposal and was not a top priority in the NCER's initial deliberations, teacher education—particularly internships—later became a chief thrust of the task force.

NCER formulated broadly-framed recommendations to restructure teacher preparation and professional development. First, NCER urged that teacher education must improve its academic content, and professional schools must equip teachers to reverse the trends of deteriorating schooling. NCER emphasized the enhancement of teachers' "practical competence," including counseling skills, to provide effective student guidance and address student behavior problems as well as the effects of internationalization and the information society on students. It also urged that student teaching be improved to strengthen preservice students' teaching and classroom management skills.

As was often pointed out by the Central Council of Education, NCER also attributed the deterioration of teacher quality, in part, to the watered-down postwar certification standards, which enabled one out of three college students to obtain certification without rigorous professional education (NCER, 1986b). For example, preservice students seeking certification for the secondary level (middle and high schools) were required to complete only 14 credits of professional studies and two weeks of student teaching. By 1984, when well over two-thirds of Japan's colleges and universities offered approved certification programs, cheap teacher certificates had proliferated. NCER sought to alter the postwar system that provided preservice students minimal grounding in teaching.

The second recommendation was to introduce internships for beginning public school teachers at all levels, a major recommendation made by NCER, which would require a substantial funding commitment by the government. NCER's characterization of Japanese education as "desolate" justified the reconsideration of internship, which had long been the conservative government's goal. The Ministry of Education's interest in internships dated back to the 1950s, when "re-education" of teachers was first recommended by the Central Council of Education (Tsuchiya, 1984), and the Teacher Education Council had proposed internships in 1962. Subsequently, these advisory councils repeated their recommendations for internships, but nothing materialized due to the lack of wide political support. The most tenacious opposition to internships came from the Japan Teachers Union, whose ideological leadership resided in the hands of members affiliated with either the Socialist or Communist party. The union argued against what it saw as control of teachers. Many years later, however, when school reforms, including internships, were deliberated by NCER, the union's political influence had declined considerably.

The internship was conceived as a mandatory year-long program designed to develop a teacher's sense of mission, pedagogical skills often identified as practical professional competence, and broad perspective. Internships would place beginning teachers on probation for one year, granting the government greater control over beginning teachers than in the past. Internship programs would be jointly developed by both the individual schools where interns were appointed and prefectural education centers for professional development. (Internships are discussed in depth in chapter 4 in conjunction with professional development.)

NCER also recommended that hiring men and women from other fields as teachers be considered to improve teaching. This new market-oriented approach to recruiting talented people would entail creating an alternate certification procedure. Specifically, the reform council proposed that the prefectural boards of education—the employers of public teachers—be authorized to grant these non-traditional recruits special teacher certification if they passed the board's screening. In contrast, the national certification law determines the qualifications of traditionally trained applicants.

Further, NCER called for *kenshu*, or teacher professional development, to be enhanced. In addition to one-year mandatory internships for first-year teachers, the reform council stressed the need to systematize and expand professional development programs for teachers to promote evolving career objectives, focusing on fifth-, tenth-, and twentieth-year teachers as well as administrators. The council also urged the effective utilization of graduate education for teachers to promote their professional development. In Japan, government-sponsored professional development programs based on such a career development model were in fact already in place when NCER's recommendation was made. Various types of professional development at the school, local, and national levels as well as graduate programs for teachers will be discussed in depth in chapter 7.

Following NCER's second report, the Teacher Education Council fleshed out its recommendations and drafted a proposal to overhaul teacher education, which was submitted to the minister of education in 1987. In essence, this proposal delineated new certification requirements to be considered by the national legislature. When approved, teacher education programs would be modified to adhere to the new certification requirements.

The Ministry of Education's Teacher Education Council had drafted a proposal to reform certification requirements in 1983, which served as a prototype for its 1987 proposal and had called for substantially raising requirements for professional studies and student teaching. That proposal, however, was tabled by the national legislature in early 1984 in anticipation of NCER's recommendations to restructure teacher education. Subsequently, the 1987 proposal to overhaul teacher education by the Teacher Education Council blended its earlier proposal with NCER's recommendations, including internships. Passage of the Teacher Education Council proposal in the legislature needed NCER's commitment and endorsement, and the higher standards were indeed approved by the legislature in 1988, with a minor amendment in 1989.

Reformers introduced some significant changes in the preparation of teachers. To improve it, they initiated advanced certification and more stringent requirements for teaching. And Japan finally began to place more emphasis on graduate preparation of teachers. Consequently, the numbers of universities and colleges that offered master's programs for teachers started to increase. Another important change in the certification system was a significant increase in required professional studies for all types of certification, with emphasis on student guidance, information technology, moral education, student activities, and clinical experience. Requirements for student teaching, however, increased only minimally, from four to five weeks (five credits) and two to three weeks (three credits) for elementary and secondary teacher candidates, respectively. Additional clinical experience, however, was expected to be provided during the internship year.

The new certification law specified three types of certification: specialist, standard (type I), and first-level (type II); there had been only first- and second-class certificates prior to 1989. The new standard type corresponded to the former first-class, and the new first level to the former second class; the specialist category was new. The specialist and standard certificates each required master's-level course work or a master's degree and a bachelor's degree, whereas the first-level certificate required only a two-year college degree. Holders of first-level certificates were expected to do additional coursework to upgrade them to standard certificates within twelve years of receiving the initial certificates. As seen in Table 3, the new law required a total of 59 credits for elementary and middle school standard certification. Credits required for professional studies were substantially increased for all types of both elementary and middle school certification, but there was only a minor change in requirements for student teaching, adding just one credit (one week) for all types of certification. In 1983 the Teacher Education Council proposed to upgrade requirements for student teaching to eight and six credits (weeks) for elementary and middle school certification, respectively. However, that proposal was altered in light of the fact that one-year internships for beginning teachers were expected to be approved. The new law required fewer credits (59) for high school standard certification, a decrease of seventeen credits: academic content requirements were reduced from 62 to 40 credits, but requirements for professional studies increased to five credits, including a minor increase in student teaching from two to three credits.

Table 3: Comparisons of Pre- and Post-1989 Certification Requirements

Elementary School Certification				
	Credit Requirements Prior to 1989		New Credit Requirements		
	First Class	Second Class	Specialist	Standard	First Level
Content Area	16	8	18	18	10
Professional Studies	32 (4 for student teaching)	22 (4 for student teaching)	41 (5 for student teaching)	41 (5 for student teaching)	27 (5 for student teaching)
Additional Content Area or Professional Studies			24		
Total	48	30	83	59	37

Middle School Certification				
	Credit Requirements Prior to 1989		New Credit Requirements		
	First Class	Second Class	Specialist	Standard	First Level
Content Area	40	20	40	40	20
Professional Studies	14 (2 for student teaching)	10 (2 for student teaching)	19 (3 for student teaching)	19 (3 for student teaching)	15 (3 for student teaching)
Additional Content Area or Professional Studies			24		
Total	54	30	83	59	35

Table 3 CONT'D.

High School Certification				
Credit Requirements Prior to 1989		New Credit Requirements		
First Class	Second Class	Specialist	Standard	N/A
Content Area	62	40	40	40	
Professional Studies	14 (2 for student teaching)	14 (2 for student teaching)	19 (3 for student teaching)	19 (3 for student teaching)	
Additional Content Area or Professional Studies			24		
Total	76	54	83	59	

The reform of teacher education in the 1980s was directed from above as in the past, and did not substantially alter the way teachers are prepared. However, professional studies and the transition to teaching via internships were strengthened. The educational restructuring was an urgent response to social change brought about by Japan's economic and industrial transformation. Japan was concerned with not only the problems of adolescent behavior with which the country was obsessed, but also the effects of internationalization and the information society upon children and adolescents as well as its transition into the 21st century. Japan's paradigm of industrial development had been based on the so-called "catch-up ideology," targeting the West as its goal. Now that it had caught up with the West, the country had to seek a paradigm of its own development, including education and teacher education.

RESTRUCTURING DRIVE IN THE 1990S

When postwar teacher education started in 1949, Japan adopted "the open certification system" under which any university or college could offer a teacher education program requiring only minimal preparation. Consequently, teacher education programs proliferated and became especially popular in the 1970s as a result of human resource procurement legislation, which made teachers' salaries competitive relative to the private sector. Private colleges and universities, which currently constitute 79 percent of all Japanese institutions of higher education, have played a dominant role in teacher education, producing the majority of certification holders at the middle and high school levels. Thus, every time the Ministry of Education's advisory councils proposed raising certification requirements, tensions grew between the Ministry, which wanted higher standards and private colleges and universities, which benefited from the existing requirements. Certification requirements, however, started to change in the late 1980s in response to social change; they will soon become more demanding as a result of another campaign to restructure teacher education in the late 1990s. Predictably, the Japan Federation of Private Universities has opposed this new campaign, claiming that it will drive private universities out of teacher education (Okuda, 1998).

Why yet another restructuring drive? Several important issues have contributed to it. First, bullying, school violence, and student absenteeism remain unabated. School violence at the middle school level declined around 1987 but surged again in the 1990s. Rates of bullying have also jumped in recent years at both the elementary and middle school levels after declining in the early1990s; some particularly cruel incidents have driven victims to commit suicide. Meanwhile, student absenteeism has been steadily increasing. There are increasing numbers of classrooms in a state of crisis, or *gakyu hokai*—a popular journalistic term which refers to a chaos in the classroom caused by students' disorderly behavior and teachers' inability to control students. The mass media have contributed to the Japanese obsession with students' disorderly behavior by frequently highlighting such incidents.

While rates of school violence and bullying are much lower at the high school level, high school students display a strong anti-authority attitude. For example, according to an international survey conducted in 1996 (Japanese Youth Research Institute, 1996), 79 percent of Japanese high school students believed that they were free to rebel against teachers, in contrast to 5.8 and 18.8 percent of U.S. and Chinese students, respectively. Eighty-five percent of Japanese students felt they were free to rebel against parents compared to only 16 and 15 percent of U.S. and Chinese students. In another international survey (Japanese Youth Research Institute, 1995), only 16 percent of Japanese high school students said they would be willing to attend to the needs of their aging parents "under any circumstances," in contrast to 46 and 66 percent of U.S. and Chinese students, respectively. These attitudes of adolescents are quite disturbing to Japan, where Confucianism and filial piety have traditionally been strong.

Second, reformers now believe that it is critical to further strengthen professional education for preservice teachers while reducing requirements in the academic content area at the secondary level. This represents a new trend, showing a contrast to the U.S. campaign to enhance teacher preparation with an increased emphasis on academic study in the arts and sciences. Confronted by growing problems of adolescent behavior, Japanese reformers are resorting to ethnopedagogy (see Chapter Two) as a way to cope with them. They emphasize education of the "heart" and a human relation-oriented pedagogy highlighting the importance of counseling, student guidance, and moral education. This trend represents a shift toward teacher education with an emphasis on a therapeutic pedagogy, and away from the academic content-dominated teacher preparation of the 1960s and 1970s.

Third, reformers believe that it is important to allow latitude in teacher education so that preservice students may have room to pursue their individual interests. In the past, preservice students' undergraduate course work was rigidly prescribed. The reformers' initiative to create flexibility in teacher education was preceded by a campaign in higher education to loosen up rigid bureaucratic control over the establishment of university curricula. The Ministry of Education deregulated the criteria for establishing curricula at colleges and universities in 1991 to provide them with latitude to develop unique and varied curricula (University Council, 1991). This deregulation also enabled colleges and universities to construct undergraduate education for preservice students without adhering to these criteria. Prior to deregulation, there were two mandatory categories in each curriculum: general education as well as a specialized field. General education was composed of study in the social sciences, the natural sciences, and the humanities. Students were expected to meet requirements in each area of general education and in specialized education. In addition, students were required to take courses in foreign languages and health/physical education. After deregulation, colleges and universities could develop their own programs without attention to these categories.

Fourth, there has been a rapid penetration of internationalization and information-based life and work, which the Japanese call *johoka* or "informationalization." Reformers believe that teacher education must be redesigned to address issues stemming from accelerating internationalization and to equip preservice students with the skills demanded in an information age.

The drive to overhaul teacher education in the late 1990s was preceded by other educational restructuring initiatives. We will briefly review them because they constitute the backdrop to the current teacher education reform campaign.

As NCER was deliberating on comprehensive educational reforms in the 1980s, the Curriculum Council completed its report proposing a major revision of the national curriculum in 1987. Based on its report, a new course of study was issued in 1989: the binding official guideline of the national curriculum. The curriculum is periodically revised every ten years, and the Curriculum Council is responsible for reviewing the existing curriculum and recommending revisions. The council's deliberation on the curricular revision paralleled NCER's initiative, and it reflected NCER's major thrust of school reform in the new course of study, emphasizing individual differences, lifelong learning, and adaptability to social change. The revised course of study pronounced "a new notion of academic competence" expected of students, or *shin garkuryoku-kan*. This notion placed a stress on students' motivation and ability to engage in what is commonly known as problem solving. Another central concept was learning for self discovery, including "identifying and inquiring into problems, making independent judgments, conceptualizing judgments, and solving them" (Ministry of Education, 1993, p. 9). Thus, students' interest and motivation to learn became a critical part of the new academic competence and evaluation of student performance. Developing these qualities of student performance was now considered a top priority, representing an important shift in the national curriculum. The Ministry of Education (1993) admitted that past emphasis had been on passive learning, concentrating on the transmission of a body of knowledge and skills to students when Japan was trying to "catch up with" the U.S. and Europe. Now that the country had gained an equal footing with the West, schooling faced new challenges.

It is relevant to note that reformers' recent rhetoric describing the notion of academic competence, reminiscent of the American progressive education introduced to Japan shortly after the Second World War, is hardly different from rhetoric used by the Central Council of Education nearly thirty years ago in its most comprehensive school reform report (Central Council of Education, 1971), which aimed to introduce the second major restructuring of schools in the postwar period. The same rhetoric, however, was employed in different social contexts: the catch-up and post-catch-up eras. Theories and methods of progressive education were popular among enthusiastic teachers and university professors when they were introduced to Japan in the 1940s and 1950s. Japanese teachers became acquainted with what is now called a "new notion" of academic competence through their exposure to progressive teaching. But the influence of progressive education in Japan precipitously declined by 1960, when the national curriculum was firmly established and the Ministry of Education assumed complete control of the nation's schools. Thus, the so-called new notion of academic competence is hardly novel in Japan, but was presented to teachers in the 1990s as if it was a new concept in the contemporary social context.

Meanwhile, the restructuring of higher education was under way, in which the newly established University Council, as an advisory body to the minister of education, played an active role by making a series of recommendations to overhaul higher education (see University Council, 1991). Deregulating the criteria for establishing university curricula was a part of its restructuring initiatives.

In 1996 and 1997 the Central Council of Education completed its latest school reform report, "Education for the 21st Century." The first part of the report (Central Council of Education, 1996) presented a broad range of reform issues, including the future of education in schools, homes, and communities; education for internationalization and an information age; and education and environmental issues. Also included in the 1996 report was a proposal to improve teacher education, which provided the Teacher Education Council with a broad framework to formulate recommendations for teacher education reform.

A theme of this report was to enhance the child's "power to live," or *ikiru chikara*, which could be attained by "balanced" education at both the elementary and secondary levels if the intellectual, moral, and physical development of the child were harmonized. Because the notion of "power to live" was not defined in the report, its operational meaning remains elusive. It seems, however, to refer to a Japanese ethos that symbolizes personal adaptive capacity required in an age of great change. The Central Council of Education's (1971) earlier report also referred to the power to live as a personal quality to promote one's life with "independent initiative and self control" in an age of rapid economic and technological transformation (p. 131).

In any event, the 1996 report enunciated the imperative to develop balanced schooling emphasizing the individual child's initiative, motivation, and interest in learning, identified earlier as an attribute of academic competence. To enhance the student's initiative, the council proposed a "comprehensive study period" at both the elementary and secondary levels, which would cross subject-matter boundaries. Students will take the initiative in organizing projects focused on, for example, issues stemming from internationalization, the information age, and environmental deterioration. The council urged that nontraditional teaching strategies should be adopted to promote individual children's academic interests, including individualized instruction, team teaching, cooperative learning, and more course options in the high school curriculum. The council also stressed that education should be designed to promote both a robust and healthy body and a "rich human quality," or *ningensei*, which is an embodiment of a shared value system. This value system includes a host of moral qualities: sensitivity to beauty and nature; respect for justice and equality; respect for life and human rights; thoughtfulness and contribution to society; independence, self control, and responsibility; and tolerance of individual differences (Ministry of Education, 1998, p. 14).

The council recommended that curriculum content at all levels be restructured by reducing it selectively to ensure a match between the curriculum and student ability, as well as to allow students greater freedom in school. The proposed reduction of the curricular content took into account an elimination of one school day each week, as Japanese students will soon attend school five days a week instead of six. Japan has been experimenting with various models of five-day weekly school attendance since 1992. A five-day attendance policy will be fully implemented in 2002, providing students more free time at home at a time when they are pressured to attend *juku*, private "cram" schools to prepare for entrance examinations.

As noted above, these recommendations are not new, but are largely recycled from previous reform reports. As suggested by a critic (Ichikawa, 1996), they hardly include fresh proposals for the next century. The council's recommendations are, by and large, measures to cope with current problems. However, its proposal to reduce the curriculum content will have substantial consequences. Following the Central Council's reform report, the Curriculum Council (1998) completed revision of the national curriculum, detailing a new framework for the next ten years. Its central goal is to "teach basics thoroughly" and rectify the past overemphasis on knowledge transmission. In effect, it has made the curriculum lean by reducing its difficult content by 30 percent. Since the late 1970s, Japan has been cutting the curriculum content, but the Curriculum Council's latest proposal represents the most drastic trimming yet. The new national curriculum will be implemented beginning in 2002.

Further, the Central Council of Education (1998) issued another report focusing on "education of the heart" for grades K-12. In chapter 2, we suggested that Japanese teachers see the heart as a basis of education, the centerpiece for self development, and a window through which one's identity and universe are communicated. The 1998 report stated that the heart has deteriorated and that this decay is reflected in the social pathology of student behavior. The report offered strategies to restore a "rich heart" by promoting the "power to live" and moral life through education in the school, home, and community. It is evident that in the view of Japanese educational reformers, deterioration of the heart as a social and emotional embodiment of the self and moral life is a fundamental issue underlying contemporary problems of student behavior. Reflecting these views, more attention has been given over the past decade to moral education and the cultivation of rich human qualities as well as human bonding, or *fureai*, and moral education has become popular at elementary and middle schools throughout the country. Power to live, education of the heart, rich human qualities (*ningensei*), and *fureai* are all ethnopedagogic terms that appeal to the minds of the Japanese in considering school reforms, and so Japanese school reforms have been framed in these cultural terms.

What has been described above is a series of reform efforts leading to the second drive to restructure teacher education within a decade after the 1989 initiative. Following the Central Council of Education's 1996 report, the Teacher Education Council deliberated on improving teacher preparation and completed its report in 1997.

We discussed why the second drive was considered necessary. We will further look at specific characteristics of the latest teacher education reform. Shulman (1987, p. 8) classifies the knowledge base for teaching into seven types:

- content knowledge
- general pedagogical knowledge
- curriculum knowledge
- pedagogical content knowledge (an amalgam of pedagogy and content)
- knowledge of learners and their characteristics
- knowledge of educational contexts
- knowledge of educational ends

The Japanese teacher preparation curriculum includes all seven areas of knowledge, but reformers placed a priority on some of these areas over others to strengthen preservice students' grounding in teaching. Content knowledge is essential, but, in their view, it had been overstressed in Japanese teacher education in the past. Thus, requirements in the content area were drastically reduced for middle school and high school certification. The rationale underlying the Teacher Education Council's report is fourfold.

First, preservice students must develop practical competencies in teaching. In other words, they must have stronger grounding in the knowledge base for teaching, especially pedagogical knowledge, knowledge of learners, and pedagogical content knowledge. In reformers' view, especially important are pedagogical knowledge and knowledge of learners and their characteristics, as student behavior has become a sustained national concern. Pedagogical knowledge includes broad principles and strategies of classroom management and student guidance; knowledge of learners is embodied in teachers' understanding of students' social, emotional, physical, and intellectual characteristics as well as their adaptive problems, manifest in such phenomena as bullying and school violence. Pedagogical content knowledge is also critical to teach a subject matter effectively. Accordingly, the Teacher Education Council proposed extending student teaching at all levels to provide a longer period for "practical experience." Preservice students are expected to gain a greater mastery of pedagogical knowledge, knowledge of learners, and pedagogical content knowledge through their extended clinical experiences.

To enhance practical competency, the council proposed to expand professional studies for all types of certification, a significant change in the teacher education curriculum. While requirements in professional studies remained the same for elementary certification in its proposal, they substantially increased for middle and high school certification. In particular, professional requirements for middle school certification more than doubled over the pre-1989 level. Notable is an increased weight on teaching methods, counseling, student guidance, and clinical experience for middle and high school certification. The council attempted to restructure the knowledge base of educational ends to enunciate the prominence of a sense of mission in teaching, including "love for teaching, pride as a teacher, and a sense of professional belongingness" (Teacher Education Council, 1997, p. 9). The council went so far as to create a new category in the professional curriculum, called "orientation toward teaching and a sense of belongingness." "Professional belongingness" refers to an orientation toward teaching informed by common professional purposes and commitment. This new category of study is designed to provide the opportunity for preservice students to inquire into the teaching profession and teachers' roles.

Second, the teacher education curriculum should exhibit flexibility. The minimum national curriculum requirement for a bachelor's degree at Japanese universities is at least 124 credits, of which preservice students must take 59 credits for standard certification in the content and professional studies areas (see table 4). Students

Table 4: Comparisons of Pre- and Post-2000 Certification Requirements

| | Elementary School Certification | | | | | |
| | Credit Requirements Prior to 2000 | | | New Credit Requirements | | |
	Specialist	Standard	First Level	Specialist	Standard	First Level
Content Area	18	18	10	8	8	4
Professional Studies	41 (5 for student teaching)	41 (5 for student teaching)	27 (5 for student teaching)	41 (5 for student teaching)	41 (5 for student teaching)	31 (5 for student teaching)
Additional Content Area or Professional Studies	24			34	10	2
Total	83	59	37	83	59	37

Middle School Certification					
	Credit Requirements Prior to 2000			New Credit Requirements		
	Specialist	Standard	First Level	Specialist	Standard	First Level
Content Area	40	40	20	20	20	10
Professional Studies	19 (3 for student teaching)	19 (3 for student teaching)	15 (3 for student teaching)	31 (5 for student teaching)	31 (5 for student teaching)	21 (5 for student teaching)
Additional Content Area or Professional Studies	24			32	8	4
Total	83	59	35	83	59	35

High School Certification					
	Credit Requirements Prior to 2000			New Credit Requirements		
	Specialist	Standard	First Level	Specialist	Standard	First Level
Content Area	40	40		20	20	
Professional Studies	19 (3 for student teaching)	19 (3 for student teaching)		23 (3 for student teaching)	23 (3 for student teaching)	
Additional Content Area or Professional Studies	24			40	16	
Total	83	59	N/A	83	59	N/A

seeking certification at colleges and universities other than schools of education at public universities must take the required credits in professional studies above and beyond their minimum total degree requirements. Reflecting the deregulation policy, the Teacher Education Council proposed to promote students' pursuit of their interests by creating a new sub-category of "additional content area or professional studies" for all types of certification. In this new category, students are encouraged to focus on topics of special personal interest.

Third, teaching must be informed by a global perspective. Men and women all over the world are closely interconnected by information technology, rapid globalization of the economic and industrial sectors, and the internationalization of work and living as well as by global issues like racial and ethnic conflicts and environmental threats. These global phenomena transcend national and geographical boundaries and invariably have an impact on the lives of children and adults in contemporary society. While the council urged that preservice students should have an opportunity to study global problems outside the field of teacher education, it proposed a seminar on global issues to sensitize students to their impact on education.

Fourth, teachers must have adaptive competencies to work in an age of change. The council proposed two new required courses for certification of all types to help develop teachers' adaptive competencies. These courses focus on computer technology and foreign languages, and will be added to the existing two required courses, the Japanese Constitution and physical education. Students may further study computer science and foreign languages outside their course work in teacher education. Incidentally, these four required courses are not counted as part of the teacher education programs shown in Table 4. The revised certification requirements shown in the figure were approved by the national legislature in 1998.

Overall, the current restructuring drive in teacher education is an extension of the first, and is designed to respond to the same educational and social problems and needs. In this sense, there is continuity between the two. The second drive, however, makes the methodological and therapeutic emphasis much more salient than the first drive. In contrast, the content area is substantially reduced at all levels of certification. Will preservice students be adequately prepared in the academic area? In the U.S., this question has haunted reformers and policy makers over the past two decades (see National Commission on Excellence in Education, 1983; Carnegie Task Force on Teaching as a Profession, 1987), leading to reforms quite different from Japan's.

The Japanese educational literature, on the other hand, indicates that policy makers and educators of teachers in Japan appear to be little concerned with this question. One possible explanation for the lack of concern is that over 50 and 85 percent of beginning middle and high school teachers, respectively, are drawn from private universities and graduate schools, where they major in specialized fields related to their teaching content area. However, 46 and 14 percent of beginning middle and high school teachers hold degrees in education from schools of education. Will they be adequately prepared in their content areas? Further, one must be concerned about the academic preparation for elementary certification in the new teacher education, which requires only eight credits in the content area. But reformers assume, perhaps correctly, that students in schools of education do plenty of course work outside education. According to a 1994 survey (Ministry of Education, 1994), 77 percent of education students at national universities earned more than 51 credits in the content area, and 20 percent earned 41 to 50 credits in content. Further, the revised curriculum has the new sub-category of content area or professional studies options that will permit students to do course work in the content area, in addition to the specified content requirements if they so choose.

Finally, there is the issue of teacher education at the graduate level. The Central Council of Education's 1996 report, from which the second campaign to restructure teacher education sprang, recommended the enhancement of graduate-level teacher education, targeting full-time teachers. Prefectural boards of education across the country, which employ public school teachers, want to hire more teachers with a master's degree or specialist certification; a recent survey by the Ministry of Education (1997), for example, indicates that 61 percent of the prefectural boards of education are interested in increasing the number of master's degree holders in teaching. Interest in graduate education for teachers began to grow only in the middle of the 1980s, when the education reform movement started, and, since then, the percentages of master's degree holders in teaching have been slowly rising. As discussed in chapter eight, the government created three national universities of education around 1980 with the explicit purpose of offering graduate education to full-time teachers. Consequently, in 1997, 4, 8, and 15 percent of elementary, middle school, and high school teachers, respectively, had a master's degree while 5, 6, and 8 percent of those cohorts of teachers each had specialist certification. Currently all schools of education at national universities and a dozen other institutions offer master's programs for teachers. About 1,000 teachers are enrolled in master's programs offered by national universities each year.

In response to the need for teacher development through graduate programs, as will be discussed in the context of teacher professional development in Chapter Seven, the Teacher Education Council (1998) drafted a proposal to expand graduate education for teachers. Its rationale is to provide greater numbers of teachers with an opportunity to develop a higher level of knowledge and skills in teaching by diversifying master's programs to meet teachers' needs.

CONCLUSION

Japan's first postwar school reform took place in the late 1940s, guided by the recommendations made by the United States Education Mission to Japan (1946), which drastically changed Japanese education. The new school system was built on a single track and egalitarian structure, which provided equal opportunity at the elementary, secondary, and higher education levels. Teacher education was incorporated into university education. Toward the end of the 1950s, the Ministry of Education centralized educational control and established a national curriculum. Guided by the "catch-up" ideology, uniform schooling for efficiency re-emerged. That coincided with the historic income doubling plan launched in 1960. This plan and the subsequent Izanagi Boom transformed Japan and Japanese lives in an unprecedented manner and made the country affluent. As the rapid economic growth of the times demanded greater human resources, high school and university education swelled, and enrollments in high schools and colleges reached 94 and 37 percent of eligible youths, respectively, in the 1970s. High school education became universal, and college education was no longer reserved for the privileged, so more and more students were driven to compete in entrance examinations.

In responding to greater needs in the industrial sector, the curricula at the elementary and secondary levels were upgraded with emphasis on math, science, and technical education in the late 1960s, creating a mismatch between student ability and curricular standards that had to be corrected in the late 1970s. Japan's high growth economy created increased stresses on its people and caused social protests against the adverse effects of rapid industrialization. Student protests against authoritarianism in higher education and the sociopolitical stability attained through high economic growth became rampant on college campuses in the late 1960s. It was in the changing social context of the 1970s that student school violence, bullying, and academic failure started to become a national concern.

Established in 1984, the National Council on Educational Reform launched an ambitious initiative to change schools to meet emerging needs of students and to consider strategies for new challenges stemming from Japan's internationalization, the information age, and other social and economic issues. The first restructuring drive in teacher education started with NCER. The requirements for teacher education, which were established in 1949 based on the open certification system, began to change substantially. Previous requirements had provided only scant grounding in teaching; hence, professional studies were beefed up, and mandatory one-year internships were introduced to improve teaching in the wake of escalating problems of adolescents with teachers, peers, and school work.

The second drive was launched in the late 1990s because those problems persisted. As a result of this drive, teacher education will become more substantial, with more demanding professional studies and student teaching. Various reform initiatives since the 1980s have pointed in the same direction, emphasizing the imperative to recognize students' diversified needs and the centrality of student learning nested in intrinsic motivation and interest; to teach basics thoroughly; to improve student guidance and broaden teachers' professional and social perspectives; and to improve teachers' practical competencies.

The content area in the teacher education curriculum has been elusive. The content area requirements for middle and high school certification were 40 and 62 credits each prior to 1989. These credits, however, could be directly and easily transferred from the students' course work completed in their specialized fields independent of teacher education. What was left in the curriculum was a total of fourteen credits in professional studies, including two weeks of student teaching. Those certification requirements had been maintained for four decades in defense of the open certification system, which enabled the majority of private universities to offer certification programs. The Ministry of Education finally prevailed in making teacher education more substantive against the protests by private universities at a time when classroom chaos, student violence, student refusal to attend school, and bullying called into question the *raison d'être* of public schools.

Teaching is generally interactive and student-centered at the elementary level. In contrast, the author's observations support a common view that it is by and large didactic and noninteractive at the middle and high school levels. Typically, forty students sit in several rows facing the teacher who talks to them from the desk, and they are expected to be attentive but passive learners, diligently taking notes. The teacher's task is to maintain classroom order and efficiently transmit knowledge to students to cover all the areas required in high school and college entrance examinations. Individualized instruction is very rare in middle and high schools. This brief description is more typical than not and epitomizes the culture of classroom teaching. In this context of classroom culture, students tend to be disruptive and resist teacher authority, especially at the middle school level. Will the new teacher education be able to deliver to schools new teachers infused with nontraditional pedagogical content knowledge, innovative teaching methods, and a broader perspective? Will these teachers be able to break the barriers of the conservative culture of teaching (discussed in Chapter Eight) so that the centrality of student learning may become the focus of teaching?

It is critical to change the culture of teaching to effectively respond to student problems. Needless to say, it is similarly paramount to change the Japanese entrance examination system, which is both a major source of stress on students and pressure driving teachers to resort to the didactic teaching too often employed in middle and high schools. Tinkering with certification requirements alone will not solve the problems facing Japanese education.

CHAPTER 4

Professional Development: Japanese Strategies

The professional development of teachers is key to enhancing the effectiveness of teaching. Strategies to enhance professional development vary among industrialized nations, reflecting the availability of resources, the historical and political context of teaching, and the culture in which teaching is embedded (see Organization for Economic Cooperation and Development, 1998). This chapter will present an analysis of Japanese practice to promote teacher development.

Darling-Hammond (1997) aptly points out characteristics of teacher learning: "Teachers learn just as their students do: by studying, doing, and reflecting; by collaboration with other teachers; by looking closely at students and their work; and by sharing what they see" (p. 319). This passage epitomizes what is involved in professional development initiatives in Japan. Darling-Hammond further suggests several strategies that result in effective professional development (p. 326). They include: experiential learning in tasks of teaching, assessment, and observation; grounding in teachers' questions and inquiry; teacher collaboration and sharing of knowledge; and sustained modeling, coaching, and problem solving (see Darling-Hammond & McLaughlin, 1995). These strategies for professional development, considered and tried in the U. S., are closely related to the approach that Japanese teachers have been using for some time. We pointed out in chapter Two that teaching is learned, transmitted, and reformulated as craft in Japan, and Japanese teachers commonly view craft knowledge as embedded in teacher-generated experience and knowledge. Given their view of teaching as craft, experiential learning, which focuses on teacher collaboration and reflection, is central to school-based teacher development and other peer-driven initiatives.

Teacher development is commonly known as *kenshu*, meaning "mastery through study." Teacher development is also referred to as inservice education. In this chapter *kenshu*, professional development, and inservice education will be used interchangeably to refer to teachers' efforts to achieve "mastery through study."

Why is teacher professional development essential? Obviously, preservice teacher education cannot fully prepare teachers to meet rising public expectations of educational outcomes against the background of a rapidly changing social, technological, and economic environment. It is essential that teachers engage in continued self-renewal to broaden their roles and responsibilities at a time of great change in schools and society. Further, as discussed in chapter Three, the fact that postwar preservice teacher education in Japan has provided only minimal grounding in teaching has led to a demand for inservice education.

As the Organization for Economic Development and Cooperation's (OECD) (1998) recent report makes very clear, industrialized countries invariably regard inservice education as critical to teacher development. There has been a paradigm shift in professional development in these countries from focusing on the characteristics of teachers and teaching to concentrating on student learning, as school reforms over the past two decades have zeroed in on student school performance (OECD, 1998). In Japan, the shift is gradual, but increasing attention is being given to student learning in professional development initiatives. Overall, however, objectives of professional development in these countries vary from updating teachers' knowledge of a subject in Germany to enabling teachers to apply top-down reforms in the curriculum in the U.K. and Japan (OECD, 1998). Attention in Japanese professional development has shifted in the latest reformed curriculum from teaching of traditional subjects to moral education and "comprehensive learning through projects," or *sogogakushu*, at the elementary and middle school levels.

The three most common types of inservice education among OECD countries are top-down, bottom-across or teacher collaborative networking, and individualist (OECD, 1998). The first mode, top-down, is widely organized by education authorities and implemented through education centers, such as prefectural education centers in Japan, regional centers in German *Lander*, and Swedish regional resource centers. The second mode, bottom-across, has also gained popularity in these countries, giving teachers a sense of ownership of professional development. It is the most extensively developed form of teacher development in Japan. In the U.S., the National Board for Professional Teaching Standards was recently established to certify accomplished veteran teachers as the benchmark of professional development (see National Commission on Teaching and America's Future, 1996; Darling-Hammond, 1997). It is governed and run mainly by teachers. The third mode, individualist, is dominant in the U.S., where individual teachers seek to enhance their professional qualifications and competencies, typically through enrollment in graduate programs. As Hawley and Hawley (1997) put it, American "teachers are largely responsible for their own professional development" (p. 238). Common providers of professional development in OECD countries include the education authorities, self-organized school development staff, networking and interschool collaboration associations, and third-party providers such as universities and institutes.

Japan has developed two dominant modes of delivery of inservice education, the top-down and bottom-across methods. The Japanese *kenshu* system has four structurally different types. The first is a top-down arrangement governing inservice education throughout the country, and it reflects the centralized, hierarchical system of Japanese education. In this type of *kenshu,* the Ministry of Education lays out a policy framework and the prefectural board of education provides teacher development programs in accordance with that framework. This structure has been extensively developed since the early 1960s. Another important part of this first *kenshu* type is directed by the National Education Center in Tokyo, which has inservice education facilities in both Tokyo and Tsukuba. The National Education Center component concentrates on leadership development for teachers and administrators. The second type of *kenshu* is long-term training sponsored by prefectural boards of education for selected full-time teachers, who enroll in master's programs at national universities on government scholarships. The third type of *kenshu* is a school-based structure in which teachers take responsibility for a model that encourages professional development through peer collaboration and management. The fourth type of *kenshu* represents large numbers of national teacher networks, which are completely independent of government control and subsidies.

In the first part of this chapter, we will discuss these four types of *kenshu* with particular attention to providers, form and content, and resource implications. In the second part, we will explore school-based *kenshu* at length. Finally, we will turn to critical issues in professional development in Japan and the U.S.

GOVERNMENT-SPONSORED INSERVICE EDUCATION

Providers of government-sponsored inservice education are primarily prefectural and national education centers. There are 47 prefectures (equivalent to states in the U.S.) in Japan, and each prefecture has an education center established and operated by its own prefectural board of education. Each education center is staffed by full-time personnel drawn mainly from the ranks of experienced teachers, many of whom are on leave from their schools for a few years with the charge to organize *kenshu* programs. Likewise, large cities—as well as each ward in Tokyo—run education centers with full-time staff under the direction of boards of education.

KENSHU AT THE PREFECTURAL EDUCATION CENTER

The basic structure of *kenshu* programs is largely the same across the 47 prefectures in Japan. The provider of professional development is the prefectural board of education, and funding for the programs is its responsibility. The Ministry of Education provides financial support for obligatory *kenshu* (explained below). The education centers vary in size and facilities, but generally they are housed in well-equipped modern buildings. Tokushima Prefectural Education Center, financed by a local, small prefecture, for example, is staffed by 55 full- and part-time professional employees and offers over 70 courses a year; Hiroshima Municipal Education Center, staffed by 28 full-time professional employees, offers nearly 150 courses each year. Education centers draw on a wide range of professionals as instructors for these courses.

There are two *kenshu* categories—obligatory and voluntary—which are organized to enhance teacher development at different career stages. The obligatory category consists of several mandatory programs for designated cohorts of teachers. Their primary purpose is to enhance career objectives based on a career development model. The first obligatory program is for all interns, or beginning public school teachers, for which thirty days are allocated a year. Its content is discussed below in the section on internships for beginning teachers. The second obligatory program targets fifth- and tenth-year teachers; five days are allocated annually. In addition, some centers, such as the Nara Prefectural Education Center, offer an obligatory program for teachers with eleven to twenty years' experience who are expected to assume leadership positions in schools. To develop leadership and managerial skills in this group of teachers, several centers offer intensive *kenshu* courses for selected personnel ranging from twelve days (73 hours) at Hiroshima to 51 days (328 hours) at Gunma. The third obligatory program is organized for administrators, including beginning instructional heads, head teachers, and principals as well as experienced principals, to brief them about changing administrative functions and issues. This program includes only short courses.

In addition, each prefectural education center offers a number of voluntary or elective *kenshu* seminars for teachers, which focus on special topics and contemporary issues such as minority education, international education, environmental education, information technology, counseling, and curriculum development. Special attention is given to issues in education stemming from social change. Lasting from three to eight days, they target teachers at the elementary and secondary levels. Further, each center provides a long-term professional development program, lasting from three months to one year. The Tokushima Education Center, for example, recruits 28 teachers for full-year *kenshu* every year. The selected teachers are granted a paid leave from school to launch research projects at the center.

The fourth category of prefectural education center *kenshu* is teacher development through "social participation"—voluntary, prolonged work experience in other workplaces than the formal educational institution, including service and manufacturing industries, welfare and medical institutions, and social (adult) education facilities. This type of *kenshu* targets experienced teachers for career enrichment. The purposes of social participation are to (Ministry of Education, 1998):

- Provide opportunity for self-actualization as a teacher by broadening the professional perspective through an exposure to workplaces other than schools.

- Provide opportunity to reflect on teaching through social participation to promote one's sense of mission in education.

• Promote sensitivity to students and parents through social participation in other workplaces where teacher participants must deal with clients, customers, and colleagues.

Kenshu through social participation started around 1990 in response to a recommendation made by the Teacher Education Council in 1987 to enhance teacher professional development (see Ministry of Education, 1998). Thirty-six prefectural and municipal boards of education offer social participation programs involving over 700 teacher participants. This type of *kenshu* is gaining popularity at a time when the Japanese public views teachers as professionally parochial and unfamiliar with the world outside the school.

Incidentally, the Japanese Employers Association or *Keidanren* also offers a program of work experience to over 500 teachers for inservice experience (OECD, 1998). The program provides a three-day attachment to one of over sixty participating companies during the summer vacation. It is jointly administered with the Japan Teachers Union, which was an anticapitalist union until recently. *Keidanren* offered a one-day course to 1,400 teachers in Tokyo in 1998.

KENSHU AT THE NATIONAL EDUCATION CENTER

The National Education Center, established in 1964 "to contribute to the national enhancement of education," operates under the direct purview of the Ministry of Education. It has a large conference facility for short-term courses in Tokyo, a small campus for social (adult) education in the suburbs of Tokyo, and a large, modern campus in Tsukuba. The Tsukuba campus is equipped with a multipurpose lecture hall, several conference rooms, seminar rooms, a computer laboratory with advanced facilities for fifty participants, a library, and computer study rooms. It accommodates over 300 participants for residential courses between a few days and three months in duration.

The Tsukuba campus concentrates on leadership development. The major features include residential courses for 200 principals and head teachers for 22 days and 200 to 300 experienced teachers for 36 days; these courses are repeated four times a year for different participants. Other, less intensive, residential courses focus on information technology in education, bullying, and student "school refusal," or truancy. Bullying and student school refusal have become widespread problems throughout the country over the past two decades. The center also offers leadership development courses for social education staff. The Tokyo center offers two-day courses for beginning principals, board of education staff, school superintendents, and directors of prefectural and municipal education centers, each enrolling 1,000 participants. The suburban social education campus specializes in *kenshu* courses for social education staff, lasting from 3 to 38 days.

INTERNSHIPS FOR BEGINNING TEACHERS

Internships for beginning public school teachers are the latest government initiative. The internship program, which began in 1989, is mandatory and enrolls all beginning teachers at the elementary and secondary levels for one year. The Ministry of Education had a sustained interest in internships, since it assumed that they were key to improving the quality of beginning teachers. The Ministry set up the internship program through a two-year pilot project designed to provide a model to local school systems, and it offers financial support for internships. The prefectural boards of education are responsible for the construction and implementation of the internship program.

Because the internship program's start was controversial, its background will be briefly discussed here. This is a program that the government had sought to institute since the 1960s (see chapter Two). During the prolonged school reform campaign launched by the government in the 1980s, internships were again proposed as an important measure to improve teaching in the midst of profound social change and its effects on schooling, such as a phenomenal increase of student resistance to teachers, violence, and bullying. Internships finally received legislative approval for implementation in 1988 (National Council on Educational Reform, 1988; Shimahara & Sakai, 1992). Internships place beginning teachers on probation for one year, which grants the government greater control than the previous probationary period of six months. During the probationary year, interns serve as teachers, but with reduced levels of responsibility. A full-time mentor for interns is appointed from among experienced teachers by the principal at every school that has two or more beginning teachers, and a part-time mentor is appointed if there is only one intern in a school.

Despite the ideological issue of government control of teachers through the internship, which was a major source of opposition orchestrated by the Japan Teachers Union and its allies (Horio, 1988; Miwa, 1988; Shimahara & Sakai 1995), this program fits the model of professional development based on craft knowledge embedded in the culture of teaching. When the internship model was introduced in schools, attention quickly shifted from internship as an ideological issue defined in the political arena to internship as a pedagogical device. As the locus of action changed from the central to the local level, neither the Ministry of Education nor the radical leadership of the union could actively influence internships. Although internships are legally required as a national program, local authorities are granted room to determine the details of their content. Thus classroom teachers have gained the capacity to interpret this new policy initiative within the framework of the culture of teaching to make it meaningful to them and to interns (Shimahara & Sakai, 1992, 1995).

From this perspective, established teachers see the induction of beginning teachers as an apprenticeship and regard it as the most effective way to learn to teach. The apprenticeship was initially somewhat informal, involving observations, consultation with the mentor, and conversations and interactions with experienced teachers (Maki, 1993; Shimahara & Sakai, 1992). But since its inception over ten years ago, the internship model has been substantially strengthened and improved. For example, in 1998 when the author revisited internship programs at both the elementary and secondary levels in Tokushima he found them to be much more systematically implemented under the guidance of a mentor than on his visits in Tokyo ten years earlier.

In essence, an internship comprises two components: an in-house induction program designed by the mentor to which about five hours are devoted weekly throughout the year, and a program developed by the prefectural education center. The in-house induction program focuses on both teaching and noninstructional roles. To develop teaching skills, interns: observe senior teachers' classes; present lessons for critique by the mentor; and consult the mentor about lesson plans, teaching materials, and student evaluation. Further, interns offer "study lessons" (described more fully below) before their senior colleagues for observation and critique. To become familiar with noninstructional roles, interns learn about the broad range of intra- and extramural responsibilities related to schoolwide programs and school-community relations. The internship component designed by the education center, on the other hand, includes: formal lectures on the legal framework and ethical foundations of teaching, human rights and minority education, moral education, classroom management, student behavior; the opportunity to broaden interns' perspectives through special arrangements to teach at schools other than their own and to visit various types of social institutions; information technology workshops; and a three-day retreat that allows interns to reflect on critical issues in teaching and to share their own experiences as first-year teachers. As an alternative to the education center's retreat, the Ministry of Education offers a ten-day retreat for which a large ship is rented for accommodation, activities, and visits to several sites. A total of thirty days is devoted to the center-based program, during which interns are relieved of their teaching responsibility.

TEACHER DEVELOPMENT THROUGH GRADUATE STUDY

Teacher development through graduate study is a recent innovation in Japan, but it has been gaining popularity. As the Ministry of Education pressed for legislation on teacher development through graduate study in the mid-1970s (see Central Council of Education, 1971), the national legislature approved its initiative to establish three universities of education where full-time teachers could pursue two years of graduate study leading to a master's degree. Subsequently, the Hyogo, Joetsu, and Naruto Universities of Education established by this legislation started enrolling students in the early 1980s. Prefectural boards of education, the employers of public school teachers, are authorized to grant selected teachers a two-year paid leave. Currently about 450 teachers across the country participate in full-time graduate study through this arrangement every year. After they have completed their studies, they are expected to return to their schools.

There is another type of graduate study at other public institutions for which full-time teachers receive a one-year paid leave from the prefectural boards of education. To complete their studies, however, teacher-students are expected to fulfill the program requirements in the second year while returning to the job. Reforms of certification standards in 1988 (see Miwa, 1992) stimulated a significant increase in programs for graduate studies at these institutions, targeting full-time teachers. The total number of teachers enrolled in this type of graduate work now exceeds 550 each year.

One of the critical issues inherent in these government-sponsored studies is the cost that the prefectural boards of education must bear, including funding for teacher salaries and for replacements while teachers are on leave. Since the cost factor has significantly constrained the enrollment of teachers at the three national universities of education and other institutions, these universities have failed to meet their enrollment goals. Moreover, the number of teachers enrolled in graduate studies is still quite limited because teachers' access to part-time study is severely restricted. Reflecting that constraint, in 1997 the percentages of elementary, middle school, and high school teachers with a master's degree were only 4.4, 8.2, and 15.3, respectively. Obviously there is a need to consider an alternative approach that would further enhance teacher development through graduate study.

In response to the demand for graduate studies, the Teacher Education Council (1998) completed a report in 1998 recommending that graduate programs for teachers be diversified to expand access to them. For example, it recommended that universities offer off-campus graduate programs as well as on-campus part-time programs to enable greater numbers of teachers to participate in *kenshu* at the graduate level.

SCHOOL-BASED TEACHER DEVELOPMENT

School-based professional development is initiated by teachers, whereas the *kenshu* programs discussed above are top-down government initiatives in which classroom teachers are only directly involved in constructing the internship. Teacher participation in mandatory government-sponsored programs is required at all levels of the teaching force, while participation varies with respect to optional government courses. In contrast, teacher initiatives and participation in school-based *kenshu* vary significantly, depending on the leadership of teachers in the schools and of subject-area associations of teachers, as well as the level of teaching. In general, school-based teacher *kenshu* is actively developed at the elementary level throughout the country; by comparison, it tends to be formalistic and inactive at the secondary (middle and high school) level. Data from our national survey (Fujita et al, 1996), however, suggest a high degree of teacher participation in in-house *kenshu* at both the elementary and middle school levels. Forty percent of elementary teachers participated in *kenshu* thirteen times or more in 1994 and 37 percent participated four to twelve times. In contrast, 24 percent of middle school teachers participated in *kenshu* thirteen times or more in the same year while 40 percent were involved four to twelve times. These high percentages indicate teacher participation in all types of teacher-planned events subsumed under inservice education, which include the intensive professional development activities discussed below.

Our interviews with middle school teachers, however, reveal that the intensification of teaching at the secondary level curtails their initiatives to promote school-based teacher development. One major source of constraint is the high school and university entrance examination, which drive classroom teachers to concentrate on traditional noninteractive and unreflective transmission of knowledge. Moreover, secondary teachers are required to perform a number of duties outside the classroom, including student placement in high schools and colleges, student club activities, and student guidance. All this leaves relatively little time to promote either in-house or districtwide teacher development. In short, school-based teacher development at the secondary level is stagnant.

We will, therefore, concentrate mostly on elementary-level school-based *kenshu* using the data that we have collected since 1989. The concept of *kenshu*, as it has developed in Japan, is largely predicated upon several premises (Shimahara, 1997; Sato and McLaughlin, 1992). The first premise is that teaching is a collaborative, peer-driven process and that it is improved through that process. Colleagues are regarded as interdependent resources, not isolated coworkers, and intersubjective process is promoted through close interaction. The desks of teachers of the same grade level at elementary schools are clustered in the staff room; teachers spend considerable time at these staff room desks every day for work, meetings, and consultation, as well as for socialization. Professional development initiatives thus actively draw on these interdependent peer resources. The second premise is that peer planning is a critical aspect of teaching and professional development. Peer planning is indispensable in a weekly grade-level meeting to review and plan lessons and extracurricular activities; an intraschool professional development program; and schoolwide programs. In other words, many of the everyday activities occurring in school require peer planning. The third premise is that teachers' active participation is a critical element of professional development and of teaching in general. This is evident in in-house *kenshu* and the implementation of cooperative management of the school, as explored in chapter Two. Basically, it is this cooperative management by teachers that provides smooth implementation of everyday routines and new initiatives.

These three premises are essential in organizing programs for professional development. School-based *kenshu* offers a structure by which craft knowledge of teaching is transmitted, shared, and reformulated through practice and collaboration with peers. One must note, however, that while these premises constitute the normative framework of Japanese teachers' ethos of teaching, they do not necessarily reflect an ubiquitous pattern of how professional development is organized. There is significant local variation, influenced by the quality of leadership and faculty in each school and district.

The most common type of teacher-generated professional development initiative is in-house *kenshu*. Aiming to improve classroom teaching, this form of staff development is organized by teachers without external official control. One of the most important faculty task groups in the school is a study promotion committee, which is in charge of the professional development program. It typically consists of several teachers representing different grade levels, including the director of academic programs and the principal *ex officio*. The committee drafts a yearly study plan, which is presented to grade-level groups of teachers for discussion and suggestion. Once the study theme and plan are accepted by the entire staff, each grade-level group discusses the process of implementation. The program generally consists of *kenkyu jugyo*, meaning "study lessons," scheduled throughout the year. These classes are observed by a large critical audience, including the entire staff and an invited advisor with expertise in the subject of the lesson. *Kenkyu jugyo* is a widespread, popular practice embedded in the culture of teaching, an ethos that Japanese teachers cherish as proven means to improve teaching.

The main purpose of study lessons is to enhance pedagogical knowledge and skills through peer collaboration, review, and critique. They are grounded in the belief that collaborative construction, reflection, and analysis in teaching are central to professional growth. Study lessons are actual classes that occur within the regular curriculum and school day. They are usually videotaped, and appointed staff take detailed notes of their observations, focusing on particular aspects of teaching. Preparation for each study lesson involves extensive peer participation lasting at least several weeks. At each grade level teachers are chosen to be observed on a rotating basis, and faculty of each grade group collaborate in helping those chosen to prepare their lessons. After the demonstration, staff members meet to review their observations and critique the class. An invited advisor makes critical comments on the class from the vantage point of his or her expertise. The advisor is usually a veteran practitioner from outside—a teacher with a fine reputation, a principal, or an instructional supervisor at the education center who is on leave from his or her school. During the review and critique session, the observed teacher and her collaborators defend the lesson plan, teaching strategies, and student interest in and comprehension of the materials presented. At the end of the academic year, records of study lessons are usually published in a school bulletin.

Teachers agree on the instrumental value of study lessons: they are perhaps the most effective way of enhancing critical reflection on teaching and thereby improving it. It is teachers' belief that they grow as classroom instructors through preparing for study lessons and undergoing intense classroom observation by their peers. This explains why study lessons are popular and common in Japanese schools. The centrality of study lessons for elementary teachers is evident in their belief that knowledge of teaching is enhanced through reflective practice and collaboration. Study lessons require the construction of a theoretical framework for a teaching unit of which study lessons are part, a sustained effort to develop teaching materials and strategies as well as a sequence of lessons leading to the study lessons, and the presence of a classroom culture conducive to the study lessons. In short, this observational approach aims to accomplish a collaborative construction of teaching, curriculum development, and an analysis of the process and structure of teaching and learning. Study classes equally benefit the observers.

The second type of professional development activity is closely related to the first type in its orientation. It consists of interschool programs organized by districtwide subject-area associations of teachers, or *kyoka bukai*, in which each school is represented. Each *bukai* organizes a study program in each subject field, among other activities, which includes a review of curriculum and a discussion of critical issues in the field. Venues for study programs are rotated among schools, and *bukai* members are invited to them. The *bukai* study program is similar to the in-house study program in terms of lesson preparation, collaboration, review, and reflection-in-action. Administrators, including principals and head teachers, participate in *bukai* activities as in in-house *kenshu* because they are considered "peers" with accumulated teaching experience in the context of transmitting and re-creating teaching as craft. Because the school is jointly managed by administrators and faculty, the absence of status distinction between administrators and faculty in inservice education is not unusual in Japan.

The pattern of professional development activities just described is typical in Tokyo, but there is some variation across the country. For example, in Tokushima Prefecture, Shikoku, where the author conducted his study of teacher development in 1998, in-house and districtwide professional development initiatives are usually organized as part of the prefectural study program for teachers at the elementary and secondary levels and are designed by the subject-area associations of teachers at the district and prefectural levels. Every year study schools are chosen in different subject fields on a rotating basis by these associations. With the guidance of the associations, teachers at the study school sites prepare and present study lessons at all grade levels for observation and discussion by peer teachers from other schools in the district or prefecture on the days of study meetings in the fall. Preparation for study lessons requires a prolonged process—usually one year of planning—including the construction of a detailed instructional plan in each of the subjects and what teachers call "exploratory" study lessons, offered several times by in-house colleagues and teachers in cooperating schools for critique and reflection within their schools. Teachers regard these exploratory study lessons as highly useful to help develop effective plans and strategies for the demonstration lessons presented at the study meetings. The board of education designates a professional development day to enable all the teachers in the prefecture to participate in the study meetings. A typical study meeting consists of an all-day program, including study lessons, presentations of case studies focused on the theme of study meetings, and a lecture by an invited guest.

In Tokushima, study meetings initiated by subject-area associations constitute part and parcel of teacher development activities organized at different levels: district, prefectural, and regional levels. Study lessons are largely organized in conjunction with these study meetings, although individual schools with strong leadership may independently conduct study lessons as part of their own teacher development initiative. Incidentally, regional study meetings occur once every two years and involve teachers in four prefectures, including Tokushima, in the Shikoku area. In addition, there are Chugoku regional (including nine prefectures) and national study meetings, which rotate among prefectures.

As an illustration of how school-based professional development is organized, we will briefly describe the *kenshu* program that Omatsu Elementary School implemented in 1998. Omatsu is a small school located in Tokushima City, with only twelve classes staffed by twelve classroom teachers and two administrators. The school focused on moral education as the study theme for professional development in 1997 and volunteered to serve as host for the Shikoku Regional Study Meeting on moral education held in November 1998.

The responsibility of the host school of the regional study meeting is to organize study lessons for observation and discussion and related events, including a lecture on the theme of the study meeting by an invited guest. When the study meeting was held at Omatsu in 1998, the school presented moral education study lessons for over 300 invited teachers from four prefectures in Shikoku. All twelve classes from first through sixth grade participated in study lessons, followed by the school's very impressive, illustrative presentation on moral education. Participants received a packet of materials, including a 168-page document titled "Program of Moral Education at Omatsu" and a 121-page study meeting bulletin, which included the framework for moral education at each grade level and units of lessons leading to the study lessons at the meeting.

The significance of such an event to teacher development is not only in the outcomes but also in the process of *kenshu* leading to the product. This process involved prolonged planning, including construction of a moral education curriculum, many faculty discussions to develop the strategies to present moral issues to students, creation of exploratory study lessons, and consultation with the subject-area associations on moral education at the municipal and prefectural levels. Omatsu faculty held a seminar to discuss how to construct a lesson plan in April of 1998; in May they organized three in-house exploratory study lessons presented by second-, third-, and fifth-grade teachers for observation, critique, and reflection. These lessons were preceded by a faculty review of the lesson plans. In June faculty organized two more study lessons and briefed the municipal subject-area association on moral education about their process in preparing for the study meeting. In July a sixth-grade teacher presented a study lesson; faculty met to discuss how to prepare a draft for the study meeting bulletin. In like manner, faculty organized three more study lessons preceded by discussions on lesson plans in October. All this effort culminated in the Shikoku Study Meeting at Omatsu in November.

The head teacher, who shared leadership with the director of the study promotion committee in developing moral education, explained the importance of a reflection meeting that occurred after each study lesson:

> At the reflection meeting, we discussed various matters: the extent to which the goals of the lesson were accomplished; how children participated in the lesson; what approach the teacher used; how she interpreted materials on moral issues and presented them to children; how she elicited children's views and feelings

on particular moral issues; how a lesson was developed to promote the moral education theme of the school. In short, these concerns centered on the question of the teacher's pedagogical approach to moral issues.

The Omatsu faculty's participation in teacher development and preparation for the study meeting was very intense and does not represent typical *kenshu*. The strategies that they used in teacher development, however, do reflect part and parcel of *kenshu* for teachers. The head teacher commented that genuine teacher development results from teachers' collaborative efforts to accomplish their shared goals. She went on to suggest that teachers' initiatives at Omatsu embodied such goals.

NATIONAL TEACHER NETWORKS

Teacher-initiated voluntary national networks designed to promote teaching have been popular in Japan. According to a survey (Otsuki, 1982), more than 47 such teacher networks developed in the early postwar period, most of which are currently active. They are independent associations committed to a shared purpose: promoting teaching, independent of government and external institutional control. Many of these national associations were initially formed as small groups of educators in the 1950s to develop an independent approach in teaching at a time when Japan's postwar education was undergoing drastic ideological and systemic transformation toward centralized control under the stewardship of the conservative government. Examples of influential associations include the Association of History Teachers, the Japanese Journal Circle of Teachers, and the Association of Mathematics Education. The Association of History Teachers is the oldest association in the teacher network movement (see Fujioka, 1992). One far-reaching, popular recent network is a loosely-knit association of teachers initiated in 1984 by an energetic and gifted elementary school teacher. Seeking a broad, collaborative basis in elementary teaching called *hosokuka* (science of teaching), this network promotes a national movement to advance teaching through sharing and critiquing individual teachers' practice (Mukoyama, 1985). Networks like these regularly hold conferences and workshops and publish magazines sold at commercial bookstores to disseminate information about their innovative ideas and practices to teachers nationally.

Currently national teacher networks hold nearly two hundred summer workshops every year, suggesting active interest in self-initiated study activities (Sato, 1992; Nihon Kyoiku Shimbun, 1998). Teacher networks hold annual membership drive meetings during the summer, drawing both elementary and secondary teachers. However, the extent to which teachers across the country participate in such meetings appears to be somewhat limited. Eighty percent of the teachers who participated in our national survey, for example, indicated that they did not take part in such meetings in 1995.

CHALLENGES IN PROFESSIONAL DEVELOPMENT

Japan has developed a model for teacher development. *Kenshu* is promoted by both government- and teacher-initiated strategies. As we have seen, the Ministry of Education and prefectural boards of education take an active part in providing a wide spectrum of *kenshu* programs targeting teachers and administrators at different career stages. Among these programs, internships for public school beginning teachers and leadership development for experienced teachers, head teachers, and principals are especially intensive. Education centers, established since the 1960s, play a vital role in promoting teacher development through the *kenshu* programs that they create for teachers. The top-down government *kenshu* system reflects the official vision of teacher development.

Teacher initiatives are equally strong on the other, bottom-across, end of the *kenshu* continuum. Enhanced by teachers without direct official sanctions, practices for school-based teacher development are by and large standardized throughout the country. District- and local-level professional organizations, earlier referred to as *kyoka bukai*, are instrumental in promoting *kenshu* via, in particular, study lessons.

Japan has developed not only a model but also standards for inservice education. The term "standard" has two meanings in this context. One refers to a pattern of practice that is established by authority or custom; the other to a degree of quality of practice. In the first sense of standard, the Japanese *kenshu* system is institutionalized and implemented nationwide. With respect to the second sense, we have to ask the extent to which Japan has developed measurements of quality for professional development. This is a much more complex issue than describing the types and content of *kenshu* activities. In this section we will discuss salient issues in professional development.

ISSUES IN TOP-DOWN KENSHU

In the postwar era, top-down *kenshu* began as early as 1945 when the Ministry of Education started a seminar on educational policy targeting educational leaders (see Maki, 1993). This was followed by the ministry's initiation of the Institute for Educational Leadership in 1948 and a succession of leadership seminars focused on different topics, such as elementary and secondary education, moral education, and student guidance and placement. *Kenshu* for leadership development by the Ministry began with these initiatives. In 1958, when the Ministry's course of study became the binding framework of the national curriculum, it offered seminars on the course of study for the first time, which continue to the present day. Meanwhile, the first *kenshu* programs at the prefectural education centers were offered in 1960 under the sponsorship of the Ministry.

It is evident that the Ministry of Education played the central role from the outset of postwar education in developing *kenshu* programs to promote its vision of teaching in Japan's centrally controlled system of schooling. The government initiatives, however, had been unswervingly opposed by the radical Japan Teachers Union until the 1980s. In the words of its former ideological spokesman (Horio, 1988), "[State-organized *kenshu*] threatens to make our teachers' desires for personal advancement directly dependent upon the power of a centralized system of administrative control. Thus, to realize their desire for higher positions within the organization of the school, teachers will increasingly have to perform successfully within government-sponsored programs..." (p. 247). In the union's view, top-down *kenshu* was a political strategy to control teachers.

Apart from this ideological conflict between the conservative government and the union, there is another problem inherent in government-sponsored *kenshu*. Teachers who participate in such *kenshu* have little input in formulating the programs, which creates a gap between school-based practitioner needs and the needs perceived by the designer of *kenshu*. This problem also applies to *kenshu* programs designed by instructional supervisors at the prefectural education center.

There are other problems with government *kenshu* programs. First, except for intensive residential courses for leadership development at the National Education Center, these programs are short and tend to be fragmentary. For example, *kenshu* for fifth- and tenth-year teachers at the education center are offered for only five days that are scattered over a period of time. Other courses are even shorter. Second, government *kenshu* programs are rarely evaluated in terms of their effects on teaching, school management, and student learning. In other words, there is little follow-up in assessing their effectiveness.

Likewise, the internship program for beginning teachers has not been evaluated since 1991. This is the most extensively implemented, costly national program among government-sponsored professional development initiatives; the Ministry of Education considers it vital in promoting teaching. Yet the program was evaluated only once by the National Institute for Educational Research (Maki, 1992)—the Ministry's research arm—in 1991, two years after the program had begun. Education centers may have informally evaluated the program, but their assessment has not been published and is not accessible to the public.

ISSUES IN TEACHER DEVELOPMENT THROUGH GRADUATE STUDY

Teacher development through graduate study has been in place for two decades since Hyogo, Joetsu, and Naruto Universities of Education started master's degree programs for teachers, and it recently received renewed attention when the Teacher Education Council (1998) proposed an expansion of graduate study for teachers in 1998. According to the proposal, 15 to 25 percent of the teaching force will be enrolled in graduate study by 2010 if its plans are implemented.

Before the council's proposal is further considered for legislation and implementation, it is important to reflect on problems inherent in the current master's programs for teachers. Sako (1998) aptly points out three major concerns with these programs. The first is the issue of access to graduate study. As mentioned earlier, most master's programs for teachers in Japan are offered on the condition that students are enrolled full-time for at least one year and that their studies are funded by prefectural boards of education. The council is now addressing this issue by proposing diversification of graduate study. The second concern is that these programs are designed to enhance individuals' acquisition of knowledge and skills. This individualist approach to teacher development, however, does not address constraints inherent in the deep-seated teacher culture that inhibit an individual from introducing change into teaching. The third concern involves the precedence of technical rationality over practical rationality in graduate study. Technical rationality views professional knowledge as the application of theory and technique derived from scientific knowledge, whereas practical rationality regards professional knowledge as grounded in teachers' practice and reflection in action. The higher status accorded to technical rationality creates a boundary between the theoretical and practical domains, relegating the latter to secondary importance.

To illustrate the relevance of the issues presented by Sako, we will draw on the focus-group interviews that we conducted at one of the universities of education in 1998, with three groups of seven graduate students each. The groups represented elementary, middle school, and high school teachers. The focus-group interviews were designed to elicit participants' views on their graduate studies and professional development. Sako's second and third concerns emerged as main themes, along with a few others.

Focus-group participants agreed that their graduate studies would not significantly affect their classroom practice due to the teacher culture. The teacher culture, in their view, is so conservative that an individual's attempt to introduce change in practice would meet resistance. The teacher group or *kyoshi shudan*, of which participants are members in their respective workplaces, represents a restraining force against change. Respondents insisted that it is essential to conform to peer expectations in order to work well with colleagues. Some even suggested that they would try to avoid making any reference to their graduate academic work when back on the job so that they would not stand out as having advanced academic credentials. In short, the impact of participants' graduate studies on their schools would be very limited.

The participants also invariably pointed out that there is a considerable gap between the "needs of professors and students," reflecting the distinction between technical and practical rationality. Put differently, professors who subscribe to technical rationality often fail to address students' interests as directly related to their teaching experiences. High school participants, for example, questioned the relevance of their coursework for classroom teaching. They also shared the view that they have few choices in their coursework to pursue their professional interests. In other words, their programs are designed without sufficient attention to their classroom needs and interests.

Another relevant theme was that participants' decisions to seek admission to the university were not influenced so much by their intrinsic professional interests as by extrinsic factors. Those factors include recommendations by principals and superintendents of schools, suggestions by colleagues, and personal interest in taking a leave from school for a variety of nonacademic reasons. In fact, few participants developed professionally relevant academic objectives before seeking admission to the university. Consequently, when they started graduate study, participants often developed a sense of mismatch between their professional interests and their programs, which they chose based on those extrinsic influences. This sense of mismatch was intensified by the emphasis placed on technical rationality in coursework.

It is difficult to determine to what extent the focus-group participants' experiences and perceptions represent the entire body of teachers enrolled in graduate programs. Nonetheless, the focus-group interviews help to raise questions and shed light on critical issues in the current graduate programs for teachers. We suggest that these issues must be systematically studied and addressed to create programs that will have a significant impact on teaching. Two-year *kenshu* for teachers through graduate study was originally proposed in an audacious school reform report issued by the Central Council of Education in 1971 (Central Council of Education, 1971), which was intended to produce the most important education reforms since late 1940s. The report called for a national commitment to enhance "standards" for teaching, with the introduction of graduate study for teachers to respond to new challenges brought about by rapid changes in the social, economic, and technological spheres. Unfortunately, the question remains: are the current graduate programs for teachers enhancing standards for teaching in the midst of social change? It hardly seems that they are meeting this goal.

ISSUES IN SCHOOL-BASED PROFESSIONAL DEVELOPMENT

We turn to issues in school-based professional development. Despite the fact that elementary teachers actively promote study lessons in the belief that these lessons significantly contribute to professional growth, there has been little documentation of the effects of study lessons on student learning and achievement. Emphasis is invariably on how teachers teach rather than how students learn. Study lessons would have a more significant impact on teaching as well as learning if they were linked to student achievement. That linkage is assumed by teachers but rarely demonstrated.

Study lessons also lack an empirical and theoretical basis for sustained, methodical refinement of practice. They are not explicitly designed to test and challenge theory and research findings. Instead, these lessons follow a well-established format throughout Japan, and teachers repeat them on different topics or subjects using the same format every year. In this regard, notwithstanding the great importance that teachers attach to study lessons, they tend to become reproductive or ritualistic events. To address some of these limitations, teachers might consider establishing a national database to be accessed by teachers and researchers throughout the country to review particular lessons, study issues in teaching, and generate an empirical basis for improving teaching. The national database might also include student performance data.

A related issue is the relative absence of school-based professional development at the secondary level, especially teacher development through study lessons, which is often attributed to the greater demands of teaching at this level. Secondary teachers are reminded daily that they must improve their teaching to promote student interest in learning. Over the past two decades, however, teachers have been preoccupied with widespread disruptive behavior in the classroom, which reflects students' lack of interest in didactic teaching—focused solely on knowledge transmission—as well as teachers' failure to address students' needs. The author's interviews with middle school teachers suggest that many would be content if students were orderly during lessons. Put differently, some teachers are not genuinely interested in promoting interactive and reflective lessons. The following interview excerpt illustrates this problem in teaching:

> *Researcher*: You mentioned that you follow a lecture format when you teach. Does this reflect a general pattern of teaching at the middle school level?
>
> *Middle school social studies teacher*: Yes. But I do not believe it is good. Put in simple terms, teaching has become completely one-way street. Basically, students sit facing the teacher, and the teacher stands facing students and talks from the desk. This is a dominant pattern in middle schools. There are teachers who use a small group discussion format, but it does not work when students become disorderly. Control is a main concern for many teachers. Teachers are afraid that if they loosen up students, they can never tell what would happen in the classroom.

School reform leaders insist that both middle and high school teachers must consider how to promote lessons that will capitalize on students' intrinsic interests, instead of unwaveringly concentrating on how to merely transmit knowledge to students. It is suggested that secondary teachers follow the lead of elementary teachers and organize study lessons that would showcase various teaching strategies. Faced with a national phenomenon characterized as a crisis in the classroom or *gakkyu hokai*, teachers must meet the challenge of reconceptualizing teaching.

A COMPARATIVE PERSPECTIVE

Professional development of teachers is a major concern in both Japan and the U.S., but the two countries' strategies to promote professional development vary, reflecting different policy contexts as well as the cultural and social embeddedness of teaching. In the U.S., local and individual initiatives are predominant and can vary significantly, whereas in Japan both teacher- and government-directed efforts are strong and, by and large, uniform. American strategies tend to emphasize an individualist model, encouraging individual initiative to upgrade professional qualifications and competencies (Hawley & Hawley, 1997). This emphasis is highlighted by the fact that American teachers actively seek enhancement of professional development through graduate study, illustrated by the evidence that over 47 percent of the teaching force currently have master's degrees. In contrast, Japanese strategies focus on collaboration and government initiatives. In the following paragraphs, we will briefly describe the types of American professional development to contrast them with the Japanese practice of professional development.

In the U.S., professional development programs include induction, a variety of staff development, and teacher development in the professional development school (PDS). Induction programs initiated in the U.S. over the past two decades are conceptually similar to the Japanese internship for beginning teachers, but they are shorter and primarily offered to prepare for state-required evaluation. The literature suggests that because these induction programs emphasize evaluation, many of them are fragmented and provide too little assistance to beginning teachers (Borko, 1986; Darling-Hammond & Cobb, 1995; Fox & Singletary, 1986). By comparison, the Japanese internship is both intensive and prolonged and not intended for evaluation of interns.

Sparks and Loucks-Horsley (1990) identify five approaches to staff development: individually guided professional development, observation/assessment, development/improvement processes, training, and inquiry. The first approach, individually guided professional development, refers to personally initiated efforts to promote professional growth through enrollment in courses offered by school districts and universities or in such funded teacher development programs as the ones offered by the Center for the Development of Teaching in Massachusetts (Nelson and Hammerman, 1966). As mentioned earlier, this individualist approach to professional development is well established and popular in the U.S. whereas it is in the incipient stage and expected to develop further in Japan. The second approach, observation/assessment, is a strategy to stimulate professional growth with feedback from supervisory personnel based on observation and assessment. This approach is rarely used in Japan, but collegial support and feedback to promote personal development is emphasized, as in school-based *kenshu*. Reflecting the importance of such support, 50 percent of elementary and middle school participants in our national survey, for example, indicated that they have colleagues who support them and serve as their "influential" models.

Initiatives such as participation in curriculum and assessment development constitute the third approach—development and improvement processes. While this approach is important and widespread in the U.S., it is not developed in Japan. As suggested by Darling-Hammond and Cobb (1995), training, the fourth approach, is a highly popular type of staff development in the U.S. Training is organized largely as short-term workshops on a variety of topics, involving experts as the source of skills and information. However, since training relies on a collection of unrelated workshops, it is often fragmented and its effectiveness is reduced (Darling-Hammond and Cobb, 1995; Miller, Lord & Dorney, 1994). Training is similar to a *kenshu* course offered by the prefectural education center in Japan, and there are comparable shortcomings in both programs.

Inquiry, the fifth approach, has emerged as a promising model of professional development focused on such activities as teacher study groups, teacher research, and teacher collaborative networks. The literature suggests that inquiry may have a meaningful and great impact on teaching practice (Little, 1993; Miller, Lord, &

Dorney, 1994). The inquiry model is related to the initiatives developed at PDSs, such as collaboration among university faculty, teachers, and interns with the intent to promote reflection, deliberation, and development; a tighter coupling of university and school; and teacher-led seminars based on collaboration with university faculty to develop, for example, instructional strategies. Stimulated by the Holmes Group of deans (1986, 1990, 1995), more than three hundred American schools of education have created programs that extend beyond the traditional confines of teacher education, and they have created PDSs to promote teacher development, including preservice education. The inquiry model is in its fledgling stage and very promising. Research indicates that there is little uniformity between PDSs regarding the processes and structure to support professional development and that the professional development initiatives at PDSs can thus far offer only anecdotal data (Valli, Cooper & Fankes, 1997). Nonetheless, the fledgling inquiry model seems very promising.

In both countries, teacher collaboration and networking are increasingly valued as strategies to promote teacher development and reflection. As Lieberman and McLaughlin (1996) observe: "Teachers choose to become active in collegial networks because they afford occasion for professional development and collegiality and reward participants with renewed sense of purpose and efficacy" (p. 63). In Japan, collegial collaboration and networks are extensively developed, but the inquiry model that is pioneered in PDSs has not yet received grassroots support. It is explored as only a theoretical interest at the university level.

In light of the American context of teaching, where collaboration is now viewed as essential in professional development, the Japanese model of peer-driven development may offer a viable and promising approach for consideration. As researchers and policy makers (e.g., Lortie, 1975; National Commission on Teaching and America's Future, 1996; Shulman, 1987) repeatedly point out, notwithstanding the aforementioned innovations, teaching in America is generally characterized by the structural isolation of individual teachers, and teaching is conducted without an audience of peers. As Cochran-Smith and Lytle (1996) put it, "the occupational culture perpetuates the myth that good teachers rarely have questions they cannot answer about their own practices or about the larger issues of schools and schooling" (p. 96).

To enhance collaboration and networking, shared teacher activities need to be developed within and across schools. We pointed out that in Japan, teaching for peer observation and analysis at the school and district levels requires peer collaboration and planning. This approach relates to the inquiry model mentioned above, but it goes beyond the limits of collaboration often seen in American schools in terms of scope and sustainability. It could, however, be incorporated into the framework of development initiatives at PDSs.

Teaching for peer observation and analysis is possible when there are networks of teachers both within and outside individual schools that envision it as a profitable effort for teacher growth. In Japan, broader networks are organized by subject-area associations within the school district or the prefecture, and professional associations at the national level. Teaching for peer observation involves sustained and systematic peer planning and inquiry focused on curricular materials, teaching strategies, and student learning. This approach would add a new dimension to professional development in the U.S. It would encourage collaboration and networking within and outside individual American schools. Teaching would be conducted before an audience of peers for analysis and critique contributing to teacher development.

SUMMARY: REFLECTIONS ON PROFESSIONAL DEVELOPMENT

Japan's practice in teacher development is promoted by both government and teacher initiatives. Government initiatives are supported by a top-down hierarchical structure in which the Ministry of Education formulates national policy on inservice education for teachers. There are several types of *kenshu* programs developed by the government: leadership development offered by the National Education Center; internships designed to provide beginning public school teachers with a supervised, reflective induction into teaching; prefectural programs organized by the education center to promote evolving career objectives; and long-term *kenshu* through graduate study. These programs address issues stemming from contemporary social change. Teacher-initiated *kenshu*, on the other hand, is strong and deeply rooted in the Japanese culture of teaching, which stresses peer collaboration. Another equally important area of *kenshu* is teacher networking at the national level. Japanese teachers are active in promoting collaborative professional development.

There are challenges to be met if both government- and teacher-initiated professional development is to improve. First, government programs tend to be fragmentary and are often viewed as impositions because they are "bureaucratic" or *kansei* formulated from above and mandatory. Teachers have little sense of ownership of professional development encouraged through government efforts. *Kenshu* through graduate study may also require restructuring to prepare lead teachers in an age of rapid social and technological change. Second, peer-driven professional development needs to broaden its perspective by restructuring its past practice and actively drawing on teacher inquiry, research, and theory. Thus far it has remained embedded within the framework of the culture of teaching that places emphasis on teaching as craft. Teacher professional development would also benefit from strong partnerships between schools and universities, as seen in the American PDS campaigns; such partnerships have been developed very little in Japan.

PART TWO

ETHNOGRAPHY OF LEARNING TO TEACH

CHAPTER 5

Learning to Teach in Japanese Schools
with Akira Sakai

Learning to teach is a complex, intersubjective process that occurs in multiple social settings, including the classroom, hallways, the teachers' room, and other formal and informal places. We have learned that beginning teachers are active participants in this process of constructing the social reality of teaching. Indeed, learning to teach is a sustained process of intense engagement in seeking advice from experienced teachers and developing strategies in response to demands and problems. The next three chapters of this book are devoted to exploring the occupational socialization of beginning Japanese teachers on the basis of the ethnographic data we collected in three public elementary schools in Tokyo. We will focus on both the cultural knowledge of teaching and how they acquired it.

In this chapter, we will discuss how beginning Japanese teachers structure teaching: the ethnographic descriptions that serve as the basis of analysis in Chapters 6 and 7. First, we will present biographical data on two beginning teachers and illuminate how they became elementary schoolteachers. Then we will investigate how they organized their classroom routines and what they were teaching students. In the last section, we will provide an overview of how they learned to teach. To understand these dimensions of Japanese teachers' socialization into teaching, we will focus primarily on two teachers from among the seven beginning teachers we studied. One is Kenji Yamada at Komori Elementary School, and the other is Yoko Kato at Taika Elementary School. Throughout our analysis we may refer to other beginning teachers when appropriate.

TWO BEGINNING TEACHERS

Kenji, Yoko, and the other five beginning Japanese teachers had only bachelor's degrees, in contrast to the American neophytes in our study, who held master's degrees. But this does not mean that these Japanese beginners had fewer qualifications than most Japanese teachers have when they are appointed. Only 1.1 percent of the men and women hired as elementary school teachers in 1989 held master's degrees (Naigai Kyoiku, Dec. 12, 1989). Most teachers at the elementary and secondary levels start teaching as soon as they graduate from their universities. Yoko was the same: she began as a first-grade teacher in April 1989, only a month after she graduated. Kenji graduated in 1988, but failed the teacher appointment examinations, so he taught at a *juku*, a private enrichment school, for a year, during which time he took the examinations again. He began teaching a fifth-grade class at Komori in 1989.

For many beginning teachers, including our research participants, their own teachers had a measurable influence on their decision to become teachers. Yoko's first-grade teacher was a significant factor in her desire to become a teacher, and Kenji's third-, fourth-, and ninth-grade teachers influenced his choice of teaching as a career. He decided to go to a teachers college when he was a high school senior. As reported by researchers (Ito & Yamazaki 1986; Kojima & Shinohara 1985), many research participants identified their role models as teachers who had influenced them during their childhood. Lortie (1975) reported the same findings with respect to American teachers. In other words, regardless of the culture, neophytes' childhood teachers are significant role models.

How did their teachers most strongly influence them in their choice of a career? The affective attributes of their teachers were felt to be more lasting than their cognitive characteristics. For example, Yoko told us that her first-grade teacher often spent a lot of time with his students in the playground and permitted them to sit on his lap. She recalled that her teacher displayed thoughtfulness to his students. She was attracted to this role model and desired to become a teacher like him. Kenji's teachers in the third and fourth grades were similarly outgoing and devoted a lot of time to their students in a variety of ways. Another beginning teacher was impressed by her teacher's patient efforts to intervene for her in solving a prolonged problem she had in getting along with her classmates.

Thus motivated in their childhood to become teachers, our Japanese beginning teachers went on to universities and took four-year teacher education programs. To become qualified as elementary school teachers, they had to attend seminars and classes on school subjects, teaching methods, the social foundation of education, educational psychology, and so on. They also had to do four weeks of student teaching when they were seniors.

After finishing these courses, they took the teacher appointment examinations conducted by the Metropolitan Tokyo Board of Education. The board establishes a hiring plan and conducts appointment examinations for about 1,500 elementary public schools in metropolitan Tokyo every year. In 1989, the year in which both Kenji and Yoko passed the examinations, the board hired 780 elementary schoolteachers. The competition was very keen; only one of every 4.2 candidates was successful (Naigai Kyoiku, Dec. 12, 1989). The board ordered Kenji and Yoko to begin teaching at their respective elementary schools in April. (The Japanese academic year begins in April and ends in March.)

The reader will recognize some differences between Japan and the United States in the ways teachers are hired and placed. In the United States, teachers are hired by local school districts, but in Japan most of them are employed by one of the 47 prefectural boards of education, under which are local, municipal-level boards of education.

Another characteristic of Japanese hiring procedures is that the educational authorities in each prefectural board of education assign beginning teachers to particular schools without consultation. Individual candidates therefore, have no choice with respect to the school at which they are to teach. In the United States, our research participants applied for teaching positions at schools of their preference. Not only do the Japanese beginning teachers have no choice, but they also do not know until late in March which school they will be going to. It is not surprising that beginning teachers are initially little aware of the special programs or the particular policies at the schools where they are assigned. In contrast, beginning American teachers make their teaching plans in light of their school's special emphases and approaches.

LEANING TO ESTABLISH CLASSROOM ROUTINES

All seven teachers we studied were hired by the Metropolitan Tokyo Board of Education in 1989. Kenji was assigned to teach a fifth-grade class in Komori Elementary School in Ota Ward, and Yoko was assigned to teach a first-grade class in Taika Elementary School in Toshima Ward.

For both of them, teaching a large number of students in one class was a big challenge. Their initial priority was to establish routines for daily activities. Routines would enable them to anticipate and monitor effectively what would happen each day. They had to establish such routines not only for the periods in which they were teaching subjects, but also for other situations in which they would be interacting with their students, whether in or out of the classroom. One of the most important tasks for beginning teachers learning to teach in Japan was to know how to set those routines, just as it was for their counterparts in the United States.

First we will describe what the routines were and then point out the features of these routines on the basis of field notes taken as we observed an entire day's activities.

ESTABLISHING ROUTINES IN FIRST GRADE

Let us first review Yoko's activities at Taika on Monday, May 22, a little less than two months after she had begun teaching. At 8:15, when we arrived, we found the principal at the school gate greeting children as they arrived. The principal's morning routine revealed a characteristic of Japanese education, the idea that teacher rapport with students through direct contact is important. At Taika, as would be true everywhere in Japan, a schoolwide assembly in the playground was scheduled. During spring this would take the form of a music assembly on Thursdays and a sports assembly on Saturdays, but otherwise, for fifteen minutes each Monday morning, all students and teachers gathered in one place to participate in schoolwide events. Yoko's first-grade students regularly participated in these assemblies, as did the older students. During each morning assembly the principal spoke to the students of his various concerns, including school goals, moral subjects, and his expectations of the students.

Yoko had arrived at school shortly before 8:00 a.m. to prepare for the day, and she had not forgotten that there was a morning assembly that Monday. At 8:30, the chimes used to punctuate the start and finish of activities sounded and a *nicchoku* teacher—a teacher assigned to be in charge of supervising the school on that day— instructed the students on the playground to form lines by class. She was followed by the principal, who stepped up onto a podiumlike wooden stand and greeted the assembly. He reported that the Taika sumo team, consisting of boys and girls, won second place in the ward's sumo tournament held the day before. He asked the team members to come forward and reminded the assembly that the goal of the school was to develop both body and mind.

At 8:45, when the assembly ended, music was turned on and students returned to their classrooms, but Yoko's and her senior colleague's first-grade classes remained on the playground to rehearse a Japanese folk dance they were to perform at the athletic festival in June. The boys wore white shirts, white pants, and white sneakers, while the girls wore white blouses, black pants, and red sneakers. The two classes were distinguished by the color of their caps, which was either red or white. With each pupil holding a large lampshade type of hat made of paper, they gathered at one corner of the playground and formed lines. At 9:05, as folk music was turned on, the children began marching toward the center of the field, where they formed two circles to begin the dance. The teachers helped the first-graders keep a proper distance between themselves as they danced and rehearsed their exit. After one more rehearsal, the teachers gathered the pupils around them to give them further instructions. Both teachers concentrated on using the exercise to develop the children's coordination and patterns of movement. When the chimes sounded at 9:30, to signal the end of the first period, the children quickly returned to their classrooms and changed their clothes. Their ability to promptly follow instructions was quite impressive, given the fact that they had become first graders only the previous month.

The classroom was a traditional four-walled classroom in which the teacher's and students' desks faced each other. Each student was assigned a desk, inside which several textbooks and notebooks were kept. Yoko had only 22 students, a relatively small class considering that the average class size is about 30 in Japan. The following school goals, in the form of mottoes, were written in large characters on a poster on the front wall of the classroom: 1) a child who is mentally and physically strong; 2) a child who is cooperative and takes the initiative; 3) a child who has a rich mind and thinks deeply. Next to this was written the school's special goal for the month of May: "Let us clean up thoroughly in accordance with our rules." (Such a display of school goals can be found in all Japanese schools. The principal and *nicchoku* teachers often remind students of these goals at school assemblies. Throughout Japan, banners with such school mottoes are often displayed in the hallways and at the entrance of the main school building, and a moral importance is attached to them.) Yoko had placed a colorful timetable next to the poster. An assignment sheet for school lunch duties was posted on one of the side walls. School lunch was to be served by the task group, with assistance from Yoko, in the classroom. She kept her work desk at the front corner of the room, facing the windows.

At 9:40, when a language arts class began, Yoko urged her class to get ready for the lesson. Two *nicchoku* (duty) students, who were assigned to be in charge of the day's classroom chores, walked to the front of the room and ordered the class to sit up straight. They called out the names of any students who were not paying attention. Yoko took the roll call and checked whether there were any messages from their parents.

The language arts class focused on practicing reading and writing *hiragana* (Japanese cursive characters), the character "mu" in particular. Having handed a work sheet to each student, Yoko wrote "mu" on the board and demonstrated the order of strokes for this character; she then instructed the class to practice the character on their work sheets, and moved around to check their work. When she found children who were not writing the character correctly, she returned to the board to show how to write it.

Although most children appeared relaxed and concentrated on their work, some did not. When Yoko saw a boy not practicing *hiragana*, she only told him, "Now is not the time to play; just practice the character." She also just called another boy's name when he spoke to someone. Moreover, when a boy, Kazu, stood up and left the classroom without her approval, she did not pay attention to him, acting as if she were not bothered by his behavior. (We were told later that a counselor at the Toshima Ward Education Center was studying this boy's antisocial behavior.) Yoko did not impose any punishment or penalty on him for having left the room.

When the chimes sounded to signal the end of the second period, students turned in their work. Normally the day's *nicchoku* students went to the front of the room to announce the end of the period, but on this day the lesson was finished without that exercise. All the children went out to the playground with Yoko for a twenty-minute break. (A twenty-minute outdoor break in the company of the teacher was a common practice at Taika and the other schools we studied.) The purpose of playing with the children, Yoko explained, was to develop close relations with them.

At 10:40 the chimes sounded for the third period, and students immediately returned to the classroom. The two *nicchoku* students stood in front of the class, shouting "Attention!" and calling out the names of those who were still making noise; and then, when everyone was quiet, they announced the beginning of the third period. Yoko began a music lesson. She was not a music specialist, but in Japanese elementary schools music specialists usually teach only upper-grade music classes, while classroom teachers usually teach them at the lower-grade levels. Yoko instructed the class to stand up and sing the school song as she played the organ. This lesson was part of rehearsing for the upcoming athletic festival. Students sang the school song in harmonious and cheerful voices, looking at the words written on a large sheet of paper Yoko had hung over the blackboard. After one round of singing, Yoko removed the sheet of paper and suggested that the class sing the song again. She told the students to sing with more energy. She then explained the meaning of the song line by line, and the class appeared to be enjoying the music lesson. Then they practiced playing a tune on the *pianica* (a kind of musical instrument).

During the lesson, however, there were several students who could not concentrate. Yoshi pushed a child in front of him, while Jiro was jumping around. That prompted Yoko to warn them to be quiet, but her warning did not include the threat of punishment. When Kazu had his legs propped up on his desk, she just called out his name. Later, he rushed to the front of the room and banged the organ keys. When told to stop it, he pulled out a white tablecloth for school lunch and wrapped himself in it and left the room. Yoko often admonished him and other misbehaving students by calling out their names, but she never resorted to punishment by isolating them from the group, a method often used by American teachers. In this classroom there were few commonly understood rules for dealing with the consequences of student offenses. But even though Kazu often misbehaved, the class did not seem particularly disturbed by it. At first sight, the class may have given the impression of being completely disordered, but in reality there certainly was order. The third period came to an end with the sound of the chimes at 11:25, and the two *nicchoku* students announced the end of the class. Some children went out into the corridor to play.

At 11:30 the *nicchoku* students announced the fourth period. Yoko told her class to open to page 17 of the math textbook, where there was a picture of five children on slides. Holding up the teacher's manual, she asked the class to explain the difference between "three children" and "a third child." A dozen students raised their hands to indicate that they were able to distinguish between them. She then told the class to color the five cars shown in the textbook and walked back and forth through the aisles to inspect the students' work. She placed a large black sheet of paper on the board and asked for volunteers to place five paper cars on it. When Yuki placed the cars on the sheet correctly, the class responded in unison, "That's right." The lesson continued, as did Kazu's deviant behavior. At 12:15 the chimes sounded to signal the end of the fourth period.

The last morning lesson was followed by a lunch period. The lunch task group went with Yoko to the kitchen to fetch meals. Back in the classroom, the children stood in line as the six lunch servers, wearing white caps and aprons just like professional cooks, handed out the meals. After lunch the children were dismissed and went home. A short time later, some sixth graders came to clean their classroom and hallway under Yoko's supervision. This brief depiction of Yoko's class reveals the characteristics of her teaching. First, repetition of routines is a major feature of her activities, which are regulated by the chimes. Students' behavior was also conditioned by the chimes punctuating the start and finish of each lesson. Educational activities in Japanese schools are structured according to a fixed time schedule that allows multiple activities (morning assembly, classes for various subjects, lunch, and the cleaning of the classroom, for example) to occur smoothly. Students had to follow the schedule while in school, and it was Yoko's responsibility to develop this response in her students. To our surprise, Yoko's students had already learned this response to the set routine by the time we observed her class in May. They were able on that Monday to leave their personal belongings and knapsacks in the classroom and go out to the playground to attend the assembly. They had already learned, too, that at the sound of the chimes they were expected to be seated at their own desks for lessons. And they had also internalized the rules that forbade them to walk around in the classroom during lessons. Most of her students could learn the appropriate way of behaving in a few months.

Second, a teacher needs to develop in students an attention pattern conducive to effective teaching. Getting the first-graders' attention and maintaining it for a sustained period is critical for her classroom management. Yoko was working hard to develop an effective attention pattern by issuing what Japanese teachers call *shiji*, instructions or directions that shape student activities. A senior colleague of hers teaching at the same grade level had suggested that developing in the children a habit of listening to the teacher was of utmost importance at this level. This required motivating them and applying *shiji* properly. A schoolwide activity, such as a sports event, was an especially good opportunity for students to learn how to listen to and follow teachers' directions. With this in view, Taika Elementary School actively promoted group-oriented activities (as most Japanese schools do). During the spring excursion trip for first graders in another elementary school we studied, several teachers accompanied more than 100 students on a train ride to visit a zoo. Both going to the zoo and on the way back, one of the major purposes of the whole experience seemed to be practicing how to form lines and how to walk in orderly ranks.

Third, her method of teaching was conventional despite her having only 22 students. Although she paid attention to individual students, her instruction was not individualized. Nor did she consider forming small learning groups (commonly called *han* in Japan), a practice often adopted by experienced teachers to promote cooperative learning. Instead, she taught the whole group, following the teacher's manual in the planning and execution of her lessons.

Fourth, the moral goals of schooling were emphasized. Yoko made a conscious display of the school mottoes and stressed the students' sitting posture. Yet, unlike beginning American teachers, she had no operational rules of classroom management. To outward appearance, she was rather incompetent in handling Kazu in the absence of such rules. But she was patient and hoped, she told us, that her patience and love for him would eventually be repaid. Operating under the assumption that he needed and wanted her attention, she often took pains to speak to him before he went home.

From the preceding description of Yoko's activities it is quite obvious that teaching is an inclusive activity. She taught all subjects (including music and physical education), helped to serve lunch, supervised students when they cleaned the classroom, and provided guidance for a child like Kazu.

Establishing Routines in Fifth Grade

We next turn to Kenji Yamada, who taught a fifth-grade class at Komori Elementary School. His routines of teaching were similar to Yoko's, suggesting that there was a great deal of continuity between the first and fifth grades. We will highlight Kenji's activities by focusing on one typical day.

Kenji arrived at school around 7:50 a.m. on Monday, May 1. Just as at Yoko's elementary school, the first day of the week at this school started with a morning assembly in the playground, and this included the entire student body and faculty. At 8:30, as each class lined up in two rows, the *nicchoku* teacher directed the assembly. Students began to sing the school song, accompanied by the school brass band set up in front of the assembly, and the school flag was raised. The principal stepped up to the podium to greet the assembly and spoke about the significance of the upcoming national holiday on May 5. He also praised the good results of Komori's track team, which had participated in a track-and-field competition. His speech was brief, but its moral symbolism was important. The principal was followed by the *nicchoku* teacher, who reminded the students of the school's goal for May, emphasizing that students should prepare for lessons every day. The assembly ended after fifteen minutes, and students marched back to their classrooms in time to the music of the brass band. All Kenji's students proceeded in orderly fashion to their classroom.

Kenji's classroom, like Yoko's, was a traditional self-contained room. The 32 students were seated at desks arranged in four rows facing the front chalkboard. The school's May goals were clearly posted on the chalkboard, as were the students' objectives (for example, "Study steadily and participate actively in physical exercise"). A wide-screen TV set was also located at the front of the room. On the rear wall was a large poster identifying several student task groups, including those charged with lunchtime, recreation, health and first aid, library, and chalkboard-cleaning duties. At the rear of the room were lockers for knapsacks, gym bags, art materials, and so on. Compared with the average American classroom, Kenji's classroom (like Yoko's) was rather plain.

At 8:50, when Kenji arrived at his classroom as the chimes were sounding, his students were seated at their desks. A *nicchoku* student shouted to the class, "Stand up," and the students rose. They then bowed to him, as he did to them. The first lesson was language arts, focusing on a poem entitled "A Horsefly" found in the thin textbook used by the class. He told the class to open to the proper page and to read the poem to themselves. After they finished reading, he asked a boy to read it to the others. Then students discussed their impressions of it for ten minutes. While they were talking about which part they liked, some students began to whisper to each other, but he didn't tell them to be quiet.

At 9:13, Kenji started reading the same poem, pausing after he had read a few lines to pose a question about the meaning of a word or phrase. He wrote on the board, "The heart of a horsefly becomes larger than a mountain" and asked what this line meant. No one answered the question. He then directed the class to form *han* (small groups) to discuss the meanings of the line among themselves.

Dividing students into *han*—cooperative learning groups—is a frequent practice at the higher levels of elementary education. It is resorted to when the teacher wants students to solve problems collectively, to be more closely involved in some task at hand, or to carry out classroom duties. It is a popular practice that is used extensively not only in schools but also in industry. In Kenji's class a *han* consisted of four students, two boys and two girls, who either sat next to one another or sat in front of and behind one another.

The students broke up into their *han* and began to talk to one another loudly. After a while the groups were asked to respond to the questions posed by Kenji. At 9:35 the chimes sounded and the lesson ended. He told the class to read over the poem three times at home. Then the *nicchoku* student ordered the class to rise and bow to the teacher to mark the completion of the lesson.

After a five-minute break the class went to the music room for a lesson given by a specialist. Meanwhile, Kenji returned to the staff room to work there. In the staff room, teachers' desks were arranged in several rows, with the desks of teachers of the same grade level clustered together to enhance interaction among them. Even the principal had his own desk there, despite the fact that his large office was located next to the staff room. In this staff room a briefing was held every morning, and all staff meetings took place in this room.

A twenty-minute break began at 10:25, when the music lesson was completed. This break provided students with opportunities to play outdoors and interact with one another in ways decided by the students themselves. Teachers did not supervise, though some of them often went out to the playground to play and interact with students as equal participants.

At 10:45, when the chimes signaled the start of the third period, Kenji's students returned to their classroom promptly, after which he came into the room. The third and fourth periods were devoted to a science lesson in the science lab, taught by Kenji. He asked his students to form a line in the hallway and walk down to the lab, which was located on the same floor. The students formed eight *han*, each of which sat around one of the twelve large blacktop tables in the lab. The class was experimenting on kidney-bean germination under various conditions and with sunlight, air, water, and temperature control. Kidney beans were germinating in the containers brought from the classroom, in a refrigerator, and in a water tank. When Kenji instructed his students to record their observations on germination on a sheet of paper, members of each *han* recorded the degree of germination of beans under different conditions. Kenji circulated in the lab to monitor their work and answer their questions. He then drew seven vertical lines on a large chalkboard in the lab to allocate space for each *han* to record the results of its experiments. The class displayed noticeable interest and involvement. Within five minutes, four of the eight *han* had written the results of their experiments on the board. When the chimes sounded at the end of the third period, he gave the class a five-minute break, but the four remaining *han* continued writing their results on the board.

The fourth period resumed at 11:35. The discussion shifted to sharing the results of each *han*'s experiments, and Kenji wrote the findings of the different *han* on the board. He asked the class how many times the results of their experiments differed from the initial predictions they had made. A girl responded by reporting her (unexpected) finding that the beans planted in a dark box grew faster than those planted in bright sunlight. He pointed out that several of the results written on the board confirmed her finding. He then asked if the findings supported the hypothesis that they formulated the previous week regarding the germination of the beans under different conditions. Student participation was high, and there was active interaction between the teacher and students.

As the discussion between Kenji and his students continued, a few students engaged in private conversations, distracting the class. He noticed them and asked one of them to explain what conclusion could be drawn by the entire experiment. When the student did not answer, he scolded him by saying, "I figured you were talking too much" and told him and his friends to listen carefully because it was something important. When they began talking a little while later, Kenji isolated them by making them sit at a table at the rear of the room. This was the first time he imposed a penalty on any of his students.

The discussion lasted for nearly thirty minutes, mainly focused on the reason beans grew faster in the dark. At the end of the discussion students started to copy the findings recorded on the board. At 12:25, when the fourth period ended, Kenji told them to clear the tables and return to their classroom with their textbooks and experiment materials.

Now it was time for lunch. The four students of each *han* pushed together their desks and spread white tablecloths over them; members on the lunch-duty roster quickly put on white aprons and caps and went to fetch the food and utensils. The food was set out on a large table at the front of the room, and students lined up for their servings, carrying them on a tray to their own places. Kenji joined them. When all were seated, they said in unison "*Itadakimasu*," a Japanese expression of gratitude for a meal and began to eat. The meal was a convivial occasion, with students conversing and having a good time as they enjoyed the meal. Kenji also chatted away with several students as he ate. After everyone was finished eating, they expressed thanks for the meal by saying "*Gochiso-sama*" ("thanks for a good meal"), returning eating utensils and leftovers to the table at the front of the classroom, cleaning their own tables, and folding up the tablecloths.

The chimes sounded at 1:10, and over the loudspeaker a student announced cleanup time to the entire school; the announcement was followed by music. Students went to their assigned cleaning areas. Kenji's class was responsible for not only its own classroom but also the resource room, the library, and the gym. Kenji remained in the classroom to participate in the cleaning. At 1:25, the loudspeaker reminded the entire student body that only five minutes remained for completing the cleaning. Kenji also encouraged his students in the classroom to finish cleaning. After cleanup time, the students spent twenty minutes playing on the playground, while Kenji went to the staff room for a rest.

The fifth period was moral education, starting at 1:50. Local school authorities did not provide textbooks for moral education, something that made Kenji feel uncomfortable in teaching the subject. He used a TV program, "Jump for Tomorrow," designed for moral education in the upper-elementary years; colleagues teaching the same grade were also using it. After he distributed printed materials for their homework, he turned the TV on at 2:00. The program was a drama that lasted fifteen minutes and that depicted a moral issue, with emphasis on honesty and integrity. He then went over the general outline of the story, asking the students about their impressions of it and writing their answers on the board. He then recounted an anecdote about something that occurred to one of the children in a neighboring class and showed how it was relevant to the TV story.

Although he planned to devote all the remaining time to a discussion of the program, the students were not concentrating, partly because they had just had lunch and felt sleepy. His questions fell on deaf ears for the rest of the period, perhaps to some degree reflecting Kenji's lack of confidence in moral education. When his students became noisy and restless, he tried to reclaim their attention several times, with little success. At the end of the lesson, he summarized the theme of the lesson by saying, "Be honest and admit it, even when you break something valuable." At 2:35, the chimes announced the end of the fifth period.

Incidentally, moral education, as an independent subject at the elementary level, was incorporated into the new national curriculum in 1961. Although the Ministry of Education has attached great importance to moral education since then, Japanese teachers have struggled for three decades with how to handle it as a subject. This reflects the tension that exists between the Japan Teachers' Union, which is opposed to it, and the Ministry of Education. It would seem that Kenji echoed the general mode of ambivalence regarding the subject. However, this ambivalent attitude is not shared by all teachers, as was evident among some of the teachers in our study schools.

When all the lessons of the day had ended, Kenji called the two *nicchoku* students to come forward and asked them to inquire if the task groups or committees had any announcements to make. Noting that there were no student announcements, he reminded the class of their homework. Normally, fifteen minutes is allocated as a period during which students reflect on problems encountered during the day. At 2:50, all the students rose, the *nicchoku* students led the others in loudly saying "Sayonara," and they all bowed to the teacher. They then prepared to walk home.

From the preceding observations we can see several similarities in Yoko's and Kenji's teaching methods, even though they taught grades that were very different in terms of intellectual, social, and biopsychological development. First, Kenji's teaching was as routinized as Yoko's. Both teachers followed the precise punctuation of activities by the chimes: class starting and finishing times and lunch and recess times were clearly differentiated. Most students in Kenji's class were more familiar with the routine set up by the school than were Yoko's first-graders. Kenji's students already knew almost everything they should do on each occasion. The schoolwide events were also similar: morning assembly, recess, lunchtime duty, and cleaning (though first-graders were exempt). This shows that, regardless of grade, common routines were institutionalized as part and parcel of the school's organization.

Second, in both classes textbooks were the main teaching materials. Yoko and Kenji used textbooks in all their subjects. A veteran teacher in another study school pointed out that the absence of a moral education textbook was the source of the difficulties teachers experienced in teaching the subject. This suggests that Japanese teachers rely heavily on textbooks.

Third, Kenji adopted a conventional lecture method of teaching, just as Yoko did. He frequently issued *shiji* or directions for developing an attention pattern. Although it is often said that the teaching in Japanese schools should be individualized, most Japanese teachers use *shiji* and follow the question-and-answer format throughout an entire class period, as the two beginning teachers did. Division into *han*, which Kenji used to promote learning, was a primary part of the lecture method.

However, it is also true that these small learning groups facilitated interaction and cooperation among students. This feature of his teaching contrasts with the American teachers' mode of teaching, which emphasizes the individualization of learning and encourages dialogue only between students and the instructor rather than interaction among students.

The fourth similarity between the two beginning teachers' teaching approaches is related to this feature of *han*. Although Yoko did not use *han* in her lessons, like Kenji she granted a variety of opportunities for her students to engage in social interaction: in the morning, before school began, and during the recess, the twenty-minute break, and the lunch period. During these times students were encouraged to take the initiative in cooperating with one another to carry out their duties and to control themselves by following rules. This reflects the Japanese philosophy of schooling at the elementary level, which puts a priority on social interaction and cooperation among students. In comparison, the American students we observed were granted much less opportunity for social interaction.

Fifth, the patterns of control Kenji and Yoko used to deal with students were similar. Both ordered their students to sit up straight and speak politely during lessons. Permissiveness toward unruly students was also a common feature. In general, neither of them imposed any penalties, but just called out the names of students who could not concentrate on the lessons.

On the basis of these findings, we can conclude that both Kenji and Yoko shared a fundamental pedagogy. The differences we found between the two were differences in the activities they engaged in and the degree of control they issued, and these were mostly related to the different grades they taught.

What Are Beginning Teachers Teaching?

From our observation of the two beginning teachers, we found that Japanese neophytes engaged in a variety of activities and established several kinds of routine. However, before we inquire into how they learned to teach, we should identify which areas of their activities were defined as teaching. As will be seen shortly, Japanese elementary education has generated its own concept of teaching, one that is significantly different from the American one. In each culture, schooling is organized on the basis of its own concept.

To obtain an overall picture of activities in a Japanese elementary school, we can look at Kenji's weekly timetable (see Table 5). It confirms the fact that his teaching was inclusive. In his fifth-grade class, besides 27 academic periods running from

Table 5: Weekly Timetable for Kenji's Class at Komori Elementary School

	Monday	Tuesday	Wednesday	Thursday	Friday	Saturday
8:30-8:45	School Assembly		Sports Assembly		Student Assembly	
8:45-8:50	Short Meeting	Short Meeting	Short Meeting	Short Meeting	Short Meeting	Short Meeting
8:50-9:35	Language Arts	Math	Language Arts	Math	Language Arts	Arts and Crafts
9:35-9:40	Break	Break	Break	Break	Break	Break
9:40-10:25	Math	Language Arts	Math	Language Arts	Language Arts	Arts and Crafts
10:25-10:45	Recess	Recess	Recess	Recess	Recess	Recess
10:45-11:30	Science	Social Studies	Home Economics	Social Studies	Math	Social Studies
11:30-11:35	Break	Break	Break	Break	Break	Break
11:35-12:20	Science	Math	Home Economics	Science	Homeroom	Gym
12:20-13:10	Lunch	Lunch	Lunch	Lunch	Lunch	Reflection
13:10-13:30	Cleaning	Cleaning	Cleaning	Cleaning	Cleaning	(12:10-12:30)
13:30-13:50	Recess	Recess	Club Activity	Recess	Recess	
13:50-14:35	Moral Ed.	Gym	(13:30-14:15)	Music	Gym	
14:35-14:50	Reflection	Reflection		Break	Reflection	
		Student Committee		Extra Period	(14:35-14:45)	
		(14:50-15:35)		(14:45-15:30)		
				Reflection		
				(15:30-15:40)		

Monday through Saturday, there were also club activities, homeroom activities, moral education, and morning assemblies. In addition, there were lunch periods and cleanup times (every day except Saturday), in which all the tasks were carried out by his students. Between the second and third periods, as well as after cleanup time, twenty-minute recesses were set up for students to play together in the playground. Table 6 indicates that Kenji's students spent more time on nonacademic activities than American students did. The table shows the number of hours spent by Kenji's students and American fifth graders in Westville Upper Elementary School (our study school) on each type of activity. Kenji's students spent 2,161 minutes per week in the school, while the American fifth-graders spent 300 minutes less—1,850 minutes total. As to time spent on academic lessons, however, Kenji's class spent as much as the American class. This suggests that Kenji's students were engaged in other types of activities as well: morning assembly, recess, club activities, homeroom activities, lunch, cleaning, and so on. In addition, the Japanese elementary school holds many events during the year, almost one every month: athletic meets, school performance days, art exhibitions, and the like. Fifth and sixth graders in most schools also go to summer camps and school trips. A considerable amount of time normally used for academic subjects is used for these activities or preparing for them. One of the significant differences between Japanese and American elementary education is the amount of time spent on these extracurricular activities.

Table 6: Total Time Spent Weekly for Each Activity in Fifth Grade

	Japan: Komori Elementary School		United States: Westville Upper Elementary School	
	Minutes	%	Minutes	%
Academic Classes[1]	1,170	(54.2)	1,200	(64.9)
Nonacademic Classes[2]	191	(8.8)	200	(10.8)
Lunch	250	(11.6)	200	(10.8)
Break and recess	315	(14.6)	250	(13.5)
Cleaning	100	(4.6)	0	(0.0)
Assemblies, meetings and reflections	135	(6.2)	0	(0.0)
Total	2,161	(100.0)	1,850	(100.0)

1.   Academic Subjects:
         Japan: language arts, math, science, social studies, music, arts and crafts, gym, home economics.
         United States: basic reading, language, spelling, activities, social studies, science, health, gym, art, computer, basic Math.
2.   Other Activities:
         Japan: moral education, student committee, extra period, club activity, homeroom activity.
         United States: activity period, open time.

But more important is the fact that Japanese teachers regard all these extra activities as being as much within the scope of teaching as are their academic lessons, while American classroom teachers tend to think that teaching is largely limited to the academic lessons in the classroom. It may be interesting to the reader to notice that Japanese teachers commonly use the term "teaching school lunch." A handbook entitled *Introduction to Teaching*, distributed to Kenji and other beginning teachers by the Board of Education of Ota Ward, illuminated the significance of teaching during school lunch as follows: "Teaching during School Lunch: Besides helping students to learn proper dietary habits, it should aim at nurturing desirable human relationships among them through eating together, as well as helping them develop physically and mentally." Because Kenji was expected to assist in accomplishing these aims, he encouraged his students to cooperate with one another in fetching and setting up the meals, and he provided them with the opportunity to chat during lunch by clustering their desks into several groups.

The first grade teachers were expected to teach students how to serve meals by themselves. We were able to observe a beginning teacher at Komori spending two periods early in May to teach his first grade students how to organize lunch service. He told them to push their desks together into three large clusters first, and appointed eight students as members of the lunch task group. He then had each of the eight students put on a white apron and white cap and led them to the wing of the building where meals were prepared. After the task group returned to the classroom with the meals, he showed them how to serve the food out to the others.

Cleaning classrooms and other places in the school is also regarded as part of education in Japan. The handbook published by the Board of Education of Ota Ward stated:

> Teaching during cleaning-up: Not to be taken as a merely utilitarian exercise, the school-cleaning activity needs to be understood as an occasion to provide education; it is a valuable activity that affects the educational efforts of the school as a whole.

The handbook emphasized that cleaning is important for students because it teaches them how to cooperate, as well as to appreciate the importance of a clean environment:

> It is very important for the students to deepen their human relations through experiencing pleasure and hard work together with their classmates. The satisfaction of having done something with others helps a child develop thoughtfulness for others as well as an attitude of working without complaint.

To achieve these educational goals, Kenji worked with his students and urged them to exert efforts in order to finish the cleanup on time.

Yoko's experience provides another example. As part of her internship program, she attended a summer seminar on recreation planning, including how to run a campfire or an orienteering exercise. The instructor at the recreation center told participants that the educational meaning of making a campfire was to encourage students to cooperate with one another and to allow teachers to integrate their students into a group. While the very fact that she learned how to run a campfire indicated that this is regarded as a relevant teaching activity, the explanation given by the instructor makes it even clearer that such an activity is as important for Japanese teachers as academic lessons. The broad scope of teaching will be explored in detail in the succeeding chapter.

On the basis of this evidence, it may be suggested that all the various activities that take place in an elementary school are defined as "teaching" in Japan. Therefore, every interaction of beginning teachers with students is evaluated from the educational point of view, and teachers themselves have to be careful not to adopt the attitude that their activities are not educational. In the next section we will explore how they learned teaching.

The Process of Learning How to Teach

Preservice Teacher Education

The opportunities for learning how to teach are divided into two stages: preservice education at a university and the period after one actually becomes a teacher. As noted above, most teachers take only four years of preservice education and only a few obtain master's degrees. During the second stage, informal learning through interaction with senior colleagues and through personal experiences while teaching, or formal learning through the official internship program offered in and out of the school, takes place. We will explore what and how the two beginning teachers, Kenji and Yoko, learned to teach in each of these stages.

As for the teacher education program in their universities, both beginning teachers were required to do course work on relevant subject matter and on teaching methods. Kenji thought that the lectures he took were not practical enough for him to teach successfully in the classroom. He suggested that his university taught him little about strategies for using materials appropriately. Nor did Yoko feel she learned anything there about how to teach, although she learned a philosophy of education that stressed that teachers should not "scold" children, but should wait patiently until they began to study of their own volition. Likewise, a beginning teacher at Ikeshita Elementary School (our study school) was not very sure how much she learned about teaching at her university. Kano (1984) reported that very few teachers felt that their preservice education had enabled them to develop the competence needed to teach successfully. In particular, many of them felt they did not learn any practical skills on how to teach in their classrooms or any knowledge of how to develop teaching materials. According to Jinnouchi (1987), one of the reasons universities did not train students effectively was that most professors tended to attach more importance to teaching the academic knowledge in each subject rather than to practical teaching skills.

However, both Kenji and Yoko identified student teaching as an exceptionally valuable preparation for teachers. Imazu (1978 & 1979) and Ito (1980 & 1981) also reported that preservice students generally felt student teaching had a considerable impact on their becoming teachers. American neophytes identified a similar impact. Yet student teaching in Japan is condensed into four weeks, a far shorter period than in the United States. Still, no matter how short it is or how it is organized, it seems to have a powerful impact upon most student teachers.

But we also found some characteristics unique to student teaching in Japan. Let us look at Yoko's case, for example. When she student taught for four weeks in her senior year, she went to her assigned school every day without attending any of her university classes at all. During the first week, after she was given a very brief explanation of the way the school operated, she was assigned two hours of classes to teach by herself. From the second week, the number of class hours she taught was gradually increased, so that by the end of the fourth week she had taught a total of 20 hours of classes. She stayed in school long after her students had gone home, to prepare for her next day's classes. Her supervisor also stayed with her, but he did not assist her unless she faced a difficult problem and sought his advice for a solution. Nor did he plan any specific program for her to follow; instead, he let her teach in her own way through trial and error.

Kenji, on the other hand, did not do as much student teaching as Yoko, although he also stayed at his school for four weeks. In the first and second weeks he observed classes taught by his supervisor; he was assigned several classes of math and language arts only from the third week on. He did not teach the large number of classes that Yoko did. Instead, he tried to take advantage of as many opportunities as possible to interact with students. Through playing with them, he remarked, he came to feel how lovable children were and how rewarding it was to be with them.

Yoko and Kenji's student teaching was entirely supervised by cooperating teachers at their assigned schools, and their university instructors gave little guidance and few suggestions during that period. The only time Yoko's university supervisor came to observe her progress was when she conducted a demonstration class in her fourth week. Kenji's student teaching was also supervised solely by the cooperating teacher.

This reveals that there is a weak connection between universities and schools with regard to student teaching. This makes student teaching an occasion for learning the routines of teaching and the patterns of interaction that exist between teachers and pupils, both in the classroom and in other areas of a school. As Yoko commented, considering the fact that during her course work at her university she had hardly any occasion to come into close contact with schoolchildren, student teaching was very helpful for her in learning how to interact with children. Kenji also felt glad that he was able to acquire some knowledge of the inner workings of a school through his student teaching. A senior teacher at Taika Elementary School agreed with both beginners about the effect of student teaching, stating:

> During the period of student teaching, a person can get some notion of how a classroom is managed throughout a whole day and can experience what it is actually like to be standing in front of children. I think these experiences have a great impact on a person's becoming an excellent teacher.... Although most student teachers are here only a few weeks, they learn a great deal from interacting with children all day long. They unconsciously internalize an appropriate attitude toward teaching.

In summary, although student teaching is one part of a larger preservice education package offered by universities, students did not find it to be an opportunity for putting into practice the academic knowledge learned from their universities; what they did find, however, was that student teaching confirmed (to their relief) that the actual patterns of teaching were just the same as the ones they had experienced in their childhood.

LEARNING TEACHING ON THE JOB

FORMAL INTERNSHIP

We now turn to the stage after the beginning teachers began teaching, to identify the most effective methods for them in learning teaching. One of the opportunities for learning how to teach made available to them was a one-year internship program for beginning teachers that had been introduced in all public elementary schools by the Ministry of Education in 1989. As discussed in Chapter 3, this program result-ed from recommendations submitted by the National Council on Educational Reform (NCER), which was established by the national legislaturein 1984. Concerned about the dramatic increase of unprecedented student behavior problems, the NCER pointed out that the Japanese school system was in a "grave state of des-olation," a "crisis" caused by pathological social conditions (NCER 1988). Characterizing Japanese education as desolate provided a strong stimulus for intro-ducing some sort of internship program (Shimahara & Sakai 1992).

The official purpose of the teacher internship program was for a teacher to develop 1) "practical teaching competence," 2) a "sense of mission" in teaching, and 3) a "broad perspective" as a teacher (NCER 1988). NCER suggested that a "sense of mission" refers to an awareness of purpose in teaching. Although the phrase has not been defined clearly, it has often been repeated and emphasized in government reform reports in the postwar era. The notion of mission is embedded in the time-honored assumption that teachers have a special moral responsibility in teach-ing (Shimahara 1991). "Broad perspective" refers to a broad social view that teach-ers are expected to develop "through exposure to business organizations and other institutions, as well as national and international events" (NCER 1988, p. 98).

With high hopes that it would achieve these purposes, the internship program was introduced in our study schools in April 1989, just as it was introduced in other public elementary schools. What we wished to see was the way the program was put into practice and how effective it might be for the beginning teachers regarding the content and methods of teaching. A handbook for the 1989 educational program published by the Metropolitan Tokyo Board of Education listed the following four areas of internship training:

1. A training program at the education center in each ward (once a week, twen-ty times altogether during the year)

2. An in-house internship program (twice a week, sixty times)

3. A five-day retreat

4. Seminars on specific themes (three seminars, fifteen times altogether)

As part of the training program held at the education center, several retired princi-pals, university professors, and experienced teachers lectured on their own experiences in teaching, human rights, home visitation by teachers, classroom management, moral education, and so on. The board of education also held workshops on the use of computers and audiovisual equipment and organized tours to public facilities in the ward. Most of the beginning teachers in our study did not regard these programs as very useful, however, because they did not feel the programs related closely to their everyday problems.

In contrast, the seminars on specific themes and the five-day retreat, which took place during the summer vacation, were valued. In the seminars, they learned the accepted ways of exchanging greetings in business settings, how to operate a video camera and a computer, and methods of educational counseling. During the retreat, the neophyte teachers learned how to organize recreational activities, for example, "orienteering." They also discussed problems in teaching specific subjects and in student behavior, and supervisors or school administrators from the ward sometimes offered suggestions for attacking these problems. For example, in the retreat planned by the Ota Ward Board of Education, 85 beginning teachers, including Kenji, participated and 20 supervisors or administrators served as their instructors. For the first three days, neophyte teachers were clustered into several groups by the grades they taught, so that they could discuss strategies appropriate to their teaching problems. Kenji felt that this discussion was very useful because he discovered that many other neophytes faced the same problems that he did. Yoko joined Toshima Ward's retreat, which was held for both beginning and second-year teachers. She also felt the retreat was valuable because she had time to talk to other beginning teachers regarding the problems she was experiencing.

But the core of the program was the in-house internship training, which the Ministry of Education required to be completed in sixty days over the course of the year. In each of the three schools we studied, a full-time supervising teacher was assigned to guide the beginning teachers. A memorandum, issued in April 1989 by the superintendent of Ota Ward Board of Education to the principals in the ward, listed the duties of the supervisor as follows:

1. First of all, the supervisor shall guide and advise the beginning teachers or interns.

2. The supervisor shall plan a training program for the interns in which approximately ten hours per week will be spent training one intern.

3. The supervisor shall observe each intern's classes on a weekly basis and give each intern the opportunity to observe classes taught by "veteran" teachers.

4. The supervisor shall offer assistance to the interns to develop their classroom management plans, to prepare lessons in moral education, to offer educational counseling, and to gain familiarity with the division of duties at the school.

At Komori Elementary School, where three beginning teachers (including Kenji) were employed, a veteran teacher, Mr. Murai, was appointed as the supervisor. He told us that, as a full-time supervisor, he was aware of his responsibilities, which included observing twice weekly the classes taught by the beginning teachers and coordinating opportunities for them to observe classes taught by senior teachers. But Mr. Murai did not always perform all these responsibilities. He taught Kenji how to fill out report cards, how to handle students during lunchtime, how to deal with emergencies, and he also briefed Kenji on home visitation and the division of work at the school. As for teaching classes and student guidance, Mr. Murai preferred to let them learn through trial and error.

The supervisor in Taika Elementary School was Mr. Ando, who was a bit more active in performing his duties. He reviewed Yoko's weekly plan of lessons and observed her classes periodically. After observing her class, he always offered her general comments such as "You taught well," which greatly encouraged her. However, he did not plan any formal meetings with her to discuss her problems in teaching unless she asked him for his advice. But she was not unhappy that he did not take greater initiative in directing her, because she felt that if he had made any detailed comments on her teaching, she would not have been able to integrate them into her framework. What she hoped he would do was to keep her headed in the right direction, so that she would not make serious mistakes.

INFORMAL OPPORTUNITIES

Both Kenji and Yoko learned more through informal occasions than through the formal internship program: typically, casual opportunities that produced cumulative effects on beginning teachers. One of the occasions in which they learned a great deal about teaching was during their actual teaching process. Yoko could not understand why students had difficulty in writing *hiragana* until she taught it to them herself. Based on this experience, she developed and modified her teaching method. She also learned from her colleagues. The most significant influence on her was Mrs. Suzuki, another first-grade teacher, who served as her model teacher. For example, when students were asked to draw a picture of morning glories during the arts-and-craft class, Mrs. Suzuki drew a model picture on the blackboard, while Yoko simply told them to look at some actual morning glories carefully and then draw them. After the class finished, Yoko found that Mrs. Suzuki's students had drawn the picture much better than her students. She then realized it was important to give them a concrete demonstration of what was wanted. Although she had believed until then that it was important to respect children's creativity, she began to realize that she had to take initiative and instruct them on how to accomplish the task at hand.

Kenji also learned about teaching from his senior colleagues, as well as through his own trial and error. For instance, when he was concerned about the poor participation of his students in the lessons, a senior colleague gave him some valuable advice. She told him how, when she taught farm mechanization in the social studies class, she was able to make the class discussion more lively by assigning them homework in which they collected information relating to the topic. Taking her advice, Kenji adopted the same strategy for his Japanese language class. On another occasion, when he observed a fourth-grade gym class taught by an experienced teacher,

Kenji noticed that the students enjoyed the exercises even though they were rather strenuous. Kenji applied the teaching method of that teacher to his own class after this observation.

In addition, to prepare their lessons better, the beginning teachers often referred to the teacher's manual. In response to the question "What did you do to prepare for the Japanese language class?" Kenji commented, "I use the teacher's manual to get hints." Likewise, Yoko prepared for her lessons by relying on the teacher's manual to make sure she did not overlook the essential points in each unit.

Furthermore, Kenji valued informal association with his senior colleagues as a means of obtaining helpful suggestions. Partly for this reason, he made it a point to participate in all the practice sessions for the annual schoolteacher volleyball or baseball competitions in Ota Ward. He also went frequently to restaurants or bars with the other teachers after the practice sessions, because in informal conversations he could get more tips about teaching.

Beginning teachers talked to their senior colleagues in informal situations, such as in the staff room or other places during recesses or after-school periods. Through these short chats with their seniors, beginners were able to learn common ideas on what to teach or how to teach, even though senior teachers did not tell them anything directly. In accordance with the sociology of knowledge of Berger and Luckmann (1966), this learning process of the beginning teachers can be defined as the process of sharing experiences with senior colleagues through interaction with them. The beginning teachers constructed a common frame of reference with their seniors, and acquired the dominant ideas on teaching that were held in their schools. Through this process, beginning teachers were able to learn a typical pattern of teaching and to develop sensitivity toward teaching so that they could determine which types of teaching were most appropriate.

One of the reasons why both Kenji and Yoko did not attach much importance to the formal internship was a shared belief that beginners had to learn teaching by themselves through trial and error. Senior teachers insisted that beginners had to agonize over their own teaching at first, because that was an essential step to learning the craft of teaching; only through this painful internal process could beginning teachers integrate their practice. A veteran teacher at Komori commented:

> It may be important to observe the teaching of other teachers, but the most important thing is to "practice" on their own. Beginning teachers have to decide which area they would like to concentrate on, and then they should work on it. If it were me, I would write out my own plan for every single lesson in one subject and keep at it at least for one year. This has been found to be a big help to me when I teach the subject the next year.

The supervisors of the beginning teachers in our study supported the view expressed by the veteran teacher. Mr. Murai, who supervised Kenji, suggested, "Beginning teachers learn best by accumulating experiences of teaching in front of children." He went on to say, "Even when they have picked up ideas from other teachers, they have to judge the value of the ideas. There will be no development in them if they just follow the advice of other teachers." Asked what he meant by "no development," he commented:

> Even though he can teach successfully this year by listening to the advice of others, he can't develop his own approach to teaching. Until he listens to others' opinions and then tries to establish his own way of teaching, he won't become a full-fledged teacher.

Mr. Ando, who supervised Yoko, also insisted, "Beginning teachers must make it on their own." In his view the beginning teachers who were in the internship program that year were being pampered. "It is better to leave them alone," he said.

Another shared tenet is that learning to teach through trial and error would be enhanced through "borrowing" or identifying useful skills and knowledge developed by experienced teachers. But the transmission of the cultural knowledge of teaching would occur incidentally. Senior teachers felt that they should not be expected to give specific information to the neophytes. At Komori Elementary School, Kenji was paired with a senior teacher as teacher representatives on the student committee, which discussed how to run assemblies and other schoolwide activities. When we asked the teacher how she, as an experienced teacher, gave advice to Kenji on the committee, she said:

> I do not give any direct guidance to Kenji during the students' committee meeting. However, when I advise the children on a more effective way of holding a discussion or on how to clarify their comments or how to proceed in their assigned work, etc., Kenji can listen to my advice. It is not necessary to guide him in front of the children; if I did, he would lose face, you see. All he has to do is make mental notes on what he might say in certain situations. . . .

As this episode suggests, experienced teachers expected the beginners to "mentally note" their observations and then to establish their approach to the problems with which they were coping.

Beginning teachers internalized the tenet of borrowing. This is evident in Kenji's comment, "Only after I try what I observe do I begin to think." In fact, when he observed classes taught by senior teachers, he did not discuss his "mental notes" with them afterwards but merely speculated on how he could apply the tips he got from the observations. Yoko also went along with the expectations of her senior colleagues and explained that she had to make her own decisions, even though she was always able to obtain advice from these colleagues.

In addition, because the supervisors of Yoko and Kenji also held these expectations, they were reluctant to actively lead them. They saw their supervisory role as something much more modest than that of "leader." Mr. Murai, for instance, defined his role as that of consultant: "In my case, as a supervisor I am more like a consultant for the beginning teachers. I do not help them as an officially designated mentor, but rather as a big brother ready to listen to their problems." Mr. Ando expressed his role as that of, in his word, *urakata* (stagehand), which is close to Murai's definition of himself. A stagehand, he said, offered assistance from backstage; the stagehandlike supervisor should offer assistance when the beginning teachers come to him with some difficulty. He believed that beginning teachers would gain confidence in their ability to teach, as well as feel at ease about teaching classes and managing their classrooms, if he continued to adopt a stagehand approach.

In a survey that we conducted of all the supervisors of elementary schools in Ota Ward, similar expectations were revealed. Of forty supervising teachers, nineteen defined their role as that of "someone who gives a minimum amount of advice so that the beginning teachers can be free to develop their independence." Furthermore, seven defined their role more conservatively by saying that they were "the senior teachers who can be consulted when necessary." In comparison, only fourteen, or one-third of the total response, defined their role as "actively guiding the beginning teachers according to a set plan."

The shared rationale for encouraging beginning teachers to learn teaching through informal occasions was that the supervision of beginners conflicted with the culture of teaching. In Japanese schools, teachers, once employed, are all regarded as equal in status; there is a tacit code among them that no teacher tells another teacher what to do to his or her face. This code, which could be termed an "egalitarian ethos," tends to inhibit direct teaching of beginning teachers by senior teachers. When we asked a teacher at Komori how he advised Kenji and the other beginners, he replied promptly, "I don't give any advice unless they ask me." Another teacher in the same school was more candid: "Do you expect me to tell them something without being first asked? Maybe it's wrong of me to hang back ... but to tell the truth I cannot figure out how much I should say to them." The tacit code made the supervisors reluctant to teach their "charges" directly. Mr. Ando at Taika expressed his reluctance as follows:

> I feel it is rather insulting to lead them by the hand step by step. They have learned about teaching in their universities already. And the principal also told me not to stand over them. At any rate, they are already to some extent mature adults. Whether a beginning teacher or an experienced teacher, he is a teacher in any case. It does not matter whether his teaching is as good as that of the others. I have no intention of tutoring them in detail just because of the introduction of the internship program. I urge them to use their own initiative.

The supervisor's orientation toward beginning teachers and full-fledged teachers, embedded in the culture of teaching, did not apply, however, to student teachers:

> Ishida, you see, is a student teacher, not a beginning teacher. So I will do more teaching as far as he is concerned. In other words, it is easy for me to teach him because he is not a full-fledged teacher yet. Also, that's the purpose of student teaching, to be trained.

> Should an accident or something happen in the class of a student teacher, it is not the student teacher but Mr. Yasuoka, the supervisor, who is responsible for it. A student teacher teaches a class under the supervision of his supervising teacher, which means that the supervisor could stop the student teacher and take over the class in an extreme case, though we try not to do such a thing.

Such a course of action is allowed in the case of a student teacher because we are the ones responsible. But we do not do the same when beginners teach a class. Because they have a teaching certificate and are assigned to a class, we just cannot say to them, "Step aside. I will teach for you." It is easier to supervise a student teacher.

This supervisor's comment marks a characteristic of the Japanese culture of teaching. He felt that it was all right to lead a student teacher step by step because the person had not become a full-fledged teacher yet. But he did not feel he could take the same position toward Kenji, because Kenji had already obtained a teaching certificate and was responsible for his class.

We should add that an agreement was reached at Komori among the principal, the supervising teacher, and the leader of the teachers union not to impose an excessive burden on the beginning teachers during the internship program (Shimahara & Sakai 1990). The Japan Teachers Union, which is the largest teachers union in Japan, criticized the internship program as a top-down rather than a bottom-up program for molding beginning teachers into a stereotyped teacher image (Miwa, 1988). Reflecting the union's policy, teachers affiliated with the union at Komori expressed reservations about the internship program.

Another feature in the learning process of the beginning teachers was that they developed an image of experienced teachers, especially dedicated and respected ones, as role models. The development of such an image eventuated through continual interaction with senior colleagues teaching the same grade. As noted above, continued interaction with more experienced teachers of the same grade helped both Kenji and Yoko learn hints that enhanced their teaching. It suffices to point out that experienced teachers' influence on the beginners was reinforced through the interaction.

Active interaction between teachers was a characteristic inherent in the organizational arrangements of the elementary schools we studied. For instance, special concerns and the rate of progress of classes were often discussed at the weekly grade-level meeting. Because most school events, such as excursions, were planned and implemented by the teachers in charge of the same grade level, they had to cooperate with one another. Through these occasions, beginning teachers engaged in recurrent face-to-face dialogue with experienced teachers.

The architectural structure of these schools also encouraged interaction among teachers teaching the same grade. For one thing, in the staff room, the desks for teachers were grouped by the grade they taught. The first thing teachers did every morning was to gather in the room to hold a short meeting, and during the recess some of them came back there to have tea or talk with their colleagues. Further, the classrooms for the same grade were located side by side on the same floor of the school building. Thus, even during a five-minute break, they were able to talk to one another.

On the other hand, as one supervisor pointed out, close-knit associations among teachers sometimes led to territorialism, so that experienced teachers had more influence over beginners than supervisors did. Partly because of this territorialism, one supervisor hesitated to supervise his intern actively, though he was responsible for her progress. He commented on the influence of himself versus that of colleagues who taught the same grade as the intern elucidates his concern:

> It's not only me, but Mrs. X and Mr. Y are also supervising her. They are keep-
> ing pace with one another. As for how much homework they should give to the
> students, they sometimes decide to give the same kind of homework. I didn't
> give her any suggestions about homework. The teachers at the same grade may
> have their own policy in regard to pacing teaching. It is a little bit difficult for
> me to decide how much I should intervene, because there is a head teacher for
> each grade who has an influence on the intern.

The learning process of Japanese beginning teachers described above is similar to the traditional apprenticeship system in Japan. An apprentice enters a workplace where, without formal training, he learns the trade through observing his master. This learning is based on intimate identification with the master, as the apprentice pays attention to his skills, knowledge, and attitudes. Likewise, the two beginning teachers, Kenji and Yoko, learned teaching not through direct instruction but by observing their senior teachers, as well as listening to them on informal occasions. Their identification with particular senior colleagues was by and large achieved through this process and reinforced by recurrent interaction with them.

The fundamentally conservative nature of the apprenticeship system should be noted. Although most senior teachers insisted that beginning teachers should develop their own approach to teaching, they also expected them to draw upon the cultural knowledge of teaching they possessed. They saw beginning teachers in a positive light when their teaching was in line with what they thought appropriate. Recall what the teacher who was on the students' committee with Kenji expected of him. She wanted him to observe her approach to handling the committee, so that he could make mental notes of what was important. Mr. Ando expected Yoko and the other neophytes at Taika to seek advice from senior teachers, even though he thought it was not prudent to give them much advice or to supervise them closely. Both supervisors and senior teachers thus expected the beginners to develop their teaching competence on the basis of what they could observe. In line with these expectations, both Kenji and Yoko largely developed their perspectives on teaching. This process of learning to teach thus contributed to maintaining the continuities of the dominant pattern of teaching among teachers.

SUMMARY

This chapter has offered a descriptive account of the routines that beginning teachers developed, followed by analyses both of their definition of teaching and of their mode of learning to teach. Because teaching at the elementary level is inclusive, learning to teach is highly challenging. The inclusiveness of teaching has evolved gradually since the Meiji Era, nearly 120 years ago, when Japan established the modern school system to contribute to the country's modernization. Because teaching initially encompassed mainly the transmission of academic knowledge, the meaning of teaching has been transformed significantly. One good example is the change in the meaning of the classroom cleanup. The regulations for elementary schoolteachers, issued by the Ministry of Education in 1881, stipulated that cleanup was necessary to maintain the classroom in a sanitary condition. At that time, the teachers were responsible for keeping the classroom clean (Ishii 1978). The educational significance of cleaning to promote cooperation was ascribed later.

Our study of beginning teachers in Tokyo suggests that the culture of teaching distinctly influenced both the process and outcomes of learning to teach. Its influence was enhanced by the patterns of intense teacher interaction facilitated by the programs of the school, a stress on cooperation among teachers, and the physical structure of the school. The influence of experienced teachers on beginners figured potently in this context. Beginners gained hints which enhanced their teaching competence through casual conversations with and observations of experienced teachers. Although the process of learning to teach was believed to be governed by an egalitarian ethos, the cultural knowledge of teaching that experienced teachers possessed was considered the primary source of guidance for neophytes, which granted higher status to experienced teachers. It was that cultural knowledge that contributed to the development of neophytes' teaching competence.

This pattern of developing teaching competence had a more significant effect on interns than did the government-initiated internship program, at least during the first year of its implementation.

CHAPTER 6

Cultural Theory of Teaching and Practice
with Akira Sakai

Japanese beginning teachers learned to teach through their enculturation into teaching. What they learned ranged from how to teach specific subjects to what general goals of teaching they should pursue. Our findings suggest that beginning teachers in Japan and the United States shared the goals of teaching embedded in the culture of teaching.

Japanese neophytes held beliefs that were isomorphic to those of their senior colleagues regarding expectations for students, classroom management, and control of students. This reveals that these pedagogical beliefs are part and parcel of the culture of teaching, and are often tacitly transmitted through occupational socialization. As Weick (1982) and Tyler (1988) point out, school organizations do not always fit the hypothesis that formal organizations are rationally organized to accomplish their goals. They saw, rather, that schools were more loosely organized than other formal organizations and needed other attributes besides rules in order to bind together all the parts of the school. Weick argues that schools need "symbol management to tie the system together." He further suggests that, "People need to be part of sensitive projects. Their action becomes richer, more confident, and more satisfying when it is linked with important underlying themes, values, and movements" (p. 675). Tyler, on the other hand, maintains that symbols alone do not suffice and that "knowledge of the background and shared assumptions of the staff becomes more important, as does their socialization into a common imagery and terminology" (pp. 88-89). Our ethnographic findings reveal that these symbols and assumptions were built up into what may be called a Japanese theory of pedagogy, and that the beginning teachers learned the theory, including the purposes of teaching. Evidently, the effectiveness of Japanese elementary education is grounded on the application of this pedagogy. It seems that it is indispensable for the versatile management of school activities, including teaching academic matters and running a variety of school events. In this chapter, we will inquire into the themes, assumptions, and ethos of Japanese teaching that beginning teachers learned: the explicit and implicit purposes of teaching and the pedagogical ethos that underscores classroom management and student control.

THE THEMES OF TEACHING IN JAPANESE ELEMENTARY SCHOOLS

What teachers expect of students is closely connected to some of the explicitly stated official goals of their schools, which are shared assumptions on which schooling is organized. The meaning and content of these goals in Japan, however, and how far they might extend, are quite different in some respects from those in the United States. Our study of American teachers revealed that American classroom teachers are mainly concerned with the students' development of cognitive skills, and pay relatively little attention to other aspects of schooling, which are addressed by specialists. It is no overstatement to suggest that elementary schooling in the United States heavily leans toward cognitive instruction. Suppose one envisages a continuum of orientation in schooling in which one end of this continuum stresses cognitive content and the other, expressivity and morality. It is obvious that on this continuum American schools lean toward the cognitive end while Japanese schools can be said to strike a balance. Japanese elementary teachers view cognitive, expressive, moral, and aesthetic content as equally vital. Thus, in terms of the cognitive aspect of instruction, Japanese teachers put considerable time and effort to teach cognitive skills and knowledge. Still, contrary to American classroom teachers, Japanese classroom teachers regard the other areas to be highly relevant, too.

Every elementary school in Japan publishes a school handbook in which the goals of schooling are stated. The relevance of these goals for our discussion is that they are not simply perfunctory official statements but reveal major themes that guide teaching. These themes include:

- To nurture healthy and cheerful children

- To educate children who take the initiative in doing their work

- To educate children who get along well and help one another.

- To nurture children who are cooperative and diligent

- To nurture children who think deeply and take the initiative

These themes encompass the cognitive, moral, expressive, and social dimensions of students' development. The goals of schooling enunciated by our study schools commonly place a priority on cooperation, a healthy body and mind, and initiative, in addition to cognitive skills. The responsibilities assumed by classroom teachers are aimed at embodying these broad goals. Cooperation and group-focused human relations are promoted through a variety of programs involving classroom teachers. We have discussed these programs in the previous chapter.

Reflecting these broad goals, the Japanese elementary school curriculum consists of three components: the subject matter area, moral education, and *tokubetsu kat-sudo*, or special activities. The subject matter area was discussed in Chapter 5, but the other areas demand further attention here. The Japanese want moral education to pervade all aspects of schooling. Hence, the course of study stipulates that moral education be provided "throughout all the educational activities of the school." It stresses that moral education is involved in all dimensions of teaching and learning, especially "special activities." There are 28 moral education themes at the elementary level and 16 at the lower-secondary level. Every year our study schools planned to cover these themes in all grades during a 35-week period (34 weeks in the first grade). Note that this is in addition to the hours of informal moral education included in special activities to be discussed shortly.

The 28 themes roughly fall into six categories. The first involves the importance of order, regularity, cooperation, thoughtfulness, participation, manners, and respect for public property. The second stresses endurance, hard work, character development, and high aspirations. Such moral attributes of human life as freedom, justice, fairness, duty, trust, and conviction are central concerns in the third category. The fourth examines the individual's place in groups, such as the family, the school, and the nation, and the world. The fifth category focuses on harmony with and appreciation of nature and the essential need for rational, scientific attitudes toward human life, and the sixth emphasizes originality.

Each school identified central goals in moral education on an annual basis. Individual teachers, too, developed their own goals for their classes. For example, Komori stressed cooperation and respect for each other as the moral theme for the school. All the teachers, including Kenji, were expected to establish common emphases and were responsible for organizing instructional materials. Unlike other subjects, no textbooks were used in moral education. Teachers often used educational television programs expressly developed for moral education and commercially available materials to promote students' discussion of moral issues.

Our study schools delineated special activities in some detail. They were designed to enhance the "harmonious development of body and mind," individual students' awareness that they are members of a group, and cooperation. The special activities include a variety of formally organized programs as part of "classroom activities," *jidokai*, (student self-governing activities), and club activities, for which 54 to 85 periods are allocated each year, depending on the grade level. The special activities also included what are commonly identified as *gakko gyoji*, or school events, which refer to such school rituals as commencements; art and sports festivals that involve parents, excursions and retreats (such as study trips, nature classrooms, and "mountain school"), and volunteer work. The principal at Komori said that school events were significant because they provided students with a sense of belonging and community. His description is fitting because school events often involve all students, the entire teaching staff, administrators, and even parents in the achievement of common objectives.

Let us further illuminate how the ethos of cooperation is conceived and embodied in other activities. Kenji worked alongside his students in cleaning the classroom and encouraged them to work cooperatively to finish it. The repeated rehearsal by Yoko's students of a Japanese folk dance for the athletic festival provided a good opportunity for them to learn how to achieve an educational objective together. Reinforcing the prominence of cooperation in Japanese schooling, a senior teacher at Ikeshita pointed out that she considered the way students interacted with their peers to be a special concern. She told us how she evaluated students:

> I evaluate them in terms of both academic and nonacademic, or life, aspects. In the nonacademic area I attach importance to how well my students are relating with each other. In their school life they function as a group, so how well they interact with peers is important. In other words, I try to determine how well they do in a group learning situation and how they can work cooperatively in the performance of group tasks in and outside the classroom.

We observed an incident where a teacher was noticeably disenchanted with what he regarded as students' lack of cooperation. All fifth-graders at Komori, including Kenji's students, were expected to get ready for a softball game on the playground. The following note, which we made during our observations, shows how Mr. Furukawa, the fifth-grade head teacher who supervised the students with Kenji, reprimanded them for being tardy and showing little cooperation during the period. Mr. Furukawa lectured them for nearly ten minutes to emphasize how essential it was to behave properly and cooperate among themselves:

> 11:30 a.m. The chimes sounded. Students were scattered around the playground. Only a few students were preparing for a softball game while others were running around aimlessly. Mr. Furukawa, a male teacher, and Kenji stood by the podium and watched them for a while. Noticing that the teachers stood by the podium saying not a word, students realized that they had to form lines in front of the podium. Several students in charge came forward to direct the others to line up. Mr. Furukawa kept watching them, leaning against the podium and waited until the students formed lines. He then had the students squat down, and he started to talk. He told the students who did not take part in the preparation to stand up, and he reproved them. He sternly questioned why they did not help out so that they could start the game earlier. He told them he was extremely disappointed with their evident lack of cooperation. As he told them to shape up, they listened in silence.

This incident is significant because it clearly demonstrates that cooperation is a very important part of teachers' shared vocabulary and that Mr. Furukawa expected the students to display it actively.

To accomplish these broad goals of schooling, both beginning and experienced teachers at our study schools were expected to participate in a gamut of programs. This is why beginning Japanese classroom teachers' responsibilities differed from those of beginning American classroom teachers. The division of work among

Japanese teachers is deliberately diffuse, so that classroom teachers may share common responsibilities. Whether or not this is an effective structure of schooling is not relevant to our discussion here; suffice it to say that this diffuse division of work is an expression of the longstanding ethos of schooling in Japan.

The cultural expectation of inclusiveness in teaching at the elementary level is justified by the broad goals of teaching. As a foreign observer (Cummings 1980) points out, Japanese parents expect elementary schools to develop the noncognitive aspects of human development, as well as to impart cognitive skills. Cummings goes on to suggest that this is not because Japanese parents leave all the educational responsibilities to schools, but because, in Japan, parents and teachers are expected to share these responsibilities. His observation is quite pertinent in view of our preceding discussion.

Azuma, Kashiwagi, and Hess (1981) elucidate this cultural notion of shared responsibilities in their study of mothers' attitudes toward the education of their children in Japan and the United States. American mothers of preschool children believed in a clear distinction between the responsibilities of mothers and those of teachers. American mothers assumed that the development of children's social attitudes is their domain of duty while teachers should assume the responsibility of teaching the cognitive domain of children's experience. In contrast, Japanese mothers presumed that both mothers and teachers should collectively assume responsibility for developing both domains. White (1987) aptly calls Japanese mothers' attitudes toward schooling "the heightened sense of collective responsibility."

ETHNOPEDAGOGY: JAPANESE CULTURAL THEORY OF TEACHING

We have illuminated the orientation underscoring teaching at the elementary level in Japan. We will now discuss how this same orientation informs beginning teachers relative to the motivational enhancement of students, focusing on time-honored shared beliefs embedded in the culture of teaching, which are part and parcel of what was called ethnopedagogy in chapter 2. Japanese teachers are adept in using it to encourage students to meet their expectations. Ethnopedagogy is a cultural theory of teaching—the tacit knowledge of teaching that Japanese teachers internalize through occupational socialization. It is invented and reproduced by teachers themselves through self-discovery, casual conversations, and inservice education. It is a widely accepted ethos of schooling in our study schools. Teachers are a fiduciary agent of ethnopedagoy and interpret teaching competence in terms of its application to motivating children. As discussed earlier, it emphasizes ligature or bonding between the teacher and students as a basis of educational process. Bonding or *kizuna* results in mutual trust, on which teachers capitalize to encourage and inspire children to learn. We noted that it is a paramount principle for promoting effective classroom management. To cultivate *kizuna*, both supervisors and experienced teachers encouraged interns to promote intrinsic, unpretentious, interpersonal experiences that engaged children.

According to Yoko:

> *Kizuna* is a primary condition for teaching and for children to learn from the teacher. If it is not developed, teaching becomes a matter of mechanical process. *Kizuna* means to me developing trust. Without it, discipline would not be effective and children would not listen to me. Teaching is based on the relationship of trust. Classroom management is impossible without trustful relationships.

An experienced teacher elaborated on her comment: "Teaching is a kind of art. Emphasis should be placed on the relationship of hearts, the nurturing of bonding between the teacher's and children's hearts." Mr. Furukawa added:

> It is important to understand children as human beings whose characteristics are expressed in their activities. It is my belief that all children can do their best and concentrate on work. But it depends on the teacher's approach and desire. I am not concerned with how to teach children; rather, I try to understand them first, by developing personal relations, *kakawari*. When I get a new class, I do not teach subject matter immediately. Instead, I play with the children intensely for a week to gain a good understanding of them. Then I will begin to know what kinds of children they are and gradually direct them toward the goals of learning on the basis of happy and trustful *kakawari* with them.

The starting point of ethnopedagogy is the teachers' appreciation of the feelings that shape children's lives—the emotional commitment by teachers to children, which leads to fostering the bond between teachers and children. Beginning teachers came to learn that effective teaching is governed by the ligature and that developing it takes precedence over technical competence in teaching. Because the ligature creates an environment where children can trust teachers, it enables the teachers to inspire the children to meet their expectations. A small handbook titled *An Introduction to Teaching for Beginning Teachers*, prepared by the Ota Board of Education (whose district includes Kenji's school), highlighted the prominence of teachers' personal knowledge of students in teaching:

> To become a classroom teacher trusted by the students, he/she must fully know the fears, worries, and aspirations of each child and deliberately and effectively plan ways to deal with the problems children have. By doing it, the teacher will promote their confidence in him/her and positive attitudes toward themselves.

It is evident that Japanese teachers, including beginning teachers, unfailingly try to cultivate students' dependency on them, which is inherent in *kizuna*, and this, in turn, fosters a sense of security and self-confidence. When Kenji attended a workshop for beginning teachers in the summer, he made the following entry in his notebook: "I must build trustful relationships between my students and myself and among students. Such relationships would make them feel they could come to school without worries." Kenji also suggested in an interview:

> In order to gain my students' confidence in me, I have to sweat with them. I think that trustful relationships will develop when I, as a teacher, let my chil-

dren see me do all I can in my encounters with them, joining them in what they are doing.

Kenji made sustained efforts to gain a personal knowledge of his students. For example, as is common practice in Japanese elementary schools, he visited each student' home to familiarize himself with his students from the perspective of their parents. He also often talked with his students during lunch time, when they were relaxed, and encouraged them to write journals and share them with him.

Yoko recognized that personal knowledge was critical in ligature with children, but for her it involved the notion of love. She commented:

> Although I am still groping, I feel that as long as I love my students, whether I am reprimanding them or playing with them, I can communicate with them. If I ever feel that my students are bothersome or annoying, whatever I say to them will be of no use. Telling them to be quiet out of annoyance would be just a waste of time.

Yoko patiently approached Kazu, the deviant boy in her class who was described in the previous chapter, believing that her love for him would eventually make him feel secure and stop acting up. She noted that when the trustful relationships between her and her children began to develop in the late spring, the children responded more enthusiastically to her expectations. Given this development though fragile ligature, she said, "When I am doing my best, they know it. When I am serious about what I do they understand my intention." She told us that *kizuna* is a relationship that reinforces the reciprocity of the emotional commitment to one another. She related one episode to illuminate it. When she told seven-year-olds to enjoy their holidays in the spring, but to be careful to avoid accidents, one of them came up to her and said, "I will be careful because I like you and want to see you again after the holidays. If I got injured I could not see you again." Even such a seemingly insignificant encounter with her children made her euphoric, because she felt she had finally begun to receive a positive emotional response from them.

It may be suggested here that in the following respects, Japanese ethnopedagogy can be differentiated from the American emphasis on emotional involvement in teacher-student interaction. First, the authority of Japanese teachers is assumed to emerge in the context of interaction with students, especially at the elementary level. Beginning teachers were encouraged to "mingle with students without disguise and pretense"—an expression often used by teachers. In contrast, our data suggest that American student teachers, as well as beginning teachers, were expected to assert their authority a priori. As White reports, cooperating teachers "universally tell" their charges, "Don't make the mistake of trying to be friends with the kids" (1989, p.183). Second, the Japanese emphasis on *kizuna* is a cultural attribute, not fundamentally a means to an end. It differs from what Jackson (1990) characterizes as the "intensity of emotional involvement" by teachers, which is guided by the explicitly instrumental purpose of developing students' individuality. In contrast to Japanese beginning teachers, American beginning teachers expected their students to be independent and self-disciplined.

CLASSROOM MANAGEMENT: AN INTERPERSONAL APPROACH

Our study explored the cognitive approach to classroom management dominant in American schools. It highlights procedures—rules and policy—as a framework for management, and the degree that students internalize and adhere to the rules manifests a measure of success in classroom management. The emphasis is put on each student's cognitive organization of rules, so that it may become a guiding principle. In sharp contrast to the cognitive approach, Japanese teachers have developed what may be called an interpersonal or affective approach to classroom management. It is embedded in ethnopedagogy and applies ethnopedagogy's tenets to management. In this approach, interpersonal relations are viewed as paramount in promoting effective management of students and their activities within and outside the classroom.

Japanese teachers define classroom management as a broad, rather diffuse domain, as do American teachers. It typically includes a plan for teaching and strategies for improving students' work and enhancing the classroom environment, constructing a comprehensive plan for relevant activities (such as picnics, sports festivals, and swimming programs), demonstration classes for parents, and what Japanese teachers call *seikatsu shido*, "guidance for living." Consistent with this description of classroom management, the Japan Society of Educational Sociology (1986) defines it as "the function of maintaining conditions for enhancing effective classroom teaching and learning through involving all aspects of a classroom" (p. 99). In any event, the Japanese teachers' belief that interpersonal relations characterized by trust and cooperation are fundamental is thought to be central to the effective implementation of such activities.

Through their "apprenticeship of observation" for a number of years as students, beginning teachers became partially acquainted with their teachers' approach to classroom management. That observation is a primary source of the latent culture of teaching that influenced the formation of beginning teachers' disposition toward teaching. As beginning teachers they become keenly aware of the need to construct and apply it effectively. The beginning teachers we studied were invariably tense and nervous in the first month or so, and they became frustrated and sometimes depressed when they were not able to handle children. In fact, it was no accident that three of the six beginners who participated in our research stayed home for a couple of days in the first month because they had a fever resulting from the tension and fatigue that they experienced in the classroom. Yoko and Kenji were understandably nervous, and both struggled at the beginning of the year. Their problem was what they perceived to be their inability to relate to children, resulting in children's inattention to lessons. Their common expression of the problem was "I cannot handle children."

Supervisors unvaryingly saw this problem as a classroom management issue. Yoko's supervisor suggested, "Classroom management is key to teaching effectively. Its purpose is to develop *shudan* [a group] and an environment where children can express their problems openly." Kenji's supervisor concurred with him, suggesting the need to create an environment to foster the "touching of the hearts" between the teacher and students. Supervisors believed that classroom management is a craft that teachers learn through their encounters with students, not an abstract plan that can be given to beginners, although such a plan is suggested in handbooks for teachers and experienced teachers have such a plan.

Our beginning teachers gradually learned to adopt the interpersonal approach to classroom management in more focused fashion. Yoko, for one, suggested that bonding between students and herself was fundamental to building a well-managed classroom, as is clear in her remark "Unless there is *kizuna*, classroom management will not be effective." Kenji also felt that to create an effective classroom, a relationship of trust must be created between himself and his students. Bonding among students, he added, is a basis on which they can get along well and develop a sense of cohesion as a group. During an interview he mentioned his plan for moving his classroom in "a good direction":

> [Good direction is when] the class becomes a cohesive group and my students come to be on good terms with one another. When this occurs, students feel relaxed, spontaneous, and active as members of the class. There will be uninhibited communication and a sense of connectedness between students and myself. To build a classroom of this nature is my ultimate goal.

Understandably, beginning teachers' views regarding classroom management are an epitome of ethnopedagogy because they saw classroom management as an application of that pedagogy.

"Good direction," however, represented Kenji's aspirations only, not what he could realistically hope to achieve soon. In what ways, then, did the beginning teachers actually try to manage their classrooms? Let us explore this question, beginning with Kenji, who had been concerned about his inability to form his students into a harmonious group. When he taught at a *juku*–a tutoring school—as a part-time teacher, he had to deal with only a small number of students attending to their academic work only, but at Komori he realized that teaching meant not only teaching academic subjects but also guiding some thirty students in how to conduct themselves in a group. Here he experienced immense difficulty.

To overcome this problem, Kenji followed a commonly-used classroom management pattern that he learned from various sources, including experienced teachers. He created *han*, small groups that could work together closely. Earlier, we saw Kenji form his class into several *han* during a lesson in the Japanese language, during a science project, and during the lunch period. To develop cooperation among students, he also created *kakari*, groups for performing classroom chores, including attending to pets, managing the library, posting notices, serving lunches, distributing handouts, and promoting recreational activities.

Meanwhile, Kenji expected that his students would participate in various schoolwide programs because their peers in other classrooms were involved in the programs. One of these programs was an excursion to Nikko, a famous national park, to which the entire fifth grade went for three days during the summer. Kenji hoped that this event would provide an opportunity for his class to achieve an identity:

Staying overnight and working together, they would bond closely and become cohesive as a class. They would also display a sense of cooperation through an experience like this. Moreover, they would always remember this trip as a happy, shared event of their elementary school days.

Also, students at Komori assembled every Friday morning to join in special programs planned and coordinated by teachers in the fourth grade and up. Games and music performances were planned so that all students could participate in one way or another. During the second semester, Kenji volunteered his class to perform a music concert, at which his students led the entire school in singing and dancing. Through these experiences, he believed that his students developed an appreciation for participation, cooperation, and group work.

However, despite these programs, all Kenji's diligent efforts, and all the expectations he harbored, problems more often than not arose among his students, his class failed to become a cohesive, cooperating group, and this affected individual students' morale and work in the classroom. He discovered that there were latent conflicts among students, which were revealed to him during his visits to their homes in May. He then learned that not only his students but also their parents were concerned about the conflicts. Kenji entertained the thought that he might discuss the problem with the students actively involved, but his senior colleague, Mr. Furukawa, advised him to discuss it openly with the entire class. Kenji cancelled a class period to bring it to the attention of the whole class:

> I was scared because I had never done this before. No experience whatsoever. At the beginning I told my students, "I myself have no idea where this discussion might take us, but I will try my best to find a solution to this problem, so let us discuss it openly."

Thereafter, however, interpersonal conflicts still lingered among his students, with added hostility between boys and girls. During the summer vacation Kenji told us that this problem took precedence over any other matters, because he thought group harmony to be an elemental condition for effective teaching and student work in the classroom. Still convinced that the interpersonal approach to classroom management would eventually work, he decided to spend more time with his students, playing with them outdoors and engaging in casual conversations with them as often as he could. He believed that this active interpersonal strategy would enable him to know his students' problems better and gain their confidence.

Turning to Yoko, she became aware of several problems of classroom management. Unlike Kenji, she did not have to deal with interpersonal conflicts, notwithstanding the constant behavior problem of one boy, which concerned her deeply. She perceived her primary problem as managing her class as a group. Although she had only 22 first-graders, an ideal number of children for individualized instruction, she never attempted to individualize their work—an idea that she did not entertain. Her challenge was in how to teach the whole group, bringing every child to the performance level of the group regardless of individual differences. To accomplish this, she organized her classroom in the most conventional fashion with all students seated in several rows facing her. She typically taught her class standing in front of the chalkboard. Her problem was how to attract the attention of these six-year-olds for a sustained period without distractions. She was aware that these students would not pay attention to uninteresting lessons and could be easily distracted by little things. So she devised lesson plans as attractively as possible, mixing difficult lessons with music, gym, and exercises for school events such as athletic festivals.

In any case, her primary concern remained how to deal with the group. Realizing that students' cooperation with her and other students and their active participation in the class would contribute to effective teaching, she began to concentrate on interpersonal relations. She felt it was imperative to focus on developing students' adaptive dispositions to the classroom environment, so that they could be distinguished by diligence, cooperation, and participation.

Like Kenji, Yoko became familiar with how the Japanese classroom was typically managed, and tried to adopt it to foster these dispositions. She recalled the relevance of *kakawari*, personal connectedness, which was accentuated by a lecturer at a retreat for beginning teachers she attended in the spring. She organized task groups to promote cooperation and made herself available to play and talk with her students. She used the *nicchoku* setup, in which two students were assigned to maintain classroom order on a rotating basis—a student self-governing system created to facilitate classroom activities. Yoko noticed that what her supervisor called "naked *tsukiai*," unpretentious engagement with students, slowly began to produce some positive results shortly before the summer vacation. Students became more attentive, showing interest in her initiatives, and, moreover, become tolerant of and even cooperative with the deviant boy.

In summary, the strategies of classroom management that Japanese teachers typically employ are part of the Japanese culture of teaching. The fact that official and practitioners' views on classroom management are remarkably compatible suggests that the Japanese classroom management ethos is widely accepted throughout Japan. *Seikatsu shido*—guidance for living—to which we referred earlier, is part of Japanese classroom management, and the teachers' network movement to develop guidance for living has been supported by both the Ministry of Education and the Japan Teachers Union, although the union's and the ministry's interpretations of it were often at variance. What is common is the belief that interpersonal relations are fundamental to good classroom management. Our beginning teachers were also committed to this belief, although they met with only limited success in adopting it in their first year.

THE PATTERN OF CONTROL

There are some salient differences between American and Japanese patterns of control. Our study shows that beginning American teachers exert a high degree of control over activity, space, and time and affirmed the legitimacy of institutional authority entrusted to them as the source of their control. In contrast, we discern a comparatively low profile of the Japanese teacher as a control agent. Control of students, however, is a ubiquitous, dominant concern of teachers in American and Japanese schools; it demands considerable attention from both American and Japanese teachers.

Ethnopedagogy, classroom management, and control strategies are closely related and cannot be arbitrarily separated, because the underlying principle governing these domains is inherent in what the Japanese perceive to be the management of ligature in students' behavior. While American teachers celebrate individualism and self-reliance as the core of American culture, which accounts for people's behavior in not only education but also economic, political, and social spheres (Bellah et al. 1985; Hsu 1963), Japanese teachers embrace group orientation and interdependence as the central cultural tenet that influences behavior in these spheres (Hsu 1975; Nakane 1970; Shimahara 1979). These contrasting creeds epitomize two distinct cultural ideologies to which people in each nation by and large conform. Inevitably, individuals adhere to the cultural ideologies to varying degrees in both cultures, especially in the United States, because it is made up of multiethnic and racial groups. Yet, as we saw, there is a remarkable uniformity in American schools in their adherence to cultural tenets. The same is true of Japanese schools.

In this section, we will look at the strategies of control that Japanese teachers employed. Control is a mechanism to establish order and to accomplish students' compliance with rules and expectations, and therefore it involves the use of power, authority, punishment, and rewards. Let us now turn to the control strategies used in Japanese schools.

Both beginning and experienced Japanese teachers believe that order is established not so much by the stipulation of rules and authority as by the development of basic habits of everyday life. They have broadly framed rules in the form of slogans, mottoes, and weekly objectives, such as "Let us keep the classroom clean" or "Let us observe the traffic laws." The expectations of the school and teachers are not codified to the extent that they are in American schools. Instead, they are communicated to students through institutionalized activities in which teachers use authority to enforce their expectations. In this regard, the teachers' creed is remarkably consistent with the policy on basic habits promoted by the Ministry of Education. The teachers assume that children's orientation toward order and control result from practice, just as the Japanese in general believe that character formation is grounded in practice. Peak (1991), speaking of preschool education, illuminates the point:

> The term "basic habits of daily life" and its ubiquity as a goal of character training in preschool education stem from Japanese assumptions about the nature of ethical behavior. Good character and morality are driven by a person's beliefs and attitudes, and these are formed from the habitual residue of the personal habits and customs of daily life. (p. 65)

The same assumptions apply to the formation of children's attitudes toward order.

In teachers' handbooks published by the local board of education and the Ministry of Education, the notion of basic habits is spelled out in relation to moral education and special activities in the course of study and as a basis for moral behavior as well as academic work. Likewise, school handbooks unfailingly refer to it as fundamental in schooling.

Both Komori and Taika Elementary Schools offered a variety of programs to develop students' basic habits; these programs ran the gamut from cleaning the classroom to outdoor activities. Likewise, the habits that Yoko's first-graders were expected to develop ranged from simple to highly complex. The former included such customs as greeting people and neatly placing sneakers in a shoebox located in the entrance where students took off their outdoor sneakers and put on indoor ones. Japanese schools always emphasize greetings and changing shoes to keep the floors clean.

A more complex behavior that her children learned from the first month of their enrollment in school was to join the entire body of students on the playground for a regular Monday morning assembly. At 8:30 a.m., when the chimes signaled the start of the assembly, all students were expected to line up promptly in several rows, grade by grade, on the school playground in less than two minutes. The *nicchoku* teacher (monitor) directed them from the podium to line up in precise lines, with a proper distance between individual students. Every child was expected to stand straight, and no talking was allowed during this process. When all students lined up in front of their teachers, the principal went up to the podium to greet them and gave a speech, which was followed by an announcement by a *nicchoku* teacher and a message by a student government representative. The whole event took less than fifteen minutes, during which first-graders stood still and paid attention to the speakers.

What is marked as relevant in a meeting like this is not only the moral messages communicated to the children, but also their attitudes and behavior in a large collective setting. When it was completed, music was turned on, and all students proceeded to their classrooms. This whole complex behavior required Yoko's first-graders to respond to the chimes promptly, form lines by responding to authority, develop the self-discipline needed to stand still and listen to the speakers, and return to their classroom in an orderly way. What is described here is how six-year-olds are expected to learn a rather complex practice of group behavior, coordination, concentration, self-discipline, and compliance with authority. This practice, in addition to other collective events, is repeated every week throughout the year.

Teachers at Taika and Komori articulated the important habits, such as the Monday morning assembly, developed through practice, and also regarded special activities (referred to as *gakko gyoji* earlier) as highly relevant for training students and teaching them the values and norms that underscore the activities. These norms always become pronounced during the group-oriented activities that are regularly organized at these schools. Cleaning is another familiar example. Performed every afternoon by all students, including first-graders, it demands diligence, coordination, cooperation, and promptness. Tardy students are singled out during the reflection meeting held before students return home. One of the big schoolwide events aimed at developing these behavioral attributes at our study schools was a sports festival held in the spring. This all-day program was carefully planned by students themselves in consultation with teacher advisors. The festival required nearly three weeks' preparation. The program consisted of several events for each class and required several rehearsals during gym periods. The reader may recall Yoko's children engaging in rehearsals. The execution of the program was coordinated by teachers and students. The festival attracted several hundred parents and community leaders, such as members of the board of education. We observed athletic festivals at both schools and were impressed with the six-year-olds, who displayed extraordinary coordination and precision in movement, and the ability to respond to their teachers' directions. Students who rejected or deviated from these norms were reprimanded by their teachers and were under pressure to conform by their peers as well. We rarely saw such students during the festival, and even the deviant boy in Yoko's class participated in the events.

In brief, a variety of schoolwide special activities were used to teach relevant norms, and peer pressure was effectively brought to bear in this type of teaching. Teachers significantly accomplished their control over students by developing their habits through the use of the school as a community or through an outside environment, such as "mountain school" or excursions. These strategies for control employed by our study school and other schools in Japan represent a sharp contrast to the pattern of control we saw in American schools.

We will turn to the pattern of control at the classroom level. We have noted beginning American teachers' high level of control over students with respect to time, space, and activity. They did not invent a high profile of control, but it reflected the collective pattern of control manifested at the school level. From our descriptions of teaching in the preceding chapter, it is evident that both Yoko and Kenji displayed a relatively low profile of control with respect to time, space, and activity. Put differently, Japanese students displayed a higher degree of control over these aspects of schooling than did American students.

When Yoko and Kenji's students came to school, they controlled use of the school playground for ten minutes before the first class began. They had a brief morning meeting, which was their space and time, and they were free to use recess time, including a twenty-minute break between the second and third periods. Most students went outdoors to play, often accompanied by teachers during the long break—one of the most animated scenes we observed at the study schools. Students managed the entire lunchtime (including serving lunch and cleaning tables), the classroom cleaning period, and the brief recess following the cleaning. In addition, students had a couple of special-activity periods each week.

Student self-governing routines are popular in Japanese schools, and their success is contingent upon the classroom teacher's competence to engage students effectively in the routines. Both Yoko and Kenji established these routines, just as experienced teachers did. The student self-governing setup included rotated *nicchoku* duties to maintain classroom order; task groups, including lunch-servicing groups; and *jidokai*, or a formal classroom period in which children's interests and concerns were discussed. While some activities designed to promote student self-management were marked by tokenism, others, such as the task force for lunch duty and *nicchoku* duty, were functional parts of life in the classroom. The symbolic meaning of student self-governing routines lies in Japanese teachers' assumption that part of the control of a classroom is shared with students.

But this does not suggest that Yoko and Kenji did not exercise enough control over students during the class. Because both adopted largely conventional methods of teaching (except when Kenji organized *han*, small discussion groups), they taught the whole class and demanded the simultaneous attention of all the students. This required a considerable degree of control in directing students to their tasks, namely, listening to the teacher, answering his/her questions, and doing work at their desks. In our beginning teachers' classrooms, students were expected to sit upright, follow directions in minute detail, and speak only when they were granted permission. Teachers reminded them if they did not display expected classroom manners and occasionally shouted admonitions if they were too noisy.

Beginning teachers undeviatingly accepted the time-honored assumption that sitting upright at one's desk and keeping a proper distance between the eyes and the book on the desk are morally correct. This posture, according to them, suggests diligent and disciplined engagement in study, and it intimates the importance of self-discipline. When we questioned Yoko's supervisor about the educational significance of this posture, he suggested that a disciplined attitude toward learning was an essential habit for a child, although he was not sure of the relationship between the child's sitting position and his or her ability to learn. He attributed the customary emphasis on correct posture to Japanese tradition. Another supervisor used a Japanese calligraphy lesson to emphasize correct posture; in the lesson he first taught students the appropriate way of holding the writing brush and the appropriate posture for writing as an elementary skill. Japanese teachers often remind students to adjust their posture if it is not considered proper. We see it as a control strategy to induce students to pay attention to the teacher.

All in all, our field notes reveal that Japanese beginning teachers were relatively patient with students when they were noisy or even failed to observe classroom manners. Yoko never isolated her deviant boy, and instead largely appealed to his sense of guilt—although she occasionally fired stern warnings at him. The noise and occasional rule breaking notwithstanding, beginning teachers generally did not attempt to keep a constant control over students' behavior and activities. It was evident in our observations that Japanese classrooms were relatively noisy, while American classrooms were distinctly quiet and orderly.

Relative to our study, the sociologist Tsuneyoshi, in her comparison of Japanese and American elementary schools (1992), points out a contrast in behavior control: in the United States teachers resort to their authority to control students, while in Japan teachers tend to appeal to students' sense of guilt. Cross-cultural findings by the psychologists Azuma, Kashiwagi and Hess (1981) suggest a similar marked difference in the ways mothers in the two countries disciplined their children. American mothers tended to issue clear and concrete directions in a firm voice, while Japanese mothers were inclined to suggest indirectly what they expected their children to do (p. 74). These contrasts paralleled the Japanese and American teachers' different control strategies: a low and a high profile of control, respectively.

SUMMARY

We have explored themes, assumptions, and domains of teaching in Japanese schools. Broadly defined, teaching in Japan is characterized by the inclusiveness at the elementary level of the cognitive, moral, expressive, and social dimensions of children's development. This definition of teaching is reflected within three interrelated categories—subject matter, moral education, and special activities—of each school's programs. It is expected that elementary teachers actively and inclusively address these aspects of schooling because of Japanese schools' emphasis on holistic education. Therefore, the diffuseness in the division of work in elementary schools is dictated by the Japanese ethos of schooling. It seems to take precedence over the technical efficiency that might stem from a well-defined division of work among teachers, as seen in the United States.

Ethnopedagogy, classroom management, and student control are closely connected in Japan. Ethnopedagogy has been developed on the Japanese assumption that ligature is basic to the enhancement of children's orientation toward schooling. It is evident from the preceding discussion that ethnopedagogy is the foundation of the Japanese style of classroom management, with its emphasis on interpersonal relations and group harmony. Japanese teachers believe that control over students can be achieved by developing students' proper habits, putting a priority on practice over the codification of rules.

The concepts of inclusive teaching, ethnopedagogy, classroom management, and student control are part and parcel of the culture of teaching in Japan. They are shared and reproduced by practitioners without the mediation of teacher educators. The beginning teachers who participated in our study partly learned them as students during their apprenticeship of observation and mainly learned them as teachers through their enculturation into teaching.

In its emphasis on human bonding, ethnopedagogy is an expression of Japanese culture. Hamaguchi (1988), a cultural anthropologist, maintains that, for the Japanese, the self is identified in relationships with others. He suggests that the self, as conceived by the Japanese, is analogous to the Japanese mother, who perceives herself as a mother through the inseparable bond with her child. He characterizes the Japanese notion of self as "contextual," the attributes of the self being interdependence and mutual trust. Hamaguchi's contextual view of self is comparable to what Lebra (1976) calls "interactional relativism":

> If the actor is primarily concerned with a social object, as the Japanese are, his actions will be governed by something far removed from unilateral determinism. The Japanese Ego acts upon or toward Alter with the awareness or anticipation of Alter's response, and Alter in turn, by responding according to or

against Ego's expectation, influences Ego's further action. If Ego talks, Alter is likely to talk back, and thus they will alternate in a chain of interaction until a conversational trajectory is felt completed. Activation of the chain cannot be attributed to either Ego or Alter exclusively but to both or to the relationship between the two. The actor is unable to locate the prime mover and is likely to be indifferent to its existence. Instead, he is more aware of influence flowing both ways between himself and his object. (p. 7)

Ethnopedagogy is closely grounded in the contextual view of self and interactional relativism. Bonding between the teacher and students is cemented in a relative social context in which students' selves are defined.

CHAPTER 7

Occupational Socialization of Beginning Teachers

with Akira Sakai

It is evident from the preceding discussion that Japanese beginning teachers learn to teach in a context of schooling that is in sharp contrast to the context of schooling in the United States. They were expected to achieve much broader teaching goals than those in American schools. In other words, the definition of teaching embedded in the Japanese culture of teaching is broad, and this makes teaching an inclusive engagement. Moreover, Japanese pedagogy is distinguished by its emphasis on the ligature, or bonding, between the teacher and students as the fulcrum for creating a conducive learning environment. Beginning teachers' success in teaching measurably depends on nurturing *kizuna* with their students.

In this chapter, we will turn to other significant dimensions of the occupational socialization of beginning teachers. Our exploration will focus on the perspectives on teaching developed by beginning teachers, including their thoughts on the transition from college to elementary school and their approaches to problems in teaching, collegial relationships, and relationships with parents and the community.

Until recently, the functionalist model dominated the discussion of occupational socialization. Brim (1969), for example, defines socialization as the process of transforming "the raw material of society into good working members" (p. 5). His view embodies the functionalist model of socialization, which assumes a given social structure to be stable and unitary. At the same time, it tends to portray the socialized person as a completely passive entity (LeCompte & Ginsburg 1987).

As Lacey (1977) writes in his critique of functionalism, a human being is nothing but "an empty vessel to be filled with the basic value orientations and customs of the society of which he will become a part" (p. 18). The functionalist model has thus omitted any analysis of how teachers react given their own perspectives vis-a-vis the expectations or influences acting on them from the outside.

In response to these criticisms, a new approach began to attract scholarly attention in the 1970s and 1980s. It includes different paradigms concerning the process of occupational socialization, all of which examine the process of socialization from the point of view that has been neglected by the functionalist model. These paradigms are usually lumped together as the "interpretative approach," but strictly speaking, they should be divided into two theoretically separate models of socialization.

One is based on symbolic interactionism. Stressing the autonomy of individuals, this model assumes that they construct their own frame of reference in response to the situation in which they are. As Reid (1986) maintains, those who adhere to this model argue that "in a social situation a person is capable of deciding what his/her needs are and how these can be satisfied, review[ing] the possible ways of achieving them, decid[ing] on the most appropriate action, undertak[ing] it and change[ing] course if [his/her] predictions prove incorrect" (p. 31). The best-known work based on this socialization model is that of Becker et al. (1961). The authors offer an account of the occupational socialization of medical students and define the students' socialization as a process of developing their own perspectives in response to the expectations and demands of their professors. Lacey (1977) modifies this position by emphasizing individual strategies for highlighting the goals that they embody in actions to cope with problems. His emphasis on strategies, he maintains, would make it possible to capture more clearly the aims or needs of actors in the actual situations they are in.

The second model within the interpretative approach is derived from the field of phenomenology. Reid (1986) summarizes it as follows: "Phenomenologists are concerned, after Schutz, with how reality is constructed through social process and how the individuals involved acquire ways of thinking" (p. 32). Representing this approach as the foundation of the sociology of knowledge, Berger and Luckmann (1966) explain how reality is socially constructed and maintained. According to this approach, occupational socialization can be seen as a process wherein individuals construct their own reality by sharing knowledge unique to the occupation through interaction with other members of the occupation. Applying this model of socialization, we (1990) offered an account of how beginning Japanese teachers constructed their social reality of teaching. We defined teacher socialization as the process whereby beginning teachers acquired knowledge of teaching and sensitivity toward it by typifying their experiences through interaction with experienced teachers.

Comparing these two models, it can be suggested that the former, the symbolic interactionist model, regards the conscious judgments of a person made from his or her own perspective to be critical, while the latter—Berger and Luckmann's model—focuses on the fact that the reality on which the person's judgment is based is itself socially constructed. In other words, Lacey attaches great importance to the intentional choice of the actor, while Berger and Luckmann shed light on the nature of the perspective by which the actor makes a choice, stressing that the perspective reflects a reality, or a common sense assumption regarding the reality, constructed through the intersubjective process.

Symbolic interactionism has attracted more attention in the study of teacher socialization than has the Berger and Luckmann approach. Taking teachers' autonomy as a primary concern, recent studies have focused on such issues as the interests of teachers and the ways in which they cope with problematic situations, and these studies have analyzed the variety of strategies that teachers adopt to deal with these situations. But it is our view that if we take the approach advanced by Berger and Luckmann, the social reality of teaching that is constructed through the intersubjective process meaningfully defines what teachers are concerned about. Especially in Japan, whose culture is significantly different from American culture, a clear grasp of the ways the social reality of teaching is constructed by Japanese teachers is essential if we are to understand the process of their occupational socialization. Without insight into this process of the construction of reality, it would be difficult to explain why some matters are regarded as problematic by Japanese beginning teachers and others are not. Furthermore, Japanese beginning teachers naturally look for the grounds of their problems, and the strategies they use to deal with the problems are also influenced by their own perceptions of the reality of teaching. They thus develop long-term perspectives on teaching through this process of reality construction, coping with specific problems as they face them.

To probe how the beginning Japanese teachers we studied constructed their own perspectives on teaching, we will first explore the extent to which the preservice education programs offered by their universities had an impact on them and how they experienced the transition from their universities to their schools.

THE TRANSITION FROM UNIVERSITY TO SCHOOL

Studies have been conducted both in Europe and in the United States on how beginning teachers experience the process of the transition from their universities to the schools where they began teaching. Veenman (1984), who reviewed the English and German literature on this subject, comments that "the transition from teacher training to the first teaching job could be a dramatic and traumatic one" (p. 143) and that this transition was often referred to as "reality shock," "transition shock," "Praxisschock," or "Reinwascheffekt." He suggests that these terms characterize "the collapse of the missionary ideals formed during teacher training by the harsh and rude reality of everyday classroom life" (p. 143). He adds that many beginning teachers learned an idealistic view of teaching from the professors in their universities, but soon after they began teaching in the schools, they were disappointed to find that it was extremely difficult to realize their ideals in the schools.

Japanese beginning teachers, however, underwent the transition from their universities to schools differently from the students reported in Veenman's article. Japanese beginning teachers maintained a significant degree of continuity by retaining the image of teaching that they formed from their actual childhood experience of schooling. Kenji displayed that continuity: his image of former teachers was a latent force that influenced his orientation toward teaching, and as a beginning teacher at Komori, he espoused an ethos of teaching that was compatible with that latent image. Because such an image was related to the pedagogical beliefs underlying ethnopedagogy, Japanese beginning teachers were inclined to weigh the teacher preparation program in terms of how effective it was in passing on that ethnopedagogy. Kenji remarked that the program at his university was not useful for learning teaching skills or for enhancing competency in understanding children, an essential part of teaching in Japan. The exceptions were the classes on educational psychology and on educational counseling, because both of them contributed to building a personal knowledge of children.

In an interview conducted before he began teaching, Kenji stated that he had chosen a suitable occupation, one to which he would be able to devote his life, even though he had encountered some difficulties during his student teaching. He gained confidence and renewed his desire to become a teacher as a result of his student teaching. In response to our question "What areas of student teaching were useful to you?" he stated:

> The fact that I became acquainted with students was very valuable. Up till that time, I was not sure about what teaching was like and whether I could perform it. I was not confident until then, but through student teaching I came to feel I really wanted to become a teacher. I learned that knowing children and developing good rapport with them is key to teaching them effectively. The children were so sweet and I felt like staying with them all the time.

Even before he had taken up a teaching position, he was exposed to some of the dominant teaching tenets shared among experienced teachers in the school and to the actual methods of teaching organization based on them. His problem, when he assumed teaching at Komori, however, was his unfamiliarity with the complexity and multiplicity of teaching. For instance, though he had some experience of teaching in front of a group of children in a private enrichment school, he had never taught more than thirty students at one time before assuming his teaching position. He found it very challenging to teach such a large number of students, because he not only had to teach academic subjects but also had to deal with the moral and expressive dimensions of students' development.

But even with this difficulty, he was able to maintain a level of motivation toward teaching. After a month at his new job, he commented: "I am so glad to be with children. It is hard to teach, but I feel like seeing them even during the weekend." After another month passed, he had this to say about teaching: "I've wanted to be a teacher since my high school days. I am quite satisfied now that I have started my teaching. It was a good choice for me, I believe."

Yoko, on the other hand, may be distinguished as one who changed her views about teaching as she moved from her university to teaching in school. However, she did not experience the reality shock that Veemnan speaks of. She was interested in the educational philosophy she studied at her university, with its emphasis on children's spontaneity and education without punishment. Before she began to teach, she believed that these pedagogical beliefs should be an underlying principle of teaching, and she wanted to teach in accordance with that principle. Standing in front of a group of children, however, she realized that controlling children was critical in effectively managing her class. She felt compelled to adopt some control strategy when dealing with her class. During the four weeks of her student teaching, she became aware of the need for control. She suggested that although it was not necessary to exercise overt control over children when she taught a small number of students, it was unavoidable when she taught a large group. After she finished her student teaching, she and her friend admitted to each other, "I can hardly teach without scolding children." "Scolding" suggested a gamut of control.

After she started her job, she recognized that there were gaps between theory and practice. Two months after she began teaching she revealed:

> I have been taught not to scold a child, but sometimes children won't understand unless they are scolded. I cannot allow them to do dangerous or harmful things to others, so I have to scold them. When I came here, I told them not to make me angry. But when they do something wrong, it's wrong. They would understand if I went up and patted them on the head, too, but it is more important to tell them outright not to do certain things. Especially in the case of first-graders, a larger part of teaching is devoted to developing their social habits rather than to teaching them academic things. In such a situation, rather than explaining, I need to tell them simply, "You must not do this." As for the academic subjects, since they are learning simple matters, they can learn as long as I go over things repeatedly. But in terms of their school life, I think I have to make them understand clearly what is allowed and what is not, even if I have to use such a control strategy as scolding.

The change in her view could be seen as a transformation from a progressive orientation to a conventional attitude toward teaching. In his research, Tanaka (1974) finds a similar change in the attitudes of Japanese beginning teachers. But it is not quite right to attribute her change to a loss of idealism, as Veenman put it. When she began teaching at Taika, Yoko learned the imperative of maintaining order in her classroom and shaping six-year-olds' expected behavior. And she legitimated the use of control strategies when they were properly applied in the context of ethnopedagogy. As discussed in the previous chapter, Yoko was exposed to that ethnopedagogy at Taika, which attaches great importance to the ligature between teachers and students and to cooperation among students. It may be suggested that she learned a different teaching "ideal," one that is more congruent with the culture of teaching, rather than implied that she lost her original idealistic view and became authoritarian. When we asked her how she viewed her experience as a beginning teacher after two months of teaching, she responded:

> I must say I had a hard time in April. Partly because of Kazu's presence in my class, I felt, "What a job!" Time passed very slowly, and I was depressed. Because I was obsessed with the idea that I had to perform my duties successfully, I was often disheartened. In May, however, after the Golden Week holidays, I began to feel that time was passing more quickly. I got used to my job and started to embrace my children as lovable and gentle.

She further commented:

> I began to feel that the children liked me, though maybe I might have been flattering myself a bit. They would come around and call me "Kato *sensei* [Teacher Kato], Kato *sensei*." And I noticed that my students were kind to Kazu, even though he is such a difficult child. Seeing such an attitude on their part makes me feel very gratified. In the month or so since I have gotten to know them better, I already feel, "How wonderful it is to be assigned to this class!" It was the right choice to be a teacher.

As Yoko put it, it was because she had not adjusted to the daily routines in the school that she was depressed during the first month of her teaching. But after she developed familiarity with them a couple of months later, she started to feel glad about choosing teaching as her career. It is evident that Yoko did not experience a reality shock, and she diligently learned shared tenets of teaching, which became a framework of her orientation toward teaching. Against this framework, she reflected on her university course work.

Other beginning teachers in our study experienced varying degrees of stress when they encountered the pressures of teaching. But their experiences did not lead to a loss of idealism about teaching. For example, one beginning teacher at Ikeshita compared what he had imagined about teaching prior to assuming teaching with what teaching actually entailed:

> I sometimes feel sorry for having made light of teaching when I was a college student. Now I realize how heavy the responsibility of a teacher is, and sometimes I worry about whether I can handle it or not. I become embarrassed when I think of it. "Why can't I be more confident?" I ask myself.

This beginning teacher was overwhelmed when he realized the importance of his role as a teacher because he had begun the job without an articulated image of teaching. Another beginning teacher at Taika agreed:

> When I am teaching, I feel that every minute the children spend at school is very important and I, as a teacher entrusted with their education, have an awesome responsibility to them. I can't cut corners. If I do, the effects show up right away.

Although this beginning teacher felt that knowing his students was important for effective teaching, in the first month or so he was ambivalent about how to enhance his personal knowledge of students. Moreover, he was pressed by a large amount of paperwork at school and various special activities. Before he assumed teaching, he was unaware of the inclusiveness of the teacher's role in a Japanese elementary school.

From the preceding discussion, we can suggest that most of the challenges that beginning teachers encountered did not result in disillusionment with teaching, but resulted in a keener awareness of the responsibility and duties expected of them; in other words, their image of teaching in an elementary school was not defined well until they became classroom teachers. Soon after they began teaching, they came to share the ethnopedagogy dominant in their schools, and from this pedagogy they derived educational beliefs different from the theories taught at their universities. It is probable that the reason few Japanese beginning teachers experienced a shock lies mostly in the fact that ethnopedagogy became a frame of orientation and aspiration in teaching.

In a similar vein, Lortie (1975) comments, "Training is not a dramatic watershed separating the perceptions of naive laymen from later judgments by knowing professionals" (p. 66). Japanese beginning teachers' transition from the universities to the classroom supports his observation. Zeichner and Tabachnick (1981), who reviewed the literature on teacher education both in the United States and in the United Kingdom, speak of the two different types of impact of professional education on teaching. One is "the liberal impact of professional education and a progressive-traditional shift in teaching perspectives" (p. 7), and the other is "the low impact of professional training and the maintenance of traditional teaching perspectives throughout professional education" (p. 8). It seems that the second type by and large reflects Japanese beginning teachers' transition from training to teaching.

Having accepted the basic cultural premises of teaching, beginning teachers gained confidence in their teaching while losing confidence in the programs offered by their universities. Jinnouchi's (1987) findings suggest that classroom teachers generally tended to distance themselves from professors, because they felt that the professors were out of touch with the actual teaching scene. Kenji's comments reflect Jinnouchi's finding:

> Well, I think it is not connected with, or—shall we say it?—is remote from, actual teaching. All I know is that we were told, "There is this theory," but we did not learn how, and in what situation, we could use the theory. We were only given a brief explanation of the theory. And that was the end of it.

We suggest several reasons for the fact that Japanese teacher education programs do not have much influence on the socialization of beginning teachers. First, most teachers in Japan obtain teaching positions immediately after four years of undergraduate education. In comparison with teachers in the United States, where more than 40 percent of the elementary public schoolteachers hold a master's degree, the period of teacher education is not long enough for Japanese teachers to become acquainted with theories in teaching and reflect on them in connection with classroom practice. However, we note that the American beginning teachers with master's degrees who we studied did not actively draw upon theory in classroom teaching.

The second reason may be found in their personal biographies. As Lortie (1975) argues, we should not overlook the apprenticeship of observation that teachers undergo as students. He maintains that their school experiences encourage them to identify with the teaching occupation, and this surely can be applied to Japanese beginning teachers. As may be recalled, the reason Yoko held her own childhood classroom teacher up as a model was that he played with children and permitted them to sit on his lap. Kenji was also deeply impressed by his own teachers, who were devoted to their students in a variety of ways. Their former teachers remained a source of guidance and inspiration for both beginners when they taught.

Third, it may be suggested that university preservice programs do not offer an effective alternative to the time-honored, indigenous pedagogy shared among practitioners. Elementary teacher candidates have also been receptive to that pedagogy for the following reason. Because the number of universities that offer elementary certification programs is limited, so the admissions requirements for elementary certification candidates to these universities are very competitive. In 1990, for example, to be admitted to the universities at which Kenji and Yoko studied, applicants had to be in the top 30 percent of all university applicants that year (Nippon Nyushi Center, 1991). When both Kenji and Yoko sought admission to their universities in 1985, they had to study just as hard. It is apparent that most college students who want to be elementary schoolteachers must have ranked relatively high in their elementary and secondary schools and must have adapted well to the dominant pedagogy when they were children.

COPING AND ADAPTATION

Although they did not experience a "reality shock" that caused them to lose their teaching ideals, these beginning teachers did encounter many difficult problems. In which aspects of teaching did they find difficulties, and how did they cope with them? We also want to explore those aspects of teaching they did not regard as problematic. By inquiring into these questions, we will discover that their interests and concerns were oriented toward certain aspects of teaching.

RELATIONSHIPS WITH STUDENTS

For beginning Japanese teachers, their relationships with students were a major concern. This is quite understandable in view of the fact that they regarded bonding with their students as crucial in teaching and felt that bonding was fostered through close interaction with students and a deep personal knowledge of students. But managing an entire class demanded use of authority and power. The beginning teachers' dilemma was how to maintain a proper balance between the centripetal forces of bonding and the control of students exercised by the teacher as an agent of socialization who is endowed with the status of authority. Beginning American teachers resolved this dilemma by valuing authority over friendship with students; friendship was encouraged on the condition that students respected the authority of the teacher. In contrast, beginning Japanese teachers believed that their authority evolved in the context of intense interactions with their students. Their belief made control problematic, especially in a managing group, although they recognized that it was necessary and indispensable.

One of the main anxieties that commonly plagued the Japanese beginning teachers was how to control students' behavior in a group setting. In Japanese elementary schools teachers interact with students in a variety of formal and informal situations both inside and outside the classroom. Their concern with control is omnipresent in such situations. The problem of control loomed large for Yoko.

When we asked her what the most serious problem she experienced during the first marking period was, she responded:

> On the whole, I would say, that of controlling a group of students. It was easy for me to deal with them individually, but I found it most difficult to manage a group of students, whether in the classroom or other places. I guess I can handle individual students without problems, but in many situations I have to deal with them as a group. I am not as yet competent enough to manage a group. This is the hardest thing for me.

Obviously, her problem was not that she could not control her students. As her following remark suggests, her dilemma was that she more often than not resorted to reprimands to control students in a group setting.

> In the beginning, I was pressing my students more than necessary to meet my expectations by issuing warnings at them. I shouted typical warnings such as, "Be quiet," "Stop it," and "Shape up." I don't like to use those words. But there were times when I was using them, even though I hated to do so.

It seems that from her point of view, the problem was that she had to rely on the control strategies that conflicted with her desire to develop close relationships with her students. Therefore, her main concern at that time was to create an environment compatible with her own expectations. As shown in Yoko's case, the problem of control beginning teachers encounter is perceived in relation to the expectations toward teaching they form on the premises of ethnopedagogy.

The beginning teachers' difficulties were revealed in their admission that they were unable to understand children well. In our interviews with beginning teachers and their supervisors, they often used the phrase "understand children." "Understand children" conveyed several overlapping meanings in the context of schooling in Japan, three of which will be mentioned here. First, it meant building a personal knowledge of students based on *kizuna* that is formed through unpretentious association with children. Second, it meant broad familiarity with students' personal lives and with the motivations underpinning their behavior in school and at home. Third, it meant knowing and appreciating children's feelings, which would enhance communication with them. In everyday conversation the phrase was used to refer to any of these meanings, depending on the topic of the conversation.

On the assumption that teachers must develop bonding with students for effective management of their work, beginning teachers were expected to know their students. In the first few months the beginners were commonly plagued by their difficulties in understanding children. For example, in the absence of personal knowledge of them, a beginning teacher at Taika did not know how to handle his students when they became confrontational toward him. A beginning teacher in Komori commented that she did not have a large enough *utsuwa*, (translated as a receptacle or a capacity), to be able to understand the feelings of her students. Likewise, Kenji's salient concern was that he was not competent at getting to know his students. He first spoke of this problem about two months after the school year had begun. He characterized his inability to understand his students as "not being able to see my students": "I cannot figure out what they are thinking about. During lessons, I am not sure if they are actually concentrating or not; they may be just pretending to do so. I still do not understand what they are really thinking." To know them better, he strove to develop personal ties with his students through close association with them in the classroom and outside. As noted in the previous chapter, his strategy for coping with this problem was to encourage each student to write a diary and share it with him daily. He explained the aim of the diary:

> I do not know what my students are doing after they go home. I can understand the children who come up to me frequently, but not the others. I wonder how they get along at home or how they spend their time after school. I want to know more about their lives through their diaries, which would reveal their private feelings.

Encouraging students to write diaries is a well-established, common practice in Japan. Senior teachers at Komori told us that diaries offered a vital communications channel between them and their students. One teacher encouraged his students to create what he called a "home-study notebook," which included reviews of lessons and preparations as well as personal notes about themselves. Students handed home-study notebooks to him every morning and he, in turn, wrote comments on them before returning them to the students before they went home. The diary entry could be just three sentences or a paragraph, but through it the teacher was able to understand his children and communicate his own feelings to them as well. One of the students he had taught from first to fourth grade had gone through 27 notebooks by the end of the fourth year.

SOCIALIZATION INTO INTERPERSONAL RELATIONS

In Japanese schools, managing interpersonal relations among colleagues is as important as managing them among students. This is especially so in Japanese elementary schools, where teachers closely associate with each other for both instrumental and expressive purposes. In contrast, in the United States, as Lortie (1975) observes, the "single cell of instruction has played a key role in the development of the American public school" (p. 15), and "schools were organized around teacher separation rather than teacher interdependence" (p. 14).

Japanese elementary school classes are not run as independently as those in the United States, because school programs, especially special activities, require teachers to cooperate closely at the grade as well as the schoolwide levels. Teachers at the same grade level meet weekly to coordinate curricular matters, such as the pace of instruction and other common activities. The entire teaching staff meets at least once a day in the faculty room. The physical and social structure of the faculty room in Japanese schools is designed to encourage beginning teachers to meet experienced teachers daily and interact with them to ensure cooperation in implementing a variety of programs. All teachers, including the head teacher, have their personal desks in the staff room, and they are arranged to promote interaction among teachers. This room is used for staff meetings, work, and relaxation. The structure of the Japanese elementary school contributes to faculty interaction in the staff room, on the playground, and in the specific floors where classrooms are clustered by grade. Moreover, professional development activities and recreational activities, which are organized regularly, provide teachers with opportunities for interaction at all levels. In short, there is extensive face to face interaction among teachers, making interpersonal relations a pivotal factor in everyday school life. Although intense interaction can create a sense of community, it can also lead to uneasiness because it exerts a pressure toward conformity, leading to judgments of each other's behavior. In any event, it is sufficient to suggest that these relations can have a significant effect on teachers' morale and effectiveness as faculty members.

Adaptation to a close-knit community was an important part of the beginning teachers' occupational socialization. Our beginning teachers displayed differential adaptation to this dimension of their induction. Here we will comment on how Kenji and Yoko responded to it. Although they were equally sensitive to interpersonal relations, they differed in their adaptation.

Concerned with interpersonal relations, Kenji actively availed himself of opportunities for association with his colleagues. He was a diligent participant in all officially-announced meetings and activities, as well as after-school recreational events. Moreover, he made a conscientious effort to accompany his colleagues to bars or restaurants after such recreational activities as baseball and volleyball practice. In his school there were several informal groups where special relationships among members of the groups developed, providing a sense of belonging and support. Kenji became a member of a group that included the head teacher, three beginning teachers, and a few other teachers. This group often met after school and socialized, sharing personal concerns. He was quite deliberate in his efforts to avoid conflicts with colleagues in his formal and informal associations with them.

Kenji also went out of his way to avoid being evaluated poorly by his colleagues—part of the covert judgment resulting from collegial interaction. A couple of examples can shed light on his strategies. He was assigned to give a "demonstration" gym class in December as part of his school's professional development program; his colleagues, as well as the principal, were to observe this class and give him feedback afterwards. In preparing for this lesson, he devised a plan for making it especially appealing to the observers. To impress the observers, he intentionally chose a lesson that his students could plunge into with enthusiasm. On another occasion, he decided to cancel an academic class in order to play with his students, as part of his plan to improve his management of students. He used the gym, where he and his students could not be readily seen by teachers, rather than the playground. He was afraid that if teachers saw him and his class out in the playground, they might not have thought that his cancellation of the class was legitimate. Therefore, to avoid veiled criticism by his colleagues he chose to be inconspicuous when playing with his students.

His sensitivity to his colleagues was quite obvious when he displayed embarrassment about his failure to control his students during a trip to a concert hall. He commented:

> I was so ashamed at the recent concert. We walked to the Komori Station to take a train and, after the train ride, had to walk again to reach the concert hall. The other two classes were walking in neat lines, whereas my students made a poor show, even though I reminded them several times. I felt so bad I could have cried then. It was only a ten-to-fifteen-minute walk, but my class couldn't keep straight lines and were so disorganized. It looked really disgraceful.

Kenji was concerned that his class might be compared with other classes: "Yes, especially in a situation like that, it bothers me. I felt that my students' behavior reflected on my poor teaching. I was really embarrassed."

What Kenji was concerned about as he interacted with other teachers was the "impression management," theorized by Goffman (1959). For an actor, acquiring and playing a certain role means employing and maintaining an expected "front," that is, "the expressive equipment of a standard kind intentionally or unwittingly employed by the individual during his performance" (p. 22). In other words, "whether his acquisition of the role was primarily motivated by a desire to perform the given task or by a desire to maintain the corresponding front, the actor will find that he must do both" (p. 27). In the process of learning his role, Kenji realized that he must maintain a proper front as a teacher in addition to acquiring the necessary skills to perform the role. Impression management was important for Kenji, especially when intense interaction and the pressure for conformity were present.

Kenji's anxiety about his colleagues and his front, however, is in part inherent in a special occupational feature of teaching. According to D. H. Hargreaves (1980), teachers find it difficult to acquire feedback on their performances to help them evaluate their competence, because their teaching roles tend to be so multifaceted and the goals of teaching tend to be so manifold and indefinite. As we noted earlier, teachers in Japanese elementary schools do not directly offer explicit advice to a beginning teacher. Hargreaves suggests that such an absence of feedback in the teaching profession brings about feelings of uneasiness among teachers about their own competence. Kenji's anxiety about his own competence as a teacher seemed to reflect these feelings of uneasiness.

In contrast, although Yoko regarded interpersonal relations as pivotal in her work, she displayed much less anxiety about her colleagues' evaluation of her behavior than the other beginning teachers we studied. Like Kenji, she was a conscientious participant in formal and informal activities organized by her school's faculty. She also joined in after-school social events. But she was much more confident with respect to teaching than the other beginning teachers and declared:

> I think the most important thing for teachers is the relationship between teachers and the children. I think you asked me about how I get along with my colleagues teaching next door, but I don't have to be so anxious about it. It may depend on who it is, but at present I am not worried about it. As long as I am able to manage my class successfully, my colleagues will support me. I'm sure the principal and vice-principal will do the same.

She gained more confidence in managing her class and teaching academic subjects during the first marking period than did Kenji. It pointed out that the difference between Kenji and Yoko with respect to their sensitivity toward their colleagues is partly linked to their different levels of anxiety about teaching. All in all, however, beginning teachers were sensitized toward the importance of interpersonal relations among colleagues during the course of the first year of teaching.

ORIENTATION TOWARD EDUCATIONAL GOALS AND TEACHER ROLES

We have pointed out that one of the salient differences in schooling between Japan and the United States is the fact that Japan has a national curriculum; this has been a feature of Japanese education since the late nineteenth century, when the nation began modernizing. Compiled by the Ministry of Education, the national course of study serves as a binding framework for curriculum construction. Textbooks are written in compliance with the course of study and are adopted for use in schools only after they have been authorized by the Ministry of Education. Given legitimacy by the Ministry, the textbook constitutes the official curriculum, which is supplemented by relevant materials chosen by individual teachers. Given this definition of curriculum, beginning teachers as well as experienced teachers assume the role of transmitter of officially legitimized knowledge to students.

Berlak and Berlak (1981) speak of "dilemmas" in teaching. They point out that there is a dilemma between treating knowledge as given and treating it as problematic. If knowledge is treated as given, teachers define it as universal and objective truth, though if it is seen as problematic, they view it as constructed, provisional, tentative, and subject to political, cultural, and social influences. For beginning Japanese teachers, knowledge is given and objective, and they invariably take the official curriculum for granted and have few personal doubts about teaching it. In their view, textbook knowledge is legitimate and indisputable. They define their role as primarily concentrated on imparting legitimate knowledge to students. There is a sharp contrast between their definition of their role as an instructor and American beginning teachers' definition of their role.

The lessons we observed in Japanese schools were unambiguously aimed at transmitting to students the knowledge delineated in the textbooks. For example, in Kenji's science class (described in chapter 5) he instructed his students to experiment on kidney bean germination under a variety of conditions. The content of the lesson, the method of conducting the experiment, and the conclusions that his students were expected to derive from it were outlined in the textbook. But because the science textbook was condensed and compact, Kenji had to consult the teacher's manual to teach the unit and devise some details of the experiment. Given this perspective on teaching, it is understandable that Yoko also heavily relied on the teachers' manual as the source of guidance. She referred frequently to it to "stay on the right track," as she put it, and infrequently referred to other sources. One of the beginning teachers' focal concerns was to teach the textbook to their students regardless of the grade level. Because the curriculum was assumed to be indisputable, they concentrated on ensuring that students learned the material in the lessons. They resorted to a variety of strategies, some of which were like those used by beginning American teachers: recitation, seatwork, small-group discussion, drill, frequent tests, and some homework.

With respect to their more inclusive teaching responsibilities, beginning teachers accept them wholeheartedly. Although they were more often than not overwhelmed by the range of teaching, they found the broad goals of teaching to be legitimate. Indeed, they were committed to "whole person" education, involving cognitive, moral, expressive, and social aspects of schooling. These goals were not only mandated by the course of study but also supported by teachers as the raison d'être of their school. In short, the preceding discussion reveals that beginning teachers were socialized into the role of teaching mandated by the course of study and broad educational goals.

BEGINNING TEACHERS' ACCOUNTABILITY

Japanese teachers' accountability is broad, since their roles are diffuse and inclusive. Their accountability is defined in the Fundamental Law of Education (promulgated in 1947) and other statutes. For example, the Fundamental Law of Education reads: "Teachers of the schools prescribed by law shall be servants of the whole community. They shall be conscious of their mission and endeavor to discharge their duties. For this purpose, the status of teachers shall be respected and their fair and appropriate treatment shall be secured." As noted in Chapter 6, one of the purposes of the nationally-mandated internship program was to promote *shimeikan*, a sense of mission. However, because such a legal definition of accountability is abstract, general, and out of context, it did not serve as a practical guide for beginning teachers. Perhaps few beginning teachers, if any, would read it. Instead, their sense of accountability seemed to evolve in the broad context of teaching as they were enculturated into teaching.

Our beginning teachers' views of accountability were affected by the Japanese practice of hiring teachers and by the national curriculum. As discussed earlier, teachers were hired as employees of the Tokyo metropolitan government (and thus designated as prefectural employees nationwide) not by a local ward or a community. Fifty percent of their salaries were drawn from national funding; the remainder came from the metropolitan government. Moreover, it was the national certification law that determined their qualifications as teachers. The law is the basic, binding framework that specifies the requirements in teacher education programs. What distinguishes Japanese beginning teachers from American beginning teachers is that the former are prefectural employees and the latter are employees of local communities. From a legal point of view, Japanese teachers are directly accountable to their prefectural board of education, whereas American teachers are accountable to their local board of education.

As mentioned above, the national curriculum is another factor that circumscribes the beginning Japanese teacher's role. Unlike beginning American teachers, our beginning Japanese teachers were not expected to construct curricula suitable to the needs of children in their school districts. They used nationally authorized textbooks as the primary teaching materials, and they were little concerned with what they had to teach. Thus, the hiring practice and the national curriculum made beginning Japanese teachers considerably less accountable to their local districts than were their American counterparts. In other words, Japanese teachers identified their accountability in terms of their responsibility to fulfill national mandates—common national educational goals and materials stipulated in the course of study. Holistic education was part and parcel of these mandates, and the inclusiveness of teaching we discussed stemmed from them, not from local needs.

Further, parents were not as strong a source of external pressure for Japanese teachers as they were for American teachers. Parents were much more accommodating to teachers, emphasizing their children's ability to adapt to the school environments. This evidently reflects Hess and Azuma's (1991) assertion that Japanese teachers and parents emphasize children's adaptive dispositions. Parents of Yoko's class expressed more concern with how their children were getting along with peers and how diligent they were at school. When another beginning teacher at Taika visited his children's homes in the spring, he was surprised to hear many mothers ask him to be "strict" with their children so they would develop disciplined attitudes toward study at school. During our study we rarely heard that parents were a source of concern for beginning teachers. In late June Kenji told us: "I was afraid I would be under pressure from conflicts with colleagues and parents. But as it is, I feel hardly any pressure from parents at all in this school." His feelings were shared by other beginning teachers. Our research supports Hess and Azuma's observation: "Adults in Japan are particularly eager to prepare the child to be diligent and to cooperate with the teacher. In the United States, more concern is focused on acquiring academic (especially verbal) skills, independence, and self-reliance" (p. 3).

However, this does not suggest that Japanese teachers were insensitive to parents. On the contrary, our observations reveal that they were considerably sensitive to the parents and actively participated in parent initiatives. In the spring, as part of the schoolwide program, beginning teachers and experienced teachers devoted five afternoons to visiting parents to gain familiarity with them and their students. Prior to the home visitation, beginners received advice from their supervisors on how to conduct it and also had a practice session at the education center as part of the internship program. Three *hogoshakai* ("parent schools"), similar to "back-to-school" night in the United States, were organized so that parents could observe classes and consult with the teachers. The beginning teachers were extremely nervous at the first parent school held in the middle of the spring. It represented their first formal face-to-face encounter with parents; our beginning teachers invariably admitted that they were quite unconfident in communicating with the parents at the first parent school. In addition, parents were invited to several school programs, including sports festivals (the most popular school events), theatrical and arts festivals, and commencements. Parental volunteers were also invited to participate in "mountain schools" and "nature classrooms," which were retreats for upper-level students that lasted two to three days. Moreover, parents were kept well informed of school events through newsletters and other forms of communication frequently sent to them.

Despite their emphasis on holistic programs, elementary public schoolteachers in Tokyo, including our beginning teachers, did not have sole responsibility for teaching children. Parents' concerns regarding their children's education were mitigated by the existence of competitive private schools and *juku*—very popular privately organized after-school institutions. There are more than 35,000 academic *juku* throughout the country (U.S. Department of Education, 1987). Beginning teachers in the fifth and sixth grades, including Kenji, informed us that more than two-thirds of their students attended *juku* after school two to six times each week. *Juku* are of various types: drilling (exam-oriented drills), enrichment (for example, piano, calligraphy, and abacus), and remedial. As a result, a first-year colleague of Yoko's who taught sixth-grade students assigned students little homework because there was little time left for them to study at home after school. Kenji's internship supervisor also told us that faculty at his school agreed to give minimum homework to students to allow them some private space and time after school.

In urban areas like Tokyo and its environs, many parents aspire to send their children to competitive national or private middle schools, because this would ensure that they would have a smooth transition to competitive high schools and then to college, despite intense entrance examinations. According to a study by Hida (1989), which included a survey of the parents of sixth-graders living in Tokyo, about a third of the parents expected their children to take entrance exams for private middle schools, and 93 percent of these parents placed their children in *juku*. The widespread existence of *juku* in Japan epitomizes the pervasiveness of parents' concerns with the intense competition during high school and with the university entrance examinations. Effects of *juku* on schooling at the secondary level are greater as university entrance examinations draw closer.

SUMMARY

Beginning Japanese teachers learned how to teach by participating in the social construction of teaching. Our ethnographic analysis supports this thesis. It is evident that the neophytes were actively involved in the reproduction of teaching, incorporating the culture of teaching into their personal frame of reference. Reproduction of teaching was possible through an intersubjective process in which beginning teachers interpreted the relevance of the knowledge of teaching to which they were exposed to solve the problems that they encountered. The beginning teachers' occupational socialization was not merely a process of situational adaptation, but also a process in which the transmission of the cultural knowledge of teaching played an important role in individual teachers' decisions on teaching strategies.

For Japanese beginning teachers, the culture of teaching they acquired through exposure to their former teachers was an important factor in their transition from university to school. It remained as a potent image in creating a linkage between their biographies and the pedagogy to which they were exposed as teachers. In contrast to the preservice education they received, ethnopedagogy was a framework that effectively guided beginners in learning to teach. It was also compatible with the earlier image of teaching that they developed while in school themselves. And that compatibility contributed to their relatively smooth transition to the schools where they taught.

These beginning teachers displayed little personal conflict with, and experienced few dilemmas in their commitment to, the goals of holistic education. This support for holistic teaching stemmed from ethnopedagogy, which they identified as a foundation of teaching and of the culture of teaching at their respective schools. It was in that context that beginners strove to become effective in attending to the cognitive, expressive, moral, and social dimensions of their students' experience.

The Japanese culture of teaching involves frequent interaction among teachers, which results from a broad range of both formally and informally organized activities. In our study, this led to close-knit interpersonal relations, which became a source of concern for beginners. Beginners were sensitive to such interpersonal relations because they were conducive to the expression of veiled judgments about peers. While the emphasis on an orientation toward human relations is expected in Japanese culture, it could become personally constraining and restrict individual diversity and freedom in the interests of conformity.

The accountability of Japanese teachers is broadly circumscribed. Our beginning teachers were accountable for implementing the national curriculum, holistic teaching, and for close communication with parents. They did not feel that parents and the district exerted significant pressure on them. The centralized control of schooling is not designed to reflect the district's voice with respect to curriculum and school policy. In this respect, the beginning teachers were somewhat immune to such pressures, if, indeed, they experienced any. All in all, the beginning teachers adapted well to the culture of teaching. Their active interest in learning the cultural knowledge of teaching through the process of interaction with experienced teachers contributed to that adaptation.

Epilogue: A Critical Reflection

Part One of this book discussed the culture of teaching in Japan, strategies for professional development, and teacher education in the context of social change. Part Two explored how beginning teachers are enculturated into teaching, Japanese pedagogy, and occupational socialization. The following paragraphs present a critical reflection on educational reforms, therapeutic pedagogy, ethnopedagogy, teacher development, and the intensification of work in teaching.

LIMITS OF TOP-DOWN EDUCATIONAL REFORMS

Japanese educational reforms are invariably top-down and tend to be traditionalist. Japan has found no other ways of launching change. The prefectural boards of education are responsible for running all the public schools and are the employers of all public school teachers. Thus, they should actively take part in school restructuring. However, despite the fact that the Ministry of Education often prods the local boards to assume greater initiative in improving and managing their own schools, the Ministry persistently resists loosening the reins of the nation's schools. The local boards, on the other hand, routinely rely on the Ministry's leadership in changing schools. The gap between rhetoric and practice looms large. Moreover, professional and academic organizations and teachers' unions are either indifferent to issues of school reform or acquiescent in government leadership. For example, although the Japan Teachers Union developed its own school reform proposals independent of the Ministry of Education until it was split into two organizations in the 1980s, it has yielded to the government-led initiatives since then.

Major school restructuring reports since 1971, when a major overhaul proposal was issued, that have included changes in teacher preparation have followed the top-down approach. School reforms are initiated by the Minister of Education, the political figurehead in the Ministry, with the submission of an agenda to an appropriate body for deliberation. This body is usually the Ministry's advisory council, such as the Central Council of Education or an ad hoc task force, the best example of which is the National Council of Educational Reform. The Vice Minister, a career bureaucrat in the Ministry, in turn appoints members of a task force. Advisory council members are also handpicked by the Ministry and are appointed for a limited period of time. In other words, the composition of a task force and the framework of deliberation are decided by the Ministry and are politically influenced. Consequently, members of the Japan Teachers Union have been excluded from such reform task forces. Generally, the Ministry appoints university presidents and professors, corporate executives, journalists, school superintendents, principals, performing artists, and the like to a task force to represent a spectrum of different professional perspectives. A prominent university president usually heads a task force or an advisory council. Appointed members, however, are generally conventional people who support the policies of the Ministry.

The conservative nature of restructuring initiatives is evident in the Central Council of Education's latest report on education for the 21st century, issued in 1996-1997. Its central theme is "power to live" or *ikiru chikara*, and the enhancement of "rich human quality," or *ningensei*, referred to in Chapter 4. "Power to live" is a very elusive phrase that has some cultural appeal but is devoid of requisite intellectual construction. Further, it lacks operational utility because there is no clear agreement on its meaning. For educational reformers, however, the term seems to represent the overall premise upon which school overhauls, including the revision of the curriculum, are based. Consequently, practitioners and the public have difficulty comprehending exactly what it constitutes. At best, it is a slogan, but not a cogent organizing principle.

To suggest another example, in response to continued, widespread students' violence, bullying, refusal to attend school, and a classroom crisis caused by students' disruptions, the Central Council of Education issued a report on the "education of the heart." The Japanese see the heart as the centerpiece of self-development and the window through which one's internal universe is viewed and communicated. School reformers see those pathological incidents as a consequence of the deterioration of the heart. Accordingly, they proposed strategies to restore a "rich heart" by promoting the "power to live" and moral life in the school, home, and community. It is interesting that reformers offered a cultural explanation for the cause of children's antischool behavior: deterioration of the heart.

In any event, education of the heart and *ikiru chikara* constituted twin themes of school restructuring in the 1990s. Further, starting in 2002, all Japanese schools will follow a new attendance schedule requiring students to be in school only five days a week instead of six. As a result, many class hours will be lost each year. Moreover, the curriculum will be reduced by an astonishing 30 percent at all grade levels. In turn, reformers introduced "comprehensive studies," which are intended to enhance students' initiative and problem solving skills in organizing projects. As a result, the curriculum in each of the major academic subjects has become considerably slimmer.

School reforms for the twenty-first century are long on rhetoric and short on preparing students for an era in which there will be immense scientific and technological development, greater globalization not only in the economic sector but also in other spheres of life, further acceleration of interdependence between as well as competition among nations, the hegemony of information in the lives of all peoples, and a continued blurring of national boundaries. Since the 1980s reformers have been so preoccupied with students' anti-school behaviors that reform measures have been largely framed to cope with them. Consequently, they have failed to pay sufficient attention to the vital question of how to prepare young people for the twenty-first century.

SWING TO THERAPEUTIC PEDAGOGY

Recent educational reforms attempted to transform teaching from a deep-seated essentialist pedagogy that stresses the transmission of knowledge toward a progressive orientation that embraces students' needs, motivation, interest, and diversity— a new orientation epitomized in what reformers called a "new view of academic competence." Whether or not this policy shift changes practice in the classroom remains to be seen.

Such a swing is echoed in reforms in teacher preparation. After open certification system was introduced in the fledgling years of the postwar era, the Ministry of Education persistently attempted to alter that system for nearly four decades without much success. Open certification is a watered-down system that granted certification on the basis of minimal teacher preparation. Recall that preservice students at the secondary level could obtain a teaching certificate when they completed only fourteen credits of professional studies and two weeks of student teaching. This led to a proliferation of teacher certificates. This certification system began to change only in the late 1980s when reformers focused on the problems of mounting student violence, bullying, and anti-school behavior as legitimate justification for redesigning teacher preparation. Certification became stratified, and teachers' practical competence was emphasized. Simultaneously, internships for beginning public school teachers were introduced. This represented the first significant drive to alter certification requirements to emphasize professional competence in teacher preparation.

This was followed by the second drive to redesign teacher preparation further in the 1990s to continue to address the same student problems. Reformers beefed up professional studies in preservice education, especially at the secondary level. For example, middle school certification now requires thirty-one credit hours in professional studies compared with fourteen credit hours required prior to 1989. In contrast, the content area requirement has been halved from forty credit hours to twenty credit hours. These changes represent a drastic shift in teacher preparation, giving prominent weight to teaching methods and a human relations-oriented pedagogy that highlights counseling, student guidance, and moral education—a swing away from academic-centered teacher preparation.

All these changes are said to be necessary to enhance teachers' practical competence. Ironically, reformers have not addressed teachers' academic competence as a problem, despite the drastic reduction in the content area requirement, a critical concern in the United States, for example.

ETHNOPEDAGOGY AND CHANGING STUDENTS

Ethnopedagogy is a central cultural theory of teaching in Japan. It emphasizes bonding and trust between the teacher and students as the basis for promoting teaching and classroom management. Ethnopedagogy highlights emotional ties in the classroom community. For experienced teachers, it is a taken-for-granted ethos that pervades teaching. Beginning teachers find ethnopedagogy to be essential in the process of learning the ropes of teaching. The reform theme of education of the heart, mentioned above, plays up the importance of ethnopedagogy.

Thus, it is understandable that both reformers and classroom teachers emphasize what is commonly called *kakawari*, or interpersonal relationships, as an indispensable condition for an orderly classroom. Teachers attribute student disruptions and *gakkyuhokai* or, classroom chaos, to the absence of *kakawari*. In their view, fostering *kakawari* in the classroom is key to restoring good classroom order. This attribution paradigm, however, does not address other critical conditions causing classroom chaos. When teachers fail to meet students' needs, students resist their authority by disrupting classroom activities, which contribute to the development of chaos. Most teachers at the secondary level still routinely use a didactic, lecture-style method, a typical whole-class teaching approach whereby the pace and level of teaching is geared to the average students. Other students feel ignored and often act as an agent of classroom chaos. Even at the elementary level, classroom chaos has become commonplace. Teachers' reliance on conventional ethnopedagogical wisdom in classroom management is no longer effective in classrooms where diverse student needs dictate a redefinition of teaching methods and classroom management.

While ethnopedagogy has been an effective, tacit theory shared by teachers, there are limitations in its application. Ethnopedagogy is a cultural wisdom embedded in Japanese group orientation. The basic tenet of ethnopedagogy is to assimilate students emotionally and socially into a classroom community in which they become homogenous members of a group. Students' resistance to assimilation and the authority that demands it is a manifestation of the need to recognize children's individuality and diversity. To respond to their resistance effectively, teachers must develop teaching and classroom management strategies that fully recognize changes in Japanese student population as complementary to ethnopedagogy.

PROBLEMS IN TEACHER DEVELOPMENT

Three issues will be mentioned in this section: teacher preparation, graduate pro-grams for teachers, and professional development strategies. The last three chapters make it plain that beginning teachers rely heavily on the intersubjective process, involving them and experienced teachers in the school setting, to learn to teach. It is through this process that beginning teachers reproduce teaching. Their preservice education, on the other hand, has little impact on first-year teachers, calling the quality of preservice education into question. No matter how reformers concoct pre-service education to emphasize the quality of teaching and practical competence, preservice education will not significantly improve unless teacher educators change the way they prepare preservice students for teaching—specifically, in the construc-tion of course content and teaching methods. It is no exaggeration to suggest that this is the most critical issue in teacher education reform. Yet reformers are primari-ly concerned only about structural issues such as the number of required credit hours and courses. What needs to be underscored here is that both reformers and teacher educators must address the process of teacher education.

This issue relates to professional development through graduate programs, which were discussed extensively in chapter 4. Teacher development through grad-uate study has been in place for two decades in Japan, and it recently received renewed attention when the Teacher Education Council proposed an expansion of graduate study for teachers in 1998. Let us reflect on one of the salient issues: the precedence of technical rationality over practical rationality in graduate study. The former is the application of theory derived from scientific knowledge, whereas the latter is professional knowledge grounded in teachers' practice. The problem lies in the fact that there is little match between teacher educators' interest in technical rationality and students' concern with practical rationality. This problem is embed-ded in students' coursework, in which teacher educators do not effectively address students' concerns and interests about classroom teaching. It goes without saying that unless graduate study for teachers is designed to promote their interests and answer their questions it has little plausible *raison d'être*. Concerted attention must be paid to this all-too-common problems so that graduate programs may be redesigned to promote knowledge of teaching and educational leadership. Expansion of existing programs will not bring about positive change in teaching unless they are also redesigned.

Turning to professional development initiatives, Japan has developed standards for professional development throughout the country. However, one must ask the extent to which the country has developed measurements of quality for professional development. There is little information available that would enable one to assess the effects of professional development programs on teaching and learning. Emphasis is always on how to teach rather than how students learn. Peer-driven study lessons, discussed in Chapter 4, an extensively developed teacher development initiative, would have a more significant impact on teaching as well as learning if they were linked to student achievement. Likewise, government-sponsored programs are well developed, but they also have shortcomings. A major problem is that they are not designed with the involvement of classroom teachers. Hence teachers tend to perceive these programs as a government imposition. To make them more effective, teachers' input in designing them is necessary.

INTENSIFICATION OF TEACHING

Finally, turning to the intensification of teaching, there are a number of issues that constrain teachers. One middle school teacher said that "there is neither beginning nor end [in his work] because it just continues." He called it the unending work of teachers. His comment does not seem to exaggerate the fact that Japanese teachers' work is highly demanding, especially at the middle school level. Our national survey indicates that teachers across the country work ten to eleven hours in school each day. As discussed in Chapter 2, intensification of teaching at the middle school level stems from teachers' work beyond classroom teaching. Especially time-demanding tasks are placing students in high schools, supervising club activities, perfoming cooperative school management, and providing student guidance. Elementary teachers' work is also demanding on time, but to a lesser extent. In any event, intensification of teaching is a pervasive phenomenon in Japan. We suggested earlier that this phenomenon is self-perpetuated in part by the culture of teaching. For example, neither the Ministry of Education nor local boards of education stipulate how extracurricular activities are organized and how much time is spent for them. However, conventional practice, which we attribute to the culture of teaching, seems to dictate the management of these activities. Seventy-five percent of middle school teachers devote substantial time to club activities (Fujita et al. 1996)—volunteered time for which teachers receive little, if any, compensation. Neither local boards of education nor school reformers have addressed the intensification of teaching, taking it for granted. Even the Japan Teachers Union does not militantly demand the improvement of work conditions any longer since its influence started to decline in the early 1980s. Is intensification of teaching teachers' "lot," or *shukumei*, as a middle school teacher suggested?

Research should be conducted to investigate how the intensification of teaching influences teacher effectiveness and the quality of teaching. It is an important question that reformers must address if they are genuinely interested in improving teaching at a time when classroom chaos is becoming commonplace in both elementary and middle schools.

A final word: Japan has a dedicated teaching force. Nine out of ten teachers across the country believe that they have a sense of mission in their teaching. But teaching is now at a crossroads. The teaching force cannot be improved only by changing the teacher education curriculum, and its improvement requires teacher educators to become change agents themselves. A faculty development program must be introduced to retool teacher educators in Japan as in England.

References

Apple, M. (1989). *Teachers and text*. New York: Routledge & Kegan Paul.

Amano, I. (1986). The dilemma of Japanese education today. *The Japan Foundation Newsletter*, 12:5, 1–5.

Atkinson, P. & Delamont, S. (1985). Socialization into teaching: The research which lost its way. *British Journal of Sociology of Education* 6: 307–322.

Azuma, H. (1994). *Japanese socialization and education*. Tokyo: University of Tokyo Press.

Azuma, H., Kashiwagi, K. & Hess, R. (1981). *Attitude and behavior of mothers and the development of children: A comparative study between Japan and the United States*. Tokyo: University of Tokyo Press.

Bagley, W. C. (1907). *Classroom management: Its principles and techniques*. New York: Macmillan.

Becker, H. S., Geer, B., Hughes, E., & Strauss, A. L. (1961). *Boys in white: Student culture in medical school*. Chicago: University of Chicago Press.

Befu, H. (1986). The social and cultural background of child development in Japan and the United States. In H. Stevenson, H. Azuma, and K. Hakuta (Eds.), *Child development and education in Japan* (pp. 13–27). New York: W. H. Freeman.

Bellah, R. N., Madsen, R., Sullivan, W. M., Swidler, A., & Tipton, S. M. (1985). *Habits of the heart: Individualism and commitment in American life*. New York: Harper & Row.

Bennett, J. W. (1988). *American education: Making it work*. Washington, D.C.: U.S. Government Printing Office.

Berger, P. & Luckmann, T. (1966). *The social construction of reality*. Garden City, N.Y.: Doubleday.

Berlak, A. & Berlak, H. (1981). *Dilemmas of schooling: teaching and social change*. London: Methuen.

Bester, A. (1953). *Educational wastelands: The retreat from learning in our public schools*. Urbana: University of Illinois Press.

Bester, A. (1955). *The restoration of learning*. New York: Alfred Knopf.

Blumer, H. (1966). Sociological implications of the thought of George Herbert Mead. *American Journal of Sociology* 71 (5): 535–544.

Blumer, H. (1969). *Symbolic interaction: Perspective and method*. Englewood Cliffs, N.J.: Prentice Hall.

Bogdan, R. & Taylor, S. (1975). *Introduction to qualitative research methods*. New York: John Wiley & Sons, Inc.

Borko, H. (1986). Clinical teacher education: The induction years. In J. V. Hoffman and U. J. Edwards (Eds.), *Reality and reform in teacher education* (pp 123–136). New York:

Brim, 0. (1969). Socialization through the life cycle. In O.Brim & S. Wheeler (Eds.), *Socialization after childhood* (pp 1–24). New York: John Wiley & Sons, Inc.

Bullough, R. V. (1989). *First year teacher: a case study*. New York: Teachers College Press.

Bullough, R. V. & Knowles, G. J. (1991). Teaching and nurturing: Changing conceptions of self as teacher in a case study of becoming a teacher. *International Journal of Qualitative Studies in Education* 4 (2): 121–140.

Carnegie Forum on Education and the Economy, Task Force on Teaching as a Profession (1986). *A nation prepared: Teachers for the 21st century*. New York: Author.

Carter, K. (1990). Teachers' knowledge and learning to teach. In W. R. Houston (Ed.), *Handbook of research on teacher education* (pp. 291–310). New York: Macmillan.

Central Council of Education (1958). *Policy for improving the teacher education system*. In Yokohama National Institute for Modern Education (Ed.) (1983), *Central Council of Education and Education Reforms* (pp. 49–55). Yokohama: Yokohama National Institute for Modern Education.

Central Council of Education (Japan) (1971). Recommendations for comprehensive reforms of school education. In Yokohama National Institute for Modern Education (Ed.), *Central Council of Education and educational reforms* (pp. 125–187). Tokyo: Sanichi Shobo.

Central Council of Education (Japan) (1971). *Basic policies for comprehensive expansion and improvement of school education*. Tokyo: Ministry of Education.

Central Council of Education (1978). Recommendations for improving teachers' quality and competence. In O. Kanda and M. Yamasumi (Ed.) (1985), *Education of Japan: Historical materials* (pp. 329–335). Tokyo: Gakuyoshobo.

Central Council of Education (1996). Education for the 21st century. *Journal of Professional Development*, 1744 (August), 159–193.

Clift, R., Houston, W. R., & Pugach, M. (Eds.) (1990). *Encouraging reflective practice in education*. New York: Teachers College Press.

Cochran-Smith, M. & Lytle, S. (1996). Communities for teacher research: Fringe or forefront? In M. McLaughlin and I. Oberman (Eds.), *Teacher learning: New policies, new practices* (pp. 92–112). New York: Teachers College Press.

Cooley, C. H. (1956). *Human nature and the social order.* Glencoe, Ill.: Free Press.

Crow, N. A. (1986). The role of teacher education in teacher socialization: A case study. Paper presented at the meeting of the American Educational Research Association, San Francisco. April.

Crow, N. A. (1987). Preservice teacher's biography: A case study. Paper presented at the American Educational Research Association, Washington, D.C., April.

Cuban, L. (1994). *How teachers taught.* New York: Longman.

Cummings, W. K. (1980). *Education and equality in Japan.* Princeton: Princeton University Press.

Curriculum Council (1998). Improvement of the curricula for kindergartens, elementary schools, middle schools, high schools, and schools for the blind, deaf, and special children. *Bulletin of the Ministry of Education,* 994, June 24.

Dahrendorf, R. (1978). *Life chances: Approaches to social and political theory.* Chicago: University of Chicago Press.

Darling-Hammond, L. & Berry, B. (1988). *The evolution of teacher policy.* New Brunswick, N.J.: Rand Corp.

Darling-Hammond, L. & Cobb, V. (1995). The teaching profession and teacher education in the United States. In L. Darling-Hammond and V. Cobb (Eds.), *Teacher preparation and professional development in APEC members* (pp. 221–240).Washington, D.C.: U.S. Department of Education.

Darling-Hammond, L. & McLaughlin, M. W. (1995). Policies that support professional development in an era of reform. *Phi Delta Kappan,* 76, 597–604.

Darling-Hammond, L. (1997). *The right to learn: A blueprint for creating schools that work.* San Francisco: Jossey-Bass.

Denscombe, M. (1982). The work context of teaching: An analytic framework for the study of teachers in classrooms. *British Journal of Sociology of Education* 1, 279–292.

De Vos, G. A. (1973). *Socialization for achievement.* Berkeley: University of California Press.

Dewey, J. (1930). *Human nature and conduct.* New York: Modern Library.

Dore, R. (1987). *Taking Japan seriously: A Confucian perspective on leading economic issues.* Palo Alto: Stanford University Press.

Doyle, W. (1986). Classroom organization and management. In M. Wittrock (Ed.), *Handbook of research on teaching* (392–431). New York: Macmillan.

Duke, B. (1986). *The Japanese school.* New York: Praeger.

Edgar, D. & Warren, D. (1969). *Power and autonomy in teacher socialization.* Sociology of Education, 42, 386–399.

Education Commission of the States, Task Force on Education for Economic Growth (1983). *Action for excellence: Comprehensive plan to improve our nation's schools.* Denver: Author.

Elbaz, F. (1983). *Teacher thinking: A study of practical knowledge.* New York: Nichols.

Erickson, F. (1986). Qualitative methods in research on teaching. In M. Wittrock (Ed.), *Handbook of research on teaching* (119–161). New York: Macmillan.

Etheridge, C. P. (1989). Acquiring the teaching culture: How beginners embrace practices different from university teaching. *International Journal of Qualitative Studies in Education, 2,* 299–313.

Evertson, C. M. & Harris, A. H. (1990). *Classroom organization and management program: Workshop manual for elementary teachers.* Nashville, Tenn.:Vanderbilt University.

Feiman-Nemser, S. and Floden, R. E. (1986). The culture of teaching. In M. C. Wittrock (Ed.), *Handbook on research in teaching* (pp. 505–526). New York: Macmillan.

Fox, S. M. & Singletary, T. J. (1986). Deductions about support induction. *Journal of Teacher Education, 37,* 12–15.

Fujioka, N. (1992). Self-initiated inservice teacher education in Japan: Development and issues. Paper presented at the Comparative and International Education Society meetings. Annapolis, March.

Fujita, H. et al (1996). Survey of teachers' lives and opinions. Tokyo: University of Tokyo School of Education.

Fujita, H. (1989). A crisis of legitimacy in Japanese education: meritocracy and cohesiveness. In J. Shields (Ed.), *Japanese schooling: Patterns of socialization, equality, and political control* (pp. 124–138). University Park, PA: Pennsylvania State University Press.

Fujita, H. (1997). *Educational reform.* Tokyo: Iwanami Shoten.

Fukutake Shoten Kyoiku Kenkyu-jo (1992). *Monograph on contemporary elementary school students.* 14. Tokyo: Fukutake Shoten.

Fukuzawa, R. I. (1966). The path to adulthood according to Japanese middle schools. In T. Rohlen and G. LeTendre (Eds.), *Teaching and learning in Japan* (pp. 295–320). New York: Cambridge University Press.

Fullan, M. G. & Stiegelbauer, S. (1991). *The new meaning of educational change.* New York: Teachers College Press.

Furhman, S., Clune, W. H. & Elmore, R. F. (1988). Research on education reform: Lessons on the implementation of policy. *Teachers College Record, 90* (2), 237–257.

Goffman, E. (1959). *The presentation of self in everyday life.* Garden City, N.Y.: Doubleday.

Goodlad, J. I. (1984). *A place called school: Prospects for the future.* New York: McGraw-Hill.

Goodlad, J. I. (1990). Teachers for our nation's schools. San Francisco: Jossey-Bass.

Goodson, I. (1995). A nation at rest: The contexts for change in teacher education in Canada. In N. Shimahara & I. Holowinsky (Eds.), *Teacher education in industrialized nations* (pp. 125–154). New York: Garland.

Goodson, I. (1992).Studying teachers' lives: An emergent field of inquiry. In I. Goodson (Ed.), *Studying Teachers' Lives* (pp. 1–17). New York: Teachers College Press.

Grant, G. (Ed.) (1992). *Review of research in education*, Vol. 18. Washington, D.C.: American Educational Research Association.

Green, M. (1973). *Teacher as a Stranger*. Belmond, Cal.: Wadsworth.

Grimmett, P. P. & MacKinnon, A. M. (1992). Craft knowledge and the education of teachers. In G. Grant (Ed.), *Review of educational research*, Vol. 18, (pp. 385–456). Washington, D.C.: American Educational Research Association.

Hamaguchi, E. (1988). *Rediscovery of "Japanese-ness."* Tokyo: Kodansha.

Hammersley, M. (1980). Classroom ethnography. *Educational Analysis*, 2, 47–74.

Haring, M. & Nelson, E. (1980). A five-year follow-up comparison of recent and experienced graduates from campus and field-based teacher education programs. Paper presented at the American Educational Research Association, Boston, April.

Hargreaves, D. H. (1980). The occupational cultures of teachers. In P. Woods (Ed.), *Teacher Strategies* (pp. 45–62). London: Croom Helm.

Hargreaves, A. (1994). *Two cultures of schooling: The case of middle schools*. London: Falmer Press.

Haruta, M. (1983). *An introduction to the educational guidance*. Tokyo: Meiji Tosho.

Hata, M. & NHK Kyoiku Project (1992). *What to do with public junior high schools?* Tokyo: Nippon Hoso Shuppan Kyokai.

Hawley, C. A. & Hawley, W. D. (1997). The role of universities in the education of Japanese teachers: A distant perspective. *Peabody Journal of Education*, 72 (1), 234–245.

Hess, R. D. & Azuma, H. (1991). Cultural support for schooling: Contrast between Japan and the United States. *Educational Researcher*, 20 (9), 2–8.

Hida, D. (1989). The new entrance examination era for junior high schools. *Journal of Nanzan Junior College*, 17, 65–90.

Holmes Group (1986). *Tomorrow's teachers: A report of the Holmes Group*. East Lansing, Michigan: Author.

Holmes Group (1990). *Tomorrow's schools: Principles of the design of professional development schools*. East Lansing, Michigan: Author.

Holmes Group (1995). *Tomorrow's schools of education: A report from the Holmes Group*. East Lansing, Michigan: Author.

Holmes Group (1989). *Work in progress: The Holmes Group one year on*. East Lansing, Mich.: Author.

Horio, T. (1988). *Educational thought and ideology in modern Japan*. Tokyo: University of Tokyo Press.

Hoy, W. (1968). Pupil control ideology and organizational socialization: A further examination of the influence of experience on the beginning teacher. *School Review*, 77, 257–265.

Hsu, F. (1963). *Clan, caste, and club*. New York: Van Nostrand.

Huberman, M. (1989). *The lives of teachers*. Translated by Jonathan Neufeld. New York: Teachers College Press.

Huberman, M. (1975). *Iemoto: The heart of Japan*. Cambridge, Mass.: Schenkman.

Hurling-Austin, L. (1990). Teacher induction programs and internships. In W. R. Houston (Ed.), *Handbook of Research on Teacher Education* (535–548). New York: Macmillan.

Ichikawa, C. (1996). Interpretation of the Central Council of Education's summary of its recommendations. *The Journal of Professional Development*, 1744, (August), 115–118.

Imazu, K. (1996). *Social change and teacher education*. Nagoya: University of Nagoya Press.

Imazu, K. (1978). Internal career of student teachers. *Bulletin of the Faculty of Education of Mie University*, 29 (4), 17–33.

Inagaki, T. & Kudomi, Y. (Eds.) (1994). *The culture of teachers and teaching in Japan.* Tokyo: University of Tokyo Press.

Inagaki, T. & Kudomi, Y. (Eds.) (1979). Occupational socialization of teachers. *Bulletin of the Faculty of Education of Mie University*, 30 (4), 17–24.

Ishii, H. (1978). A history of school cleaning. In Y. Okihara, (Ed.), *School cleaning: It's role in the formation of character* (pp. 67–89). Tokyo: Gakuji-shuppan Co.

Ishii, H. (1981). Developmental process of professional orientation of students of the Faculty of Education. *Bulletin of the Faculty of Education of Shizuoka University*,31, 115–128.

Ito, K. & Yamazaki, J. (1986). Research on anticipatory socialization in the teaching profession. *Bulletin of the Faculty of Education of Shizuoka University*, 37, 117–127.

Jackson, P. W. (1990). *Life in classrooms*. New York: Teachers College Press.

Janesick, V. (1978). *An ethnographic study of a teacher's classroom perspective.* East Lansing, Mich.: Institute for Research on Teaching, Research Series No. 33.

Japan Society of Educational Sociology (1986). *New dictionary of sociology of education.* Tokyo: Toyokan Publishing Co.

Japanese Youth Research Institute (1995). A survey on high school students' attitudes toward care for parents in Japan, China, and the U.S. Quoted in The Central Council of Education's report on education of the heart, *Monthly Journal of the Ministry of Education*, supplementary issue, 1459, April 1998.

Japanese Youth Research Institute (1996). A survey on communication media. Quoted in *Monthly Journal of the Ministry of Education*, supplementary issue, 1459, April 1998.

Jijitsushin (1998). *Educational data land, '98–'99: A data book of educational statistics.* Tokyo: Jijitsushin.

Jinnouchi, Y. (1987). Preservice and in-service teacher training in career development. *Japanese Journal of Educational Research*, 54 (3), 300–309.

Johnson, W. R. (1989). Teachers and teacher training in the twentieth century. In D. Warren (Ed.), *American teachers: Histories of a profession at work* (pp. 237–256). New York: Macmillan.

Kaigo, T. (Ed.) (1975). *Education reforms: Postwar Japanese education reforms, vol. 1.* Tokyo: University of Tokyo Press.

Kano, Y. (1984). *A study on the development of teaching competence*. Kagawa University Studies on Educational Practice, 2, 29–37.

Kataoka, T. (1992). Class management and student guidance in Japanese elementary and lower secondary schools. In R. Leestma and H. J. Walberg (Eds.), *Japanese educational productivity* (pp. 69–102). Ann Arbor, Mich.:University of Michigan Press.

Kiefer, C. (1976). The danchi zoku and the evolution of metropolitan mind. In L. Austin (Ed.), *The Paradox of progress* (pp. 279–300). New Haven: Yale University Press.

Kinoshita, S. (1983). *Postwar curriculum*. In M. Okazu (Ed.), *The encyclopedia of curriculum* (pp. 25–36). Tokyo: Shogakkan.

Knowles, J. G. (1992). Models for understanding pre-service and beginning teachers' biographies: illustrations from case studies. In I. Goodson (Ed.), *Studying teachers' lives* (pp. 99–152). New York: Teachers College Press.

Kojima, H. & Shinohara, S. (1985). A study of the development of career consciousness of college students: An analysis of career consciousness of the students at the Faculty of Education, 34, 281–296.

Kudomi, Y. (Ed.) (1994). *Japanese teacher culture*. Tokyo: Taga Shuppan.

Lacey, C. (1977). *The socialization of teachers*. London: Methuen.

Lambert, M. (1985). How do teachers manage to teach?: Perspectives on problems in practice. *Harvard Educational Review*, 55, 178–184.

Lebra, T. S. (1976). *Japanese patterns of behavior*. Honolulu: University of Hawaii.

LeCompte, M. & Ginsburg, M. (1987). How students learn to become teachers: An exploration of alternative responses to a teacher training program. In G. W. Noblit & W. T. Pink (Eds.), *Schooling in social context: Qualitative studies* (pp. 3–11). Norwood, N.J.: Ablex Publishing Co.

Lessinger, L (1970). *Every kid a winner: Accountability in education*. New York: Simon & Schuster.

LeTendre, G. (1996). Shido: The concept of guidance. In T. P. Rholen and G. LeTendre (Eds.), *Teaching and learning in Japan* (pp. 275–294). New York: Cambridge University Press.

Levine, R. & White, M. (1986). *Human conditions: The cultural basis of educational development*. New York: Routledge.

Lewis, C. (1995). *Educating hearts and minds*. New York: Cambridge University Press.

Lewis, C. (1989). From indulgence to internalization: Social control in the early school years. *Journal of Japanese Studies*, 15 (1), 139–157.

Lieberman, A. & McLaughlin, M. (1996). Networks for educational change: Powerful and problematic. In M. McLaughlin & I. Oberman (Eds.), *Teacher learning: New politics, new perspectives* (pp. 63–72). New York: Teachers College Press.

Liguana, J. (1970). *What happens to the attitudes of beginning teachers?*. Denville, III: Interstate Printers.

Little, J. W. (1993). Teachers' professional development as a climate of education reform. *Educational Evaluation and Policy Analysis*, 15 (2), 129–151.

Lortie, D. (1975). *School teacher: A sociological study*. Chicago: University of Chicago Press.

Maguire, M. & Ball, S. (1995). *Teacher education and education policy in England*. In N. Shimahara and I. Holowinsky (Eds.), *Teacher education in industrialized nations* (pp. 225–254). New York: Garland.

Maki, M. (1992). *A survey of internships for beginning teachers*. A research report. Tokyo: Kokuritsu Kyoiku Kenkyusho.

Maki, M. (1993). Development of effective internship programs for beginning teachers. Research report of the National Institute for Educational Research. Tokyo:Kokuritsu Kyoiku Kenkyusho.

Maki, M. (1988). Implementation of internship for beginning teachers. *Educational Law* 75: 17–29.

Mardle, G. & Walker, M. (1980). Strategies and structure: Critical notes on teacher socialization (pp. 73–86). In P. Woods (Ed.), *Teacher strategies*. London: Croom Helm.

McCulloch, G. (1998). *Classroom management in England*. In N. Shimahara (Ed.), *Politics of classroom life* (pp. 85–106). New York: Garland.

McPherson, G. (1972). *Small town teacher*. Cambridge, MA: Harvard University Press.

Mead, G. H. (1934). *Mind, self, and society*. Chicago: University of Chicago Press.

Miller, B., Lord, B. & Dorney, S. (1994). *Staff development for teachers: A study of configurations and costs in four districts*. Newton, MA: Educational Development Center.

Ministry of Education (1980). *Japan's modern educational system: A history of the first hundred years*. Tokyo: Ministry of Education.

Ministry of Education (1982). *Understanding and guiding children: a resource book for educational guidance at an elementary school*. Tokyo: Okurasho Insatsu-kyoku.

Ministry of Education (1989a). *Education in Japan*. Tokyo: Gyosei.

Ministry of Education (1989b). *Outline of education in Japan*. Tokyo: UNESCO Asian Cultural Center.

Ministry of Education (1992). *Basic survey report on schools*. Tokyo: Mombusho.

Ministry of Education (1993). *Creation and development of the curriculum based on the new notion of academic competence*. Tokyo: Mombusho.

Ministry of Education (1994). *A survey on teacher preparation*. Tokyo: Mombusho.

Ministry of Education (1997). *A survey on roles of institutions of teacher education and graduate schools*. Tokyo: Mombusho.

Ministry of Education (1998). Central Council of Education's report on education of the heart. *Monthly Journal of the Ministry of Education*, supplementary issue, 1459, April 1998.

Ministry of Education (1998). *Survey concerning teachers' long-term social participation*. Tokyo: Ministry of Education.

Miwa, S. (1988). The problematic internship program. *Educational Law*, 75,11–16.

Miwa, S. (1992). *Comprehensive study of teacher education curriculum under new certification law*. Research report. Chiba-shi: Chiba University.

Miyasaka, T. (1959). *Educational guidance and moral education.* Tokyo: Meiji Tosho.

Morita, Y. (199 1). *Sociology of school refusal phenomena.* Tokyo: Gakubunsha.

Mukoyama, Y. (1985). *The science to improve teaching.* Tokyo: Meiji Tosho.

Munby, H. (1986). Metaphor in the thinking of teachers: An exploratory study. *Journal of Curriculum Studies,* 18, 197–209.

Munby, H. (1989). Reflection in action and reflection on action. Paper presented at the meeting of the American Educational Research Association, San Francisco, April.

Naigai Kyoiku (Domestic and Foreign Education), Bi-weekly newspaper, December 12,1989.

Nakamura, T. (1998). *A history of Showa Japan, 1926–1989.* Tokyo: University of Tokyo Press.

Nakane, C. (1972). *Japanese society.* Berkeley: University of California Press.

Nakasone, Y. (1984). Seven-point proposal for education reform. Quoted in L. Schoppa (1991), *Education reform in Japan* (pp. 214–215). London: Routledge.

National Commission on Excellence in Education (1983). *A nation at risk: The imperative for educational reform.* Washington, D.C.: U.S. Department of Education.

National Commission on Teaching and America's Future (1996). *What matters most: Teaching for America's future.* New York: Teachers College Press.

National Council on Educational Reform (I 986a). *Summary of second report on educational reform.* Tokyo: Government of Japan.

National Council on Educational Reform (986b). *The outline of deliberations,* No. 3. In Gyosei (Ed.) (1986), *National Council on Educational Reform and educational reforms,* No. 3 (pp. 231–376). Tokyo: Gyosei.

National Council on Educational Reform (1988). *Reports on educational reforms: Four reports.* Tokyo: Okurasho Insatsukyoku.

National Council on Educational Reform (1988). *Recommendations for educational reform.* Tokyo: Okurasho Instasukyoku.

Nakatome, T. (1988). How to develop the internship program for beginning teachers. *Educational Law,* 75, 17–29.

National Center for Education Statistics (1993). *America's teachers: Profile of a profession.* Washington, D.C.: U.S. Government Printing Office.

National Science Foundation (1983). *Educating Americans for the 21st century: A report to the American people and the National Science Board.* Washington, D.C.: Author.

Nelson, B. S. & Hammerman, J. K. (1996). Reconceptualizating teaching: Moving toward the creation of intellectual communities of students, teachers, and teacher educators. In M. W. McLaughlin and I. Oberman (Eds.), *Teacher Learning: New politics, new perspectives* (pp. 3–21). New York: Teachers College Press.

Nihon Kyoiku Shimbun (1998). *The comprehensive list of educational study meetings for summer 1998.* Japanese education weekly. June 20.

Nippon Nyushi Center (1991). *The 1990–1991 university entrance examination research.* Tokyo: Yoyogi Zeminaru.

Nishi, K. (1988). *A teacher who is able to see children: How to develop ability and sensitivity in understanding children*. Tokyo: Kyoiku Shuppan.

Nosow, S. (1975). Students' perceptions of field education. *Journal of College Student Personnel,* 16 (6), 508–513.

Okuda, Y. (1998). The need for the open certification system for the 21" century. In T. Urano and T. Hata (Eds.), *Teacher education at a time of transformation* (pp. 63–75). Tokyo: Dojisha.

Organization for Economic Cooperation and Development (1998). *Staying ahead: Inservice training and teacher professional development*. Paris: Organization for Economic Cooperation and Development.

Otsuki, T. (1982). *The history of postwar voluntary education movement*. Tokyo: Ayumi Shuppan.

Peak, L. (1992). *Learning to go to school*. Berkeley: University of California Press.

Petty, H. & Hogben, D. (1980). Explorations of semantic space with beginning teachers: Study of socialization into teaching. *British Journal of Teacher Education,* 3, 19–37.

Pollard, A. (1982). A model of classroom coping strategies. *British Journal of Sociology of Education*, 3, 19–37.

Reid, I. (1986). *The sociology of school and education*. London: Fontana Press.

Reid, I. (1989). Order in Japanese society: Attachment, authority, and routine. *Journal of Japanese Studies,* 15 (1), 5–40.

Rohlen, T. P. (1983). *Japan's high schools*. Berkeley: University of California Press.

Rohlen, T. P. (1989). Order in Japanese society: Attachment, authority, and routine. *Journal of Japanese Studies*, 13, 5– 40.

Ross, E. W. (1987a). *Preservice teachers' responses to institutional constraints: The active role of the individual in teacher socialization*. Albany, N.Y.: The State University of New York at Albany, Department of Teacher Education.

Ross, E. W. (1987b). Teacher perspective development: A study of preservice social studies teachers. *Theory and Research in Social Education,* 5 (4), 295–243.

Russell, T. (1989). The roles of research knowledge and knowing in-action in teachers' development of professional knowledge. Paper presented at the meeting of the American Educational Research Association, San Francisco, April.

Ryan, K. (1986). *The induction of new teachers*. Bloomington, Ind.: Phi Delta Kappan Educational Foundation.

Sakai, A. (1998). Intensification of teaching and contemporary culture of teaching. In K. Shimizu (Ed.), *Educational ethnography* (pp. 223–248). Tokyo: Sagano Shoin.

Sakai, A. & Shimahara, N. (1991). An inquiry into the process of learning teaching methods: Sociology of knowledge on teaching. *The Journal of Educational Sociology*, 49, 135–153.

Sako, S. (1998). School-based inservice education and the perspective and role of universities. In H. Nishinosono (Ed.), *A study concerning distance education for inservice education based on the utilization of the internet* (pp. 22–28). Monograph. Naruto: Naruto University of Education.

Sato, M. (1992). Japan. In H. Leavitt (Ed.), *Issues and problems in teacher education: An international handbook* (pp. 156–168). Westport, CT: Greenwood Press.

Sato, N. (1996). Honoring the individual. In T. P. Rohlen and G. LeTendre (Eds.), *Teaching and learning in Japan* (pp. 119–153). New York: Cambridge University Press.

Sato, N. & McLaughlin, M. (1992). Context matters: Teaching in Japan and the United States. *Phi Delta Kappan,* 73 (5), 359–366.

Sarason, S. B. (1971). *The culture of the school and the problem of change.* Boston: Allyn and Bacon.

Schofield, J. (1982). *Black and white in school.* New York: Praeger.

Schön, D. (1983). *The reflective practitioner.* New York: Basic Books.

Schön, D. (1987). *Educating the reflective practitioner.* San Francisco: Jossey-Bass.

Schön, D. (Ed.) (1991). *The reflective turn.* New York: Teachers College Press.

Schoppa, L. (1991). *Education reform in Japan—A case of immobilist politics.* London: Routledge.

Sharp, R. & Green, A. (1975). *Education and social control.* London: Routledge and Kegan Paul.

Shimahara, N. (1979). *Education and adaptation in Japan.* New York: Praeger.

Shimahara, N. (1986). Japanese education reforms in the 1980s. *Issues in Education,* 4 (2), 85–100.

Shimahara, N. (1991). Teacher education in Japan. In E. Beauchamp (Ed.), *Windows on Japanese education* (pp 178–205). New York:Greenwood Press.

Shimahara, N. (1993). Teacher education reforms: Salient issues in a sociopolitical context. Paper presented at the Rutgers Invitational Seminar on Education, Rutgers University, New Brunswick, N.J.

Shimahara, N. (1992). Overview of Japanese education: Policy, structure, and current issues. In R. Leestma & H. Walberg (Eds.), *Japanese educational productivity* (pp.7–33). Ann Arbor: Center for Japanese Studies, University of Michigan.

Shimahara, N. (1997). The culture of teaching in Japan. *Bulletin of the National Institute of Multimedia Education,* 14 (1), 37–60.

Shimahara, N. (1998). Classroom management: Building a classroom community. In N. Shimahara (Ed.), *Politics of classroom life: Classroom management in international perspective* (pp. 215–238). New York: Garland.

Shimahara, N. (1999). Japanese initiatives in teacher development. *Bulletin of Research Center for School Education, Naruto University of Education,* 14:1, 29–40.

Shimahara, N. & Sakai, A. (1990). Teacher internship and educational reform in Japan. *Bulletin of the Faculty of Education of University of Tokyo,* 30, 83–93.

Shimahara, N. & Sakai, A. (1992). Teacher internship and the culture of teaching in Japan. *British Journal of Sociology of Education,* 13 (2): 147–162.

Shimahara, N. & Sakai, A. (1995). *Learning to teach in two cultures: Japan and the U.S.* New York: Garland.

Shinoda, H. (1979). Teacher certification law and teacher education. In H. Shinoda and T. Tezuka (Eds.), *History of schools* (pp. 193–202). Tokyo: Daiichi Hoki.

Shintani, T. (1983). Classroom and school management. In J. Nagaoka, (Ed.), *School management* (pp. 187–202). Tokyo:Yushindo.

Shulman, L. (1987). Knowledge and teaching: Foundations of the new reform. *Harvard Educational Review*, 58, 1–22.

Sikula, J. (1990). National commission reports of the 1980s. In W. R. Houston (Ed.), *Handbook of research on teacher education* (pp 251–283). New York: Macmillan.

Smith, R. J. (1983). *Japanese society: Tradition, self, and the social order*. New York: Cambridge University Press.

Smyth, J. (1989). Developing and sustaining,- critical reflection in teacher education. *Journal of Teacher Education,* 40, 2–9.

Sparks, D. & Loucks-Horsley, S. (1990). Models of staff development. In W. R. Houston, H. Haberman, and J. Sikula (Eds.), *Handbook of research on teacher education* (pp. 234–250). New York: Macmillan.

Spindler, G., Spindler, L., Trueba, H. & Williams, M. D. (1990). *The American cultural dialogue and its transmission*. London: The Falmer Press.

Spradley, J. P. (1980). *Participant observation*. New York: Holt.

Stevenson, H. W. & Stigler, J. W. (1992). *The learning gap*. New York: Summit Books.

Tabachnick, B. R. & Zeichner, K. (1984). The impact of the student teaching experience on the development of teacher perspectives. *Journal of Teacher Education,* 35, 28–36.

Tabachnick, B. R. & Zeichner, K. (1985). *The development of teacher perspectives: Final report*. Madison, Wisc.: University of Wisconsin Center for Education Research.

Takano, K. (1998). *Teacher education movement in England*. In T. Urano & T. Hata (Eds.), *Teacher education at a time of transformation* (pp. 161–172). Tokyo: Dojisha.

Tanaka, I. (1974). The process of occupational socialization of beginning teachers: A school organizational approach. Research Bulletin of the Faculty of Education of Kyushu University, 20, 137–152.

Teacher Education Council (1983). *Recommendations to improve teacher education and the certification system*. In O. Kanda and M. Yamazumi (Eds.) (1985), *Education of Japan: Historical materials* (pp. 372–357) . Tokyo: Gakuyoshobo.

Teacher Education Council (1987). *Policy for improving teacher quality and competence*, Nos. I and 2. In M. Tsuchiya (Ed.) (1988), *How do teacher certification and inservice education change?* (pp. 58–109 and pp. 136–145). Tokyo: Rodojunposha.

Teacher Education Council (1997). *Report on strategies to improve teacher education for a new age: First report*. Tokyo: Mombusho.

Teacher Education Council (1998). *Draft report on teacher development through master's programs*. Tokyo: Mombusho.

Teacher Education Council (1998). Reforms of teacher education for an emerging age:An interim report on teacher education enhanced through graduate study at the master's level. Tokyo: Ministry of Education.

Tominaga, K. (1979). *The structure of Japanese stratification*. Tokyo: The University of Tokyo Press.

Tominaga, K. (1990). *Modernization of Japan and social transformation.* Tokyo: Kodansha.

Tobin, J., Wu, D. Y. H. & Davidson, D. H. (1989). *Preschool in three cultures.* New Haven: Yale University Press.

Tsuchiya, M. (1984). *Japanese teachers: Teacher education, certification, and inservice training.* Tokyo: Shin Nihon Shuppan.

Tsuchiya, M. (1984). *Postwar education and teacher training.* Tokyo: Shin Nippon Shinsho.

Tsuneyoshi, R. (1992). *Personality formation: A Japan-U.S. comparison of the hidden curricula.* Tokyo: Chuo Koron Sha.

Twentieth Century Fund Task Force on Federal Elementary and Secondary Education Policy (1983). *Making the grade.* New York: Author.

Tyler, W. (1988). *School organization: A sociological perspective.* London: Croom Helm.

United States Department of Education (1987). *Japanese education today.* Washington, D.C.: U.S. Government Printing Office.

United States Department of Education (1984). *The nation responds: Recent efforts to improve education.* Washington, D.C.: U.S. Government Printing Office.

United States Department of Education (1988). *Fifth annual wall chart of state education statistics.* Washington, D.C.: U.S. Government Printing Office.

United States Department of Education (1993). *America's teachers: Profile of a profession.* Washington, D.C.: U.S. Government Printing Office.

United States Education Mission to Japan (1946). *Report of the United States Education Mission to Japan.* In H. Passin (1965), *Society and education in Japan* (pp. 264–287). New York: Teachers College Press.

University Council (1991). Reform reports on university education. In Higher Education Study Group (Ed.) (1991), *Toward diverse developments of universities* (pp. 1–174). Tokyo: Gyosei.

Villi, L., Cooper, D. & Frankes, L. (1997). Professional development schools and equity: A critical analysis of rhetoric and research. In M. Apple (Ed.), *Review of research in education* (pp. 251–304). Vol. 22. Washington, D.C.: American Educational Research Association.

Veenman, S. (1984). Perceived problems of beginning teachers. *Review of Educational Research,* 54 (2), 143–178.

Waller, W. (1967). *The sociology of teaching.* New York: John Wiley.

Weick, K. (1982). Administering education in loosely coupled schools. *Phi Delta Kappan,* June, 673–676.

Weinstein, C. (1991). The classroom as a social context for learning. *Annual Review of Psychology,* 42, 493–525.

Wells, K. (1984). *Teacher socialization in the educational organization: A review of the literature.* Seattle: University of Washington.

White, J. J. (1989). Student teaching as a rite of passage. *Anthropology and Education Quarterly,* 20 (3), 177–195.

White, M. (1987). *The Japanese educational challenge.* New York: Free Press.

Yamaguchi, S. (1980). The modernization of curricular content and its critique. In Y. Shibata (Ed.), *The making of curriculum* (pp.190–206). Tokyo: Gakushu Kenkyusha.

Yanagi, H. (1984). Modern problems of the curriculum. In S. Sato and H. Inaba (Eds.), *School and curriculum* (pp.46–52). Tokyo: Daiichi Hoki.

Yokohama National University Institute for Modern Education (Ed.) (1983). *Central Council of Education and educational reforms*. Tokyo: Sanichi Shobo.

Yuki, M. (1992). Teacher behavior and intention in education for preschoolers. In T. Kuze & M. Nishito (Eds.), *Human Relations*. Tokyo: Fukumura Shuppan.

Zeichner, K. (1984). *Individual and institutional influences on the development of teacher perspectives*. Madison: Wisconsin Center for Education Research.

Zeichner, K. & Gore, J. M. (1990). Teacher socialization. In R. Houston (Ed.), *Handbook of research on teacher education* (pp. 329–348). New York: Macmillan.

Zeichner, K. & Tabachnick, B. R. (1981). Are the effects of university teacher education "washed out" by school experience? *Journal of Teacher Education*, 32 (3), 7–11.

Author Profile

Nobuo K. Shimahara is a Professor of Education and Anthropology at the Graduate School of Education and a member of the faculty of the Graduate School at Rutgers University. He has taught at Rutgers since 1968 and has served as a visiting professor at several Japanese universities, including Nagoya University, Naruto University of Education, the National Institute for Multimedia Education, and the University of Tokyo. He has published many books and articles. His recent publications include: *Learning to Teach in Two Cultures: Japan and the United States* (with Akira Sakai, 1995), *Politics of Classroom Life: Classroom Management in International Perspective* (as editor, 1998), and *Ethnicity, Race, and Nationality in Education* (as co-editor, 2001).

Index